A Teacher's Inside Advice to Parents

Praise for *A Teacher's Inside Advice to Parents*

"Robert Ward has written a clear, practical guide for parents to help their children thrive academically and emotionally in partnership with their teachers. If you are worried that your child is not reaching his or her true potential, I urge you to read this book. Through Ward's leadership, love, laughter, and learning approach, parents, children, and teachers form a winning team." —**Naomi Manzella**, parent and library media specialist, Norwood School, Maryland

"*A Teacher's Inside Advice to Parents* necessarily connects parents with teachers as allies in their joint mission of educating youth. The unassuming voice of master teacher Robert Ward provides parents with resonating wisdom and pragmatic tips on how to provide the optimal conditions for their children to flourish in the classroom and in life." —**Sarah Wu**, parent, Palo Alto, California

"Robert Ward's credibility as a teacher, writer, and mentor speaks volumes in his latest book, *A Teacher's Inside Advice to Parents*. He shares fresh insights and solutions for both parents and educators in supporting youth in today's educational setting. Currently a classroom teacher himself, Ward's discussions are relevant and right on target. I had the pleasure of being mentored by him, and his passion for teaching knows no bounds and is always infectious. While other teachers spent their lunch hours complaining about the educational system, a group of us hung out in Mr. Ward's classroom brainstorming ways to be more effective to our students and their families. He is like a breath of fresh air in a sometimes negative arena and brings with him a positive outlook on every area of teaching, parenting, and nurturing children." —**Tami Pearsall**, parent and instructor, California State University, Northridge

"I have worked with hundreds of educators during my thirty-two years in education, and I can count on one hand those with Robert Ward's level of expertise. I worked with him for over twenty years, and it was a pleasure to see his level of commitment and consistent quality of instruction. He knows very well that parents are crucial partners in educating children, and this is the book to facilitate that process." —**Lorna Bounds**, parent and retired assistant principal, Los Angeles Unified School District, California

"Robert Ward has found a way to bring parents and teachers together to help students find greater success and satisfaction in the classroom, as well as at home. In this book, both parties will discover complementary approaches to nurture and educate children, while also lowering the frustrations of all involved." —**Dr. Donald C. Helvey II**, parent and teacher, Meridian School, Utah

"From one parent to another, one thing I'm sure of is that 'it takes a village to raise a child.' As a mother of three, my greatest allies have been my children's teachers. *A Teacher's Inside Advice to Parents* will give you the tools to be a better partner in your child's education." —**Linda Armstrong**, parent, Los Angeles, California

"Robert Ward was an inspiration to me during my first year teaching at a very challenging school in South Los Angeles. He is a teacher who managed to be gentle and caring, while also firm. His high expectations raised up all of his students and set a model for the rest of us to follow. Now that I am a parent, I am even more impressed by his structured, supportive approach. Parents and teachers alike can benefit from his lessons to help all children thrive." —**Ingrid Brennan**, parent and teacher, Oxnard Union High School District, California

"Having dedicated his life to teaching, there is no one more qualified than Robert Ward to help parents become powerful, positive advocates for their own children. Ward's practical wisdom shows parents how they can help their children develop into responsible, healthy, independent individuals." —**Steven Ford**, veteran English teacher, Los Angeles Unified School District, California

"Invaluable insight for parents on how to better collaborate and communicate with the classroom! You will come to rely on Ward's menus of essential questions parents can ask their children, their teachers, and themselves in order to transform the home–school connection into the rewarding experience it was meant to be." —**Katie Hong**, parent and assistant principal, Los Angeles Unified School District, California

A Teacher's Inside Advice to Parents

How Children Thrive with Leadership, Love, Laughter, and Learning

Robert Ward

ROWMAN & LITTLEFIELD
Lanham • Boulder • New York • London

Published by Rowman & Littlefield
A wholly owned subsidiary of The Rowman & Littlefield Publishing Group, Inc.
4501 Forbes Boulevard, Suite 200, Lanham, Maryland 20706
www.rowman.com

Unit A, Whitacre Mews, 26-34 Stannary Street, London SE11 4AB

British Library Cataloguing in Publication Information Available

Library of Congress Cataloging-in-Publication Data

Names: Ward, Robert, 1964–
Title: A teacher's inside advice to parents : how children thrive with leadership, love, laughter, and learning / Robert Ward.
Description: Lanham, Maryland : Rowman & Littlefield, 2016.
Identifiers: LCCN 2016033683 (print) | LCCN 2016037838 (ebook) | ISBN 9781475822892 (cloth : alk. paper) | ISBN 9781475822915 (electronic)
Subjects: LCSH: Parent-teacher relationships. | Teacher-student relationships. | Education—Parent participation.
Classification: LCC LC226 .W37 2016 (print) | LCC LC226 (ebook) | DDC 371.19/2—dc23 LC record available at https://lccn.loc.gov/2016033683

∞™ The paper used in this publication meets the minimum requirements of American National Standard for Information Sciences—Permanence of Paper for Printed Library Materials, ANSI/NISO Z39.48-1992.

Printed in the United States of America

Contents

Foreword

Each year I have the honor and pleasure of traveling throughout the state of California as part of my position with a national program where I visit schools to determine whether they are worthy of being recognized as high-performing. This acknowledgment requires schools to show evidence of making strides to improve student academic performance, of responding to the developmental (social, physical, emotional, and intellectual) needs of students, and of possessing the proper organizational support that a school, district, and community provides for all of its children.

Many times I walk away from these experiences in awe of what professional educators are doing to nurture and enlighten children. Yet I also wonder what more could be done to support our students if we knew a little more about them and their families and if teachers and parents knew how to more effectively work together and communicate with one another.

Often when I am speaking at a school and celebrating its success, I am approached afterward by parents, elected officials, and community representatives with questions that leave me wondering: How did we neglect to inform these people of the great things happening at this school, and how is it possible that the parents did not already know about all of the programs and options available to them to support their child's developmental and academic needs?

A Teacher's Inside Advice to Parents: How Children Thrive with Leadership, Love, Laughter, and Learning bridges the chasm that often exists between teachers, parents, community members, and others truly interested in the education and raising of children. This book is an experienced-based tool for parents and teachers to examine ways to improve learning for all students and to better understand the process of nurturing children—both at home and at school.

Parents often struggle when meeting with teachers and other school personnel to discuss issues that may be impacting their child's behavior and/or academic performance and at the same time may be causing frustration for all involved. Of course, many teachers face these same concerns with their students and often act out of a lack of information about the child and their home life.

A Teacher's Inside Advice to Parents addresses these issues from the perspective of a classroom teacher currently working in one of the most challenging school districts in the United States that serves students with a wide variety of needs and talents. Teacher and author Robert Ward has created a classroom environment of tolerance, empathy, exploration, creativity, security, and the joy of learning where students daily embrace the demands of scholarship and are rewarded with the pride that comes from progressively accomplishing at high levels the tasks set before them.

His classroom is not just confined to its four walls, but is connected to a larger world that he opens to his students. Through discussion, inquiry, collaboration, and community, his students share and develop their own ideas and insights. Students entering Mr. Ward's class know they are in a safe space where all are equal and treated with respect. His students are challenged to push themselves to higher levels of understanding and to see the potential for themselves now and in the future—and isn't this what we want for all students?

This book lays out a very clear guide for parents and teachers to create cohesive home and school environments where children feel empowered, are encouraged to dream, and become active participants in their own learning and fulfillment rather than passive zombies waiting to fill in workbooks and complete computerized tests. Through positive interaction and close connections among teachers, parents, and students, the educational and developmental success for all children can essentially be assured.

This book provides the groundwork for supporting our classrooms and advancing the relationship among all who should be committed to improving the lives of our children at home and at school. Read it! Believe it! Embrace it!

Dr. Irvin Howard
Professor Emeritus, California State University, San Bernardino
Past President, The National Forum to Accelerate Middle Grades Reform
Director of Grant Programs, California League of Schools

Acknowledgments

Growing up in the 1970s as the eldest of four boys in a modest suburban tract home on the outskirts of Los Angeles was idyllic in many ways. As long as my brothers and I did our homework, completed our chores, and ate our vegetables, we were free to roam the streets and explore the surrounding hills until dusk, to pedal our Big Wheels and bikes with the wind in our helmetless hair, to wrestle each other unharnessed while riding in the back of the family station wagon, and to attend fantastic neighborhood schools that were not bounded by fences or patrolled by police.

Most moms were there when their children arrived home from school, and many dads could support a family on a high school education. Phones had dials and were tethered by cords. TV shows were watched either live or not at all. Essays were pecked out on typewriters, letters handwritten in flowing cursive were mailed, and the only web I cared about was the one downloaded by Charlotte.

Times certainly have changed and will continue to do so, wiping away some things we now long for and altering others that were long due for an overhaul. What has not changed, however, are the ways parents and teachers successfully motivate and nurture children. In fact, in a world that is increasingly more accessible yet overwhelming, interconnected yet isolating, and enticing yet unfulfilling, kids need more positive adult influence and interaction than ever, both at home and at school.

I therefore dedicate this book with love and gratitude to my mom, dad, and school teachers for their generous gifts of leadership, love, laughter, and learning. This book is my way of giving back and paying forward what all these caring, conscientious adults have given me.

I would also like to express my appreciation to my editor at Rowman & Littlefield, Sarah Jubar, for her initial belief in me as a writer and for her invaluable support and guidance along my journey to becoming a published author. What began as an ordinary teacher submitting an unsolicited manuscript and trying to turn his writing dream into a reality has evolved into a collaboration between Sarah and me on three books! Her expert advice has made me a clearer, more confident writer, and this book in particular would have never happened without her encouragement and faith in me and my ideas.

Preface

The Powerful Influence of Parents and Teachers in Partnership

Envision a world in which parents and teachers are allies who routinely work together in a harmonious collaboration of mutual respect, reciprocal trust, shared understanding, and common goals. Imagine how much more the children could achieve in such an ideal situation and how much happier both parents and teachers would be for it.

Far too often and for far too long, however, this sublime scenario has not been the case. Just ask any disgruntled, dissatisfied parent who has had less than positive experiences with the education system. For that matter, just ask any disparaged, demoralized teacher who has had less-than-pleasant encounters with parents or with how they are perceived by the public.

Unfortunately, neither one will be very hard to find, nor will each hesitate to tell you their side of the story. Yet when discord, disillusionment, and distrust between the home and the classroom fester, everyone suffers—most of all, the kids.

Speaking of the kids, also imagine homes where children and their parents are usually united and seldom at odds. Visualize as well classrooms where students and their teachers are primarily partners and almost never in opposition.

Far too often and for far too long, however, these additional ideal scenarios have not been the case. Just ask any overwhelmed, anxious, or indecisive parent *or* teacher who has experienced less than smooth sailing while nurturing and educating children. Ask any upset, apprehensive, or addled child who has endured a series of less than supportive situations with adults. Regrettably, none of these people will be so hard to find either, and they each also will not hesitate to tell you their side of the story!

Of course, it matters not which side thinks they are right. Nothing will change, and no relationships or results will improve until someone takes charge and works toward sensible solutions that make everyone's lives better.

Thus, envision parents and teachers being on *the same team*, using similar methods, working toward similar goals, and consequently achieving *the same remarkable results* with *the same kids* whom they all care for. Imagine all those children who are fortunate enough to be surrounded by adults who know exactly how to persuade them to increasingly exercise self-control, develop self-confidence, explore self-fulfillment, and expand their self-efficacy. As a result of all this shrewd adult influence and direction, these self-actualized kids would not just be functioning well, they would be thriving both at home and at school—and on a routine basis.

On the other hand, parents and teachers know all too well what happens when a *child* decides to be in charge. Yet if properly persuaded, there is no reason why kids should not feel like they are in charge much of the time, both at home and at school—not in charge of the adults, of course, but in increasing charge of their own wise choices and the resulting pleasant consequences such mature and measured decisions bring. From "using their words" to using their manners to using their heads, children gradually learn from their adult role models to better manage their emotions, their attitudes, their actions, and their outcomes.

Children who feel a developing sense of self-determination are not chronically upset, apprehensive, or addled; they are more consistently serene, secure, and sure. And aren't these the very qualities parents and teachers want to cultivate in kids?

Savvy parents and teachers engender this type of satisfaction in children by customarily meeting their elemental needs. The essential structure, support, stimulation, and skills these perceptive adults provide for children help kids become steady and strong. As a result, parents and teachers who know precisely how to motivate children are no longer overwhelmed, anxious, or indecisive; they are remarkably capable, confident, and calm. And aren't these the attributes every parent and teacher craves for themselves in order to live up to being the kind of role model all children deserve?

Therefore, every child requires intentional and informed adult leadership to steer them toward the comforting feelings of self-direction and stability. In turn, a child's healthy sense of autonomy and reassurance causes them to feel emboldened and empowered to become their best. And isn't this progressive growth in responsibility, efficacy, independence, faith, and fulfillment the ultimate goal that parents and teachers work toward developing in the children they cherish?

Conversely, if the significant adults in their lives chronically leave them wanting and disenchanted in the most fundamental ways, children will eventually react. If their days at home or school are filled with excess, insufficiency, inconsistency, or chaos, kids will retaliate. They will fill this vacuum in competent adult leadership either by seizing control and acting out or by guarding their own precious sense of control and protecting themselves with aloofness or invisibility.

Rebellion, withdrawal, and retreat in children are all symptomatic of the adults in their lives relinquishing their authority and power to positively motivate and guide them. What parents and teachers must realize, however, is that these are the kids who need adult direction and nurturing the most. Their current negative reactions may seem to indicate that the last thing these kids want is more adult involvement, but do not be fooled. These children in fact are aching for strong and stable adult influence and connection.

If you have ever had to deal with bouts of resistance and defiance, reluctance and distance, or alienation and disengagement from your children—and *every* parent and teacher has to from time to time—this book will offer sound approaches to significantly lessen their frequency, length, and severity.

If you are currently in the midst of kids who persistently act out, act aloof, or act invisible, this book will also assist you with proven methods to bring your children back into a healthy relationship of cooperation, closeness, contentment, and accomplishment with you.

The fact is, *all kids* are always waiting for the adults in the room, be it the living room or the classroom, to act their age and to take conscious and decisive action in meeting their fundamental needs. No matter how some will protest or pretend, every child wants the important adults around them to provide the leadership, love, laughter, and learning they require in order to help them live constructive, rewarding lives, both in the present and in the future.

Once parents and teachers accept that they absolutely need each other, embrace the fact that they do indeed share common goals, and acknowledge that they always accomplish so much more when working in tandem, they then have little difficulty in getting children onto their collective team. Even any currently upstart, angry, or apathetic kids do not stand a chance. More to the point, in such a consistent and cohesive scenario, those same troubled and troubling children finally have *every chance* at success and satisfaction.

In fact, all kids would have little reason to act out or hide out in the first place. For what is there for children to rebel against or to retreat from when they are receiving much the same types of reliable leadership and loyalty, sincere encouragement and acceptance, frequent enthusiasm and excitement, and dependable guidance and glory both at home and at school?

Therefore, the time for moving from imagination and idealism to reality and practicality is at hand. This book contains the insight and strategies any parent can use to immediately begin working in concert with their children's teachers to ensure a fruitful educational experience that flows seamlessly from home to school and back again. Know that it is never too late to begin to considerably affect how a child performs and progresses in any setting, but also be aware that the window of optimal opportunity continues to shrink the longer kids have to wait for the adults to get their acts together, both collectively and individually.

This book will also emphasize that education and academic achievement are only a part of what great parenting and teaching offer to children because learning is but one-fourth of what kids require from adults. If parents should expect much more from their children than just good grades, then they should also expect more from their children's teachers than just delivering a good education. In fact, good grades may never come—and if they do, they will not be worth much—if both parents and teachers are not equally as focused on providing children with the other three-fourths of what they need most: structure, emotional support, and inspiration.

Thus, this book takes a uniquely comprehensive approach to how adults must thoroughly motivate children. It places *equal emphasis* on adults supplying kids with four elemental necessities. It is absolutely possible for all parents and teachers, regardless of circumstance, to provide children with positive and persuasive discipline, warm and trusting relationships, joyful and meaningful experiences, *and* challenging yet comprehensible learning opportunities so each child can flourish and realize their individual promise. These are the nonnegotiable adult duties this book will thoroughly explain, parents will find transformative, and children will welcome.

Parenting and teaching can all too easily go awry, however, whenever adults do too much or too little in attempting to meet children's elemental needs. So this book will also point out that half measures, false starts, and extremes only hold kids back and hamper their ability to navigate and succeed in a world where some adults chronically overcompensate, overindulge, or overwhelm them—often completely unintentionally!

Obviously, parents and teachers who are overzealous, overbearing, oblivious, indifferent, or otherwise preoccupied do more harm than good to children—but most do so not out of malice but often because they do not know any other way. Thus balance and consistency will be this book's guiding principles for parents and teachers to learn to provide children with *just enough*. With such appropriate adult support, kids feel confident in spreading their wings progressively further as they impress us, as well as themselves, with their newfound capabilities.

Hence, the most effective parents and teachers take their leadership roles seriously. They employ commonsense, comprehensive, and consistent action and intervention to ensure that in the most essential ways the children they are responsible for are not left waiting, wanting, or without guidelines and guidance.

The part that may be startling but ultimately heartening is that those parents and teachers who are currently effective with kids are not any more caring or intelligent than any other adult who takes on the awesome honor of rearing and educating children. In fact, the adults who currently feel overwhelmed, anxious, and indecisive—if not completely stymied—as they continually struggle with properly motivating kids, care *just as* deeply, are *just as* smart, and seek to do the "right" things *just as* much as anyone else.

Unfortunately, where nurturing children is concerned, even the strongest of commitments and the best of intentions, though important, are not enough. Even love in and of itself is not enough. This book will demystify what effective parenting and teaching actually look like and will clearly show you how to become just as persuasive with your own children as those all-star parents or topnotch teachers you may constantly compare yourself to.

In fact, the very best parents and teachers whom you may be measuring yourself against still make mistakes, still question themselves, and still have some really bad days with the children they care so deeply about—and if you ask them, they will gladly tell you all about how they are far from perfect or how it is far from easy. Know that these successful adults are also still looking to do the "right" things for kids just as much as those who currently struggle; for if one is not careful, success itself can breed its own stressors and pressures.

Therefore, every parent, from those desperate for insight to those who routinely seek additional perspective, can benefit from the clarity and composure this book offers because confidence also comes from the confirmation that you are actually on the right track. Reassurance and validation for those who are already achieving success in the sometimes daunting and always demanding jobs of parenting and teaching are just as important as fresh understanding and sound direction are for those who currently wrestle with persuading kids toward obedience, openness, originality, and optimal achievement.

In this book, you will recognize many people, including yourself. You will recognize ways in which you parent your children, ways in which others parent theirs, and ways in which your parents raised you—and all in ways that may alternately delight or distress you. However, this book will never chide you; it will only guide you.

In these pages, you will also recognize your own children, the children of others, your children's teachers, and those who have taught you—again, in ways that may cause you to cheer or to cringe. The focus, however, will not be on dwelling on the past, assigning blame, or feeling less-than but on moving ever forward. Although meeting the essential needs of children is always a serious, stringent endeavor, your exhausting, eventful days can soon be ruled with a newfound calm and courage as you learn to more thoroughly enjoy leading, nurturing, mentoring, and coaching your kids.

If many wonderful teachers can manage, inspire, engage, and educate a classroom of students—sometimes with totals in excess of 150 students per day, repeated throughout a career spanning approximately thirty years—and accomplish all this with an inexhaustible combination of grace and enthusiasm, all parents can find similar aplomb and excitement in closely interacting with their children throughout their youth and beyond.

Even other people's children who play large and small roles in your life will benefit from your newly acquired expertise in giving all kids what they truly need. You and these other children will reap the rewards of your consistently affirmative encounters as you automatically approach all kids with an evenness and eloquence that are irresistible and eminently appropriate.

This parental poise, self-confidence, and joy are the very best gifts that you can bestow upon your own children, as well as upon yourself. Just as a classroom full of students deserves a sure and serene teacher, your entire family will benefit from parents who are assured and astute. Your tranquil yet passionate parental demeanor will set the positive and productive tone for the all-too-brief time you are privileged to spend with your kids through their childhood and adolescence. Everyone will tell you that it is all "gone before you know it." So, wouldn't it do your whole family a world of good if you could slow down and savor a lot more of it?

Therefore, there is not a moment to lose or a minute to waste when it comes to nurturing and educating children to their full potential. Of course, the success of this vital endeavor depends greatly upon adults realizing their *own* full parenting and teaching potentials and joining forces to maximize their collective positive impact.

Introduction

Capitalizing on Commonality while Honoring Individuality

I am not a parent myself. Yet as an English teacher at a public middle school in South Los Angeles for over two decades, I have educated, closely interacted with, cared deeply about, and, yes, "parented" more than 3,000 children much like your own.

In fact, the children I have taught are more like your own than you may realize. You see, as unique and as precious as every parent's child certainly is, my large sample of students viewed over a long period of time has taught me one undeniable truth: where it matters most, all children are basically the same because they all essentially need the same things.

Now, I bet you are thinking: "This man obviously does not know my child. Where does he come off presuming to negate how remarkable and marvelously complex my child is? Besides, he is not even a parent himself!"

I completely understand because I react in much the same way when I receive edicts on curriculum and instruction from bigwigs far removed from the classroom: "No one knows my students better than I do! How dare they try to tell me how to teach and interact with kids they know nothing about? When was the last time these people even stepped foot in an actual classroom, let alone educated and supported a room full of children on a daily basis?"

Parents and teachers have these automatic, protective instincts when it comes to the children they are responsible for because their sense of duty is inextricably mixed with profound caring and love. A teacher's care for their students is not the same as a parent's love, but doesn't every parent want teachers who cherish and champion all students equally and enthusiastically?

Then we must capitalize on our common concern for and commitment to children and use each other's insight to our collective advantage, not as a means for mistrust. It is completely true that no one will ever know your child better than you. In fact, your personal expertise is one of your parenting strengths, so your intuition and experience will be honored as an essential component of what this book advocates for on behalf of all children.

Nothing about your child will be negated or dismissed here. Instead, the focus is upon you providing for your own children what every kid needs most, all with the direct intention that by so doing you will maximize the *individual*, incredible potential of each of them. One major component of this book is to celebrate what is indeed remarkable about every child, especially yours, as well as to attend to the very complexities that make each child unique.

So when I boldly restate that where it matters most, all children are *basically* the same because they all essentially need the same things, this assertion also fully acknowledges that some kids need more than others, especially at different times and in different ways. What you will happily discover, however, is that those ways are most often simply a matter of a parent or teacher bestowing a child with a bit more leadership or love or laughter or learning than they had already been faithfully supplying to all children all along.

Once adults know the four fundamental, universal needs of children, they can use this knowledge to be sure they are continually furnishing kids with the essential building blocks required not merely for all children to get by, but to shine and to soar—eventually all on their own and all in their own singular ways! Moreover, the occasions when a child actually requires more from a parent or a teacher will be fewer and farther between if that child's most elemental needs have been tended to from the beginning.

In order to illustrate this proactive approach to children, this book will explore the following questions:

- What if the emphasis in parenting and teaching abandoned its fixation on showering kids with "more"?
- What if, where kids were concerned, the adults let go of vying to be "original" or agonizing about "perfection" and instead concentrated on finding that Goldilocks sweet spot where they focused on supplying all children with what is "just right"?
- What if there actually is a universal, baseline equilibrium that is thoroughly compelling and deeply fulfilling for every child?
- What if all parents and teachers share a common starting point and touchstone to which they can always return and that guarantees every child receives not only what they deserve but also what they truly require in order to realize and reap their very best?
- And what if all this sameness and equity is not confining or constricting at all? What if it is really a vital means to the end goal of every child becoming who and what is satisfying and meaningful to themselves?

- Finally, what if this approach actually frees parents, teachers, and kids to appreciate and enrich individuality, both in themselves and in others, precisely because those same adults and children are in a natural state of balance and grace?

A DUAL FOCUS

This book will show you that you can have it both ways: you can respect fundamental truths about children while at the very same time prizing and cultivating what is exceptional about each individual. Hence, this book will on one hand reveal the commonalities between the classroom and the home, as well as the general similarities among all children. On the other hand, it will also advocate for attending to the specific needs of each child, as well respecting the wisdom and wishes of each particular parent and teacher.

Even while employing common approaches, there is plenty of room in parenting and teaching for the use of personal styles. It is entirely possible to balance conventional wisdom and consistency with diversity and creativity. These seeming sets of opposites do not contradict each other; rather, they maintain what we know already works well with all children, while allowing for the flexibility and personal touch that enable growth, change, and ingenuity in order to support kids in the distinct ways they need us most.

In fact, skilled teachers maintain this dual focus every day with much success. They do not constantly run from child to child and individually tutor thirty students per class because this is not only impractical, it is unnecessary. Teachers instead provide the core curriculum to the whole group while also making sure to fill in gaps and re-explain or to accelerate and enrich, as each student may demonstrate the need.

Also keep in mind that the kids who require more help or more challenge often change with each subject or each aspect of each lesson. Moreover, this teacher attention is not just about academics. Don't you want your child to receive the same quality grade-level instruction as their peers nationwide, while at the same time expect that their individual requirements—including their ever-changing social, emotional, and soulful needs—are given proper attention?

We must finally get the job of parenting and teaching as right as possible instead of merely doing the opposite of what the last generation did to us. Instead of being reactionary or thinking that we are so much more enlightened than those who came before us—those who, despite any shortcomings, had their hearts in the right place for kids just as much as we all do—we should concentrate on some elemental truths about interacting with and raising children.

A TEACHER'S "PARENTAL" OBLIGATIONS

Regardless of whether a classroom teacher is actually a parent raising their own children at home, know that all of the teachers you entrust your child to each school day are legally bound to act as a substitute parent for as long as your child is in their care. The specific term, *in loco parentis*, means the teacher is temporarily acting "in place of the parents." Of course, this temporary yet important period when students are in a teacher's care actually adds up to a significant portion of their young lives.

During the approximately 180 days per year your children spend in school, about half of their waking hours for half of the calendar year are being directly supervised and significantly influenced by their teachers. Of course, this routine plays out for at least twelve of the most influential, tumultuous years of your child's life. Furthermore, the reach of teachers often extends way past the last bell into homework and studying time, so teachers and parents must work together to also make all this after school time as productive and even pleasant as possible.

Hence, a relationship of trust, collaboration, and consistency between parents and every single one of their children's teachers, year after year, is essential if that much critical educational and developmental time is going to be utilized to its full potential.

PARENTS AND TEACHERS ARE NATURAL ALLIES

It is self-evident that parents and children garner the benefits of a great teacher but also pay some kind of price for anything less than a sterling teacher. Likewise, teachers and children share the advantages of committed, capable parents, but also suffer consequences when parental responsibility and efficacy falters.

Therefore, parents and teachers must be allies who share common expectations, methods, and goals. The unhappy alternative is mutual blame and suspicion between home and school, which result in the children receiving mixed messages about how they should behave, struggling with mixed emotions about whom they should trust, and receiving a mixed bag of an education—none of which is close to what parents, teachers, or the children actually want!

Of course, none of this confusion, consternation, and concession is necessary because parents and teachers are natural allies who share the same love, concern, and high hopes for every child with whom they come in contact. We just need to take a moment to see this situation clearly, and this can best be accomplished by putting ourselves in each other's shoes and taking the time to see each party's personal perspective.

So, if I as a teacher am willing to invite parents into my world of the classroom—warts and all—I hope you will allow me the privilege to peek into your world and to describe a typical parent's point of view. I will also take you into the not-so-incomprehensible world of children. I assure you that this process will be illuminating and ultimately empowering.

I will not, however, presume to tell you exactly how to raise your children. I would take great umbrage at a parent telling me precisely how to run my classroom and specifically what or how to teach. Therefore, this book will suggest and offer sound direction, but it will not dictate every detail of good parenting or expound on the whole history of nurturing children. Its scope is broad and thorough, but this book does not claim to be exhaustive or the last word on what encompasses great parenting. That last word is respectfully reserved for you as your parenting evolves and blossoms in the ways that work best for you and your children.

Instead, this book will clearly point out the four underlying areas where the classroom and the home intersect and how parents and teachers can use this nexus as common ground to beneficially influence the kids they care for. You will also discover that everything you already know and will ever learn about effective parenting will find a happy home within the philosophy of this book. Because its core ideas are expansive and universal, this book welcomes and complements all your personal decisions and discoveries as a parent. Hence, its approach is applicable and adaptable to children of all ages and backgrounds, as well as to all settings.

THE FOUR Fs OF EFFECTIVE TEACHING: THE FIRM, FAIR, FASCINATING FACILITATOR

I consider myself an expert at motivating children, especially the neediest and most challenging ones. I also have vast experience with students of a wide variety of cultures and socioeconomic backgrounds. I have taught kids in crisis, kids with challenges, and kids who had every convenience and comfort. However, the one commonality between them all was a chance at a successful, satisfying school experience that would also lead them to a bright future.

Thus, my mission has always been to increase the odds of fortune and fulfillment for every one of my precious students, every day. In myriad ways, many of them have greeted me more behind in the game of chance than others, but as far as I am concerned, that game is always far from over. Besides, as they each first enter my classroom, all of my students have just got a new coach—and this guy is always intent on training an entire team of winners.

It has not always been easy, and I cannot say it has always been a pleasure. Yet it has been my great privilege to make the most impact I can in the little time I have with each student, and that aspect of education is always immensely gratifying. There have been good days and bad days, even good years and bad years; but I daresay I have done my damnedest, and I have done a great deal of good on behalf of children.

The teaching philosophy that has enabled me to become a highly effective educator for all of my students is embodied in what I call a **firm, fair, fascinating facilitator** (the Four Fs of Teaching). These four aspects of my teaching persona are the main tools I rely on, year after year, to positively, thoroughly, and consistently motivate my students. I have learned from a wealth of firsthand experience that every child needs a potent combination of structure, encouragement, engagement, and plain old excellent teaching in order to find fulfillment and achievement in school and in their daily lives.

Using my firm, fair, fascinating facilitator strategies, I have also mentored hundreds of teachers at various stages of their careers so they could be fully effective in any classroom setting and at any grade level. Know that there are masterful teachers in every school, from the lowest-performing to the highest-performing. Whether they consciously know it or not, all of these great teachers use the same four central methods to influence their diverse students toward advantageous ends.

While I have written two books for teachers on this powerful philosophy of education (i.e., *The Firm, Fair, Fascinating Facilitator: Inspire Your Students, Engage Your Class, Transform Your Teaching* and *The Teacher Tune-Up: A Workbook and Discussion Guide for How to Become a Firm, Fair, Fascinating Facilitator*), this book was written specifically for parents. It has been tailored for practical and immediate use in the home and is a natural, necessary extension of my two teacher books' central ideas and strategies. Thus, pertinent points from those books will be echoed herein, both directly and indirectly.

This book also draws frequent parallels to the classroom so parents gain a clearer picture of what excellent teaching really looks like. Guided by such insight, parents can then choose to complement and mirror the ways teaching and parenting converge so their children receive consistent, comprehensive attention to their four most essential needs. Education is at its core a threefold partnership between teachers, students, and parents, and it is high time parents were welcomed and valued as equal and informed collaborators with the classroom.

THE FOUR ESSENTIAL CLASSROOM ELEMENTS

The most sensible, balanced, and integrated approach to teaching incorporates processes to attain the following four essential classroom elements:

1. Student cooperation
2. Student participation
3. Student engagement
4. Student academic progress

Because they are each *equally important*, a thoroughly effective teacher attends to all four of the student attributes above: attitude, action, affect, and achievement. For what parent does not want their child to respectfully behave, willingly contribute, enthusiastically invest, and increasingly accomplish while at school? For that matter, wouldn't all this positivity and productivity in your children be desirable in much the same ways while they are at home?

STUDENTS' FOUR BASIC NEEDS

Teachers who seek to work in concert and in harmony with their students—without bullying, coddling, placating, or pandering to them—must create and maintain a classroom climate that meets the needs of the *whole* student. In order to consistently progress toward realizing their every dazzling possibility, all children not only require multiple methods of support from their teachers, they crave four sets of basic needs. The commonsense, multidimensional approach of the Four Fs of Teaching works because it meets the essential needs of all students by consistently motivating them on four fundamental fronts:

1. **Firmness** provides the students' needs of **safety, security, and structure**, which engenders courteous student cooperation and expedites orderly classroom management. This decorum and sense of stability maximizes time on task and ensures learning for all.
2. **Fairness** fosters the students' needs of **caring, community, and recognition**, which supports a strong teacher–student rapport and eager student participation. This warm, supportive, and encouraging environment promotes the sense of belonging and acceptance which emboldens kids to take risks, express their ideas, and try their best.
3. **Fascination** delivers the students' needs of **purpose, passion, and pertinence**, which evokes sustained student engagement and investment. This quest for discovering meaning, meeting challenges, and making connections provides kids with the direction and inspiration necessary for finding personal fulfillment both in and out of school.
4. **Facilitation** furnishes the students' needs of strategic, differentiated **academic direction, assistance, and feedback**, which elicits increased

student achievement and independence. This progressive command of deep and thorough comprehension, insightful analysis, and critical thinking prepares students to meet the rigors of college and career.

THE CONNECTION BETWEEN THE CLASSROOM AND THE LIVING ROOM

A firm, fair, fascinating facilitator simultaneously supplies these indispensable student necessities because in order to reach their full potential in school and everywhere else, every child requires leadership and limits, understanding and encouragement, meaning and inspiration, *as well as* excellent instruction and coaching. Thus, all effective teachers focus their energy to these four basic motivators. The Four Fs have it all because our children need it all!

Take away or neglect a single component and expect decidedly diminished results. I have tried and have failed miserably by taking shortcuts or by emphasizing one motivator over the others. Thus when inspiring children, balance among four primary motivators is the only path to thorough success and satisfaction.

Think about the advantageous effects such a comprehensive teaching approach would produce for your children. Students in a Four Fs classroom are cooperative, comfortable, captivated, *and* comprehending, and parents can readily see this influence in their children's grades and in their enthusiastic attitudes about their teachers and school in general.

Therefore, parents no longer need to wonder: "What would cause my child to frequently act up in one teacher's class but not another's? Why would my child be reluctant to participate or be withdrawn in one class but not another? Why would my child find one class utterly boring and useless but not another? Why would my child earn poor marks in one class but not another?"

One accurate answer to all these questions is that some teachers intentionally inspire respect, consciously establish a rapport, purposefully create relevance, and strategically expedite academic rigor for each of their students, while other teachers do not possess the proper insight and skills to motivate their students to similarly constructive ends. It is not that every teacher does not want to achieve the same sort of favorable results the Four Fs of Teaching deliver—it is that they simply do not as yet know how to find that achievement for themselves.

Of course, any school situation that does not provide kids with their fundamental needs is in no way acceptable. Yet I also well know that many teachers are desperate for practical help. They yearn to do better for your children, but as parents know, desire devoid of clear direction and sound strategies does not get you very far with kids. Believe me, I was one of those struggling, ineffective teachers way back when, and I wish I had known then what I know now.

Oh, my heart was always in the right place, but that alone does not entice thirty twelve-year-olds to simmer down long enough to take roll, let alone galvanize them to behave like serious scholars who volunteer eagerly, invest enthusiastically, and answer intelligently. Instead, teachers' hearts in such predicaments tend to break quite quickly—not to mention the hearts of the students who are secretly hungry to respond appropriately if the adult in the room just knew what the heck they really needed and could use that influence to his and their best advantages.

So, I came to write the two books for teachers because I discovered that a consistent, comprehensive approach to inspiring children and meeting their four essential needs is rarely if ever discussed in education. There is a lot of lip service dedicated to the educational flavor of the month—be it discipline, relationships, engagement, or instruction—but always in isolation and never as the integrated, balanced approach I know as the only truly effective answer.

Consequently, if a well-intentioned but woefully incompetent teacher like me could not only improve but could eventually engender startling student success, even with some of the most defiant, desperate, demoralized, and dependent kids around, then it was incumbent upon me to share this insight with my fellow teachers. Yet what also became clear to me early on is that much of what works for teachers in the classroom also works for parents at home.

By extension, if things are working well at home, things work better in the classroom. I wish my students' parents also had known then what I know now. That shared wisdom and common approach would have made things a whole lot better for all of us!

Therefore, the straightforward and thorough path for parents to transform into potent motivators themselves and to subsequently transform their own children into cooperative, contented, creative, and capable individuals is through a commitment to using four similar approaches to those that great teachers consistently and cohesively employ with their students.

In essence, teachers need to act more like the best of parents, and parents need to act more like the best of teachers because, as will be explicated throughout this book, their goals for children are nearly the same. Furthermore, if all children have the same basic needs all of the time, the means to meeting those needs and to reaching those goals should be similar as well.

THE FOUR Ls OF EFFECTIVE PARENTING: PROVIDING YOUR CHILDREN WITH LEADERSHIP, LOVE, LAUGHTER, AND LEARNING

I know from long and varied experience that the parents who give their children the greatest chance at and best head start for success in school are the ones who, whether they realize it or not, continually reinforce the very same motivators that highly effective teachers also use in their classrooms. In fact, long before their children began school, these savvy parents have been a version of the teacher I just described as a firm, fair, and fascinating facilitator.

Thus, all parents are wise to try out corresponding classroom techniques for themselves at home. Then, as you begin to persuade your children toward the same type of courteous cooperation, close interaction, active involvement, and increasing skill and intelligence that successful educators do, these remarkable results will reliably delight and reenergize you. These positive outcomes may even initially astonish you: "*Wait a second. My child is actually ... ?*"

Yes, even your child can actually .... But only if you adopt and adapt similar aspects of classroom motivation by consistently providing your children with a potent combination of **leadership, love, laughter, and learning** (the Four Ls of Parenting), which influence children by generously and responsibly supplying them with the following four fundamental necessities:

1. **Leadership** provides the guidelines, routines, and limits children require in order to feel a soothing sense of **safety, security, and structure**. This stability produces kids who are respectful, cooperative, and self-regulating so they can flourish in an orderly and serene home where love, laughter, and learning flow abundantly.
2. **Love** offers the **attention, patience, and acceptance** that create a strong bond of trust between parent and child. This close, nurturing relationship fosters the self-assurance and sense of belonging that will support your child throughout their life. A parent's unwavering understanding, encouragement, and recognition leads to the inner confidence every kid needs to thrive.
3. **Laughter** adds the elements of **joy, excitement, and adventure** to your life as a family. This infusion of fun and frolic breaks up the mundane but necessary routines and obligations that rule most days. This joy also works on a deeply personal level as each member of the family is inspired to explore their individual interests, pursue their passions, and develop their talents. Parents provide each child with positive options and opportunities, as well as actively and appropriately engage in their children's activities, in order for their kids to find meaning, purpose, and direction for their lives.

4. **Learning** supplies children with the **knowledge and skills** vital for a contributing, self-sufficient life. These tangible, practical competencies include the academic, vocational, avocational, and general life skills parents directly develop in their children in order for them to feel useful, essential, and accomplished. The parent's job as coach also extends to preparing their children for formal education, as well as continually supplementing and reinforcing what is later learned in school. This broad range of educational experiences that occur both in the home and at school not only ensure a child's successful future, they also develop their crucial sense of self-efficacy.

A COMMON, CONSISTENT APPROACH THAT ALSO VALUES THE INDIVIDUAL

It is a fact that all children respond well to the consistent combination of a parent's leadership, love, laughter, and learning and that all students react favorably to teacher who is a firm, fair, fascinating facilitator. Yet even while using the same basic approach with every child, each of the Four Ls of Parenting and Four Fs of Teaching also emphasize a child's individuality:

1. The parent's **leadership** and a teacher's **firmness** influence children's courteous attitudes and cooperative actions by establishing common rules and routines for all kids to follow. Yet these adults will also periodically adjust their requirements and restrictions depending on the maturity of each child, and they will customize their discipline approaches when necessary. For example, a child who is more prone to acting out with rebellion must be handled differently than a child who tends to withdraw or retreat.

   All kids ultimately need adults who are the boss. However, this adult authority is less about control or conformity and more about fostering an atmosphere where children happily participate in established norms, cheerfully help out, and willingly stay within limits, all with the direct intention that doing one's fair share and cooperating allow nurturing, fun, and learning to prevail in the ways each child enjoys them most.
2. Thus, the **loving** parent and the **fair** teacher strive to give children what they each need at the time instead of merely treating all situations or children exactly the same, even as the amount of caring remains consistently high for all. Being on a child's side and supporting them through their successes and stumbles necessitates listening, paying attention, and truly knowing them as distinct human beings who are constantly evolving. Kids require a close, nurturing bond with adults who understand them as the special people they are.

3. Similarly, a parent uses the metaphor of **laughter** much the same as the teacher uses **fascination** to inspire the particular passions that each child expresses. Parents and teachers are delighted to see where each child's talents and interests take them. They use the power of choice, challenge, and collaboration to encourage and embolden each child to dream bigger, reach further, and aim higher—and to have a ball while doing so!
4. In addition, the parent who takes their children under their wing to expand their **learning** acts the same as the **facilitating** teacher in advancing each child's academic and practical progress. Tailored instruction, assistance, and feedback help each child to move forward, no matter from where they began or whatever may currently hinder their progress.

EMBRACING PARENTS' INDIVIDUALITY AND RESPECTING THEIR AUTONOMY

I am a staunch advocate of preserving a wide variety of parenting and teaching styles. Since we are dealing with, valuing, and actively nurturing children who are each distinct individuals, we are right to demand a wide variety of approaches that stand at the ready for when kids express specialized needs. Parents should neither look for their children's teachers to be exactly the same each year, nor should teachers look for parents or their students to be precisely alike.

You are the expert when it comes to your children, especially in terms of how you tailor this book's methods to your children's ages and maturity levels. No single book can be all things to all parents in every conceivable situation, but the Four Ls of Parenting are solid enough to endure and adaptable enough to grow along with all of your children, all at your discretion.

If anything needs to be changed or added to the ways you already parent your children, it will be because you made that informed decision for yourself. Providing your children with a steady stream of leadership, love, laughter, and learning is not some parent "program" requiring rigid fidelity. Instead, it is a structure onto which you can hang the best of what you have to offer your kids and a guidepost to which to return when you yourself need bearing and re-inspiration.

The main tenets of effective parenting and teaching are fluidity, flexibility, and faith in one's personal consideration, and you should never settle for anything less as the captain of your home. Parents do not need to feel any more pressure than they already unduly place upon themselves or any more judgment than others unjustly place upon them.

Even so, basic uniformity and broad consensus are also necessary because these commonalities provide adults with sound direction and commonsense goals. We can all agree to disagree on the fine details, but what parent or teacher does not long for cooperation and respect from children? What parent does not yearn for a supportive bond of trust and close communication with the kids they care about? What teacher does not dream of kids finding their own meaning, direction, and joy in their lives? Both parents and teachers have high expectations for every child's capable and contented life in and out of school.

If it is easy to agree on these four integral tenets of rearing and educating kids, then it is crucial that each of these powerful motivators be given equal emphasis. Neither leadership nor love nor laughter nor learning is any more or less important than any of the other three when it comes to preparing kids for a full and rich life. In fact, all adults will maximize their beneficial impact on children when all four avenues of influence are used consistently and concurrently.

ENJOYING THE RIDE

This book, just like any honest parent or teacher will tell you, will never claim that meeting the needs of children and inspiring them toward success is easy or simple. Yet, at its core and if approached in a strategic way, *being an effective adult for kids is not nearly as impossible or as complicated as it may sometimes seem*—not for parents and not for teachers.

This book will allay any possible fears of failure or of not measuring up because it is all about restoring parental confidence through increased clarity and strengthened capability. There is plenty of room for the mistakes we adults will make with children—over and over again. There is room as well for kids to shock, disappoint, and scare us along the way. Dealing with children is nothing if not a rollercoaster ride from which it seems you can never get off.

However, this journey will also be exhilarating, pleasantly surprising, and even self-affirming as you ride out the highs and lows right beside your child—at times with you both clutching each other in solidarity, other times with each of you closing your eyes in solitary dread, but more often holding each other's hands high in spectacular thrill and soaring triumph. Parenting or teaching will never be boring or predictable, but this book will significantly lessen the insidious worry and doubt we all go through while trying to give children our very best.

Therefore, parents and teachers now need to collectively harness our sway over our children and be fundamentally the same in the ways we motivate them. You will find our common goals and methods refreshing, comforting, and empowering as we realize we all truly are in this together!

Part I

GAINING PERSPECTIVE

Chapter 1

Motivation Is Always the Answer

Common teacher complaints about their students, voiced mostly in private exasperation to their colleagues at school and to their significant others at home, are as follows:

- "He just can't keep his mouth shut."
- "She won't ever address me in a respectful manner."
- "He is constantly distracted and can't pay attention."
- "She never volunteers and won't even try."
- "He just can't be bothered and couldn't care less."
- "She won't take anything seriously and just counts the minutes until the bell rings."
- "He is so smart, but he can't pass my class."
- "She won't do any work."

Whether or not the parents themselves are also privy to these teacher concerns—even when expressed a bit more diplomatically—the fact remains that "can't" and "won't" must quickly be changed into "can" and "will." The unhappy alternative is defeated teachers, disappointed parents, and dysfunctional children who cheat themselves and others out of a valuable and validating school experience.

What do we mean anyway when we say a child "can't" do something? Do we mean that this kid does not yet possess the academic skills to accomplish a certain task? If so, it is the teacher's job as a facilitator to sharpen those skills as much as they can. More often, however, the fact is this child can certainly do what the teacher has asked—and at the very least, all kids can try. It is just that this kid *refuses* to do it or to make even the slightest attempt. Right then. Right there. For that particular teacher.

Know this from the start: Children can turn cooperative, courteous behavior on and off like a faucet. Are there special needs children who may be exceptions to this rule? Sure, but only to varying degrees. No matter what an Individual Education Plan may state or leave out, there is always capacity for progressive, often impressive, growth in every child.

"Never" and "impossible" are not words that Four Ls parents and Four Fs teachers give credence to because they know that daily doses of leadership, love, laughter, and learning are precisely what all children need to maximize their potential. Furthermore, each individual's potentiality must always be approached with boundless ambition, high hopes, and expansive expectations! These parents and teachers begin with this anticipation for advancement and eagerly await marked improvement for every child because they are certain that the kids they care for are regularly receiving from them what all children need most in order to succeed.

Therefore, in the vast majority of situations, by and large, for the most part, more often than one would expect, and even in the most difficult of cases, kids are perfectly capable of doing whatever, sometimes even more than, what their teachers ask them—be it concerning behavior, attitude, peer interaction, participation, focus, engagement, effort, or achievement. Along the way and if need be, expectations can be adjusted, and interventions can be added or intensified; but as long as adult effort and attention always remain consistent and comprehensive, children will inevitably rise to the occasion.

THE POWER OF PERSUASION

Of course, motivation is the only truly dependable resource parents and teachers can use to get children to do what ultimately is in their own best interests, especially with the kids who up until now have not been buying what their parents and teachers are selling. Motivation is the answer because the end goal is for children to progressively motivate *themselves* so that during those times when they are beyond our supervision, we can realistically expect that they will make their own wise choices more often than not.

By persistently meeting children's essential needs, we are constantly teaching them that these are the needs they themselves must attend to first—*before* merely indulging in what they may think they want in the moment—because these are the things that will truly protect, comfort, satisfy, and sustain them. All the rest pales in comparison. It is not that all the rest is inherently dangerous or bad, but the sooner kids see in practice that what you have to offer is equally as good and is often better than what they presume to desire, the sooner that they can seek these wonderful enticements all on their own.

The following examples are but a few select ways proper adult influence through the Four Ls of Parenting and the Four Fs of Teaching transform children.

- **The persuasion of leadership and firmness:** Once children realize that the feelings of reassuring stability and soothing safety trump those of wanton risk or precarious thrill, they begin to make saner decisions for themselves. Especially when adventure and excitement are regularly featured in your laughter-filled home and in their fascinating classrooms, kids are not nearly so desperate or tempted to throw caution to the wind when alone or with their peers.
- **The motivation of love and fairness:** Once kids internalize that trust, independence, and privacy are earned and then enthusiastically granted, they more often factor in their parents' and teacher's needs into their own. They begin to see that pleasing themselves and pleasing their parents and teachers do not have to be mutually exclusive. This give-and-take and win-win attitude teaches children the rewards brought by their patience, openness, reliability, and consideration.
- **The inspiration of laughter and fascination:** Once children embrace that their personal joy and fulfillment are just as important to their parents and teachers as they are to themselves, they are more willing to pursue passions that move them forward in positive and productive ways. They are also more willing to cooperate with your leadership and to act responsibly when they know that they will be recognized and rewarded for doing so.
- **The impact of learning and facilitation:** Once children accept that all forms of education directly influence not only their future success but their current feelings of self-efficacy, they are more prone to put forth the requisite effort and attention to the tasks and skills adults are constantly telling them are important. They soon realize that hard work and persistence are gratifying in and of themselves, especially as the validation of private pride dances with glory of public honor.

Thus, parents and teachers should expect increased improvement for every child, no matter their current challenges or present accomplishments. Of course, such positive, progressive growth will only happen with proper adult influence, plenty of time, and the appropriate responses from the kids themselves, the details of which will be explained throughout this book.

POSITIVE RESULTS WITH CERTAIN TEACHERS BUT NOT WITH OTHERS

It is instructive to revisit this question: *Why would the same child perform positively in one class with one teacher but perform poorly with another?*

Whether this disparity is between elementary teachers from one school year to another or between class periods with different teachers in a single year of secondary school, what is the deciding factor between student success and failure? Does one teacher simply have a "magic touch" that another does not? This variation in outcomes goes much deeper than a child simply being interested in or naturally good at one subject over another. Who or what is actively driving certain children toward satisfaction and advancement?

IN MY CLASSROOM: PLEASANT PARENT CONFERENCES

I began to figure out this difference in student outcomes during parent conferences. After my tenth year of teaching, all I could tell the majority of my students' parents was that their child was a delight and that I had bright expectations for their child's future. Imagine what a pleasure those encounters were for me, the parent, and the student!

Yet, so much of the time the parent would look at me incredulously and remark, "Are you serious? *My son*? I just came from meeting with four of his other teachers who said he was a nightmare in their classes. That's what all his teachers have ever said about my son. He is failing every class but yours."

I then would assure them that their son indeed was a respectful, hard-working gentleman for me during a two-hour block of English, while his other teachers only had the pleasure of his company for one hour. I also would emphasize to the parent, as well as to the student, that there was no reason why he could not behave in every class, every day, and that both the parent and the child should settle for nothing less—and oh, so much more!

WHO IS TO BLAME: THE TEACHER OR THE STUDENT?

The tendency to place blame and find fault so often distracts us from working toward finding a solution. Nonetheless, you may be asking yourself, "When there are serious management, participation, engagement, or achievement issues with the exact same students in one teacher's classroom but not in another's, who is to blame: the teacher or the students?"

Here are two perspectives: On one hand, that ineffective teacher is to blame because clearly the students can be motivated toward positivity and productivity because the exact same children do so in another effective teacher's class every day. That unsuccessful teacher is at fault for not finding the means to initiate and maintain agreeable behavior and academic accomplishment. On the other hand, the students are to blame because there is no excuse for them not to behave or to accomplish when they clearly can and do so elsewhere.

Oh, we can try to help. We can appeal to the child's stake in their own learning, and you may have found yourself having some of the same conversations with your children as their teachers have: "It only hurts you, not your teacher, and does nothing to help your future when you choose to misbehave or to be lazy."

Or we can appeal to their better nature: "There is simply never an excuse for misbehavior or inattention. Even if you *think* your teacher is bad, weak, new, or doesn't care, you obviously know better and therefore should do better."

Yet savvy teachers do not make such pleas to their Jekyll and Hyde-like students because it is futile. Kids only behave when they want to or when they are directly motivated to do so—right then and there. Appealing to some higher moral order or to some far off future never works with adolescents who are only concerned with *now*. Impulse control unfortunately is one of the very last phases of brain development. The bottom line is: When the opportunity for misbehavior, sloth, or inattention is allowed to exist, even the "best" of kids will seize upon it.

The solution then, of course, is for teachers to very strategically veer their students toward much more efficient and advantageous ends and to do so on four very intentional fronts. Hence, the firm, fair, fascinating facilitator was born. For if a teacher's students' brains are still developing in their capacity to self-regulate, then in the meantime, their wise and experienced teachers will just have to act as their students' surrogate prefrontal cortexes!

In other words, if students sometimes make decisions that ultimately are not in their own or others' best interests, then the teacher must find a way to guide them to make better decisions that in fact are equally and ultimately as satisfying to them as acting on their own whims. This is a crucial lesson children learn directly from their parents' and teachers' daily motivating actions rather than from mere words—and without which, kids will not learn much else.

IN MY CLASSROOM: THE HONORS INFLUENCE

As a further example of how the vast majority of children are perfectly able to control themselves and can be motivated to perform more beneficially, consider the following: A few times when I have reached my limit with a kid who has proven himself a class destroyer who constantly instigates bad behavior in his classmates, I have conducted an experiment where I have bent the rules a little bit.

I call the boy's parents and ask for their permission to temporarily move him into my honors English class. I explain, "Let us see how your son acts when he is away from his friends and surrounded by positive peer role models, both in terms of behavior and scholarship."

The parents are always eager to see the results of my plan! I then arrange for a simple switch of only two of this boy's classes, one of which is with another one of his current teachers who has agreed to our crafty investigation. All his teachers remain the same; just two of his class periods are swapped. I also inform the counselor of our temporary, "off the record" move.

What has always ended up happening is that once I make this class change, this kid with whom I had yet to make any headway instantly is put off guard and unsure just how to act now that he is out of his comfort zone and in a completely foreign environment—even though it is the same classroom with the same teacher as before!

This kid just as quickly abandons his disruptive behavior while in this new class period. He intuitively knows that these honors students not only will be completely unresponsive to his antics, they will look down upon him for his base behavior. Suddenly, he is offered no clout or cheers from his classmates for being uncooperative or a clown. Oh, he still acts like the same old knucklehead everywhere else on campus, but not in this new, constructive environment.

After an adjustment period where he now longs *not* to be noticed as he attempts to get his bearings, this kid then actually begins to slowly match his new peers' beneficial behavior by working diligently and even sometimes daring to intelligently participate in class discussions. He is used to being a leader, but in this setting he begins putting those skills to better use. This kid who even I had thought could simply not be persuaded to behave and on whom I had been about to completely give up has proven me wrong!

However, the Four Fs have proven themselves right yet again; it was just that this particular boy needed the motivation of more positive peers, as well as his teacher. He always had the potential in him, and now that he has seen it in action he can never go back—especially not with his teachers and parents capitalizing on his progress. And once he does go back to his original class, I will have used his absence to lead those students away from being mere followers so that he reenters a class that is now acting remarkably similar to the one he just left.

This is why the classroom environment a teacher creates is so very crucial to success. Can't all teachers strive to make all of their classes perform like an "honors" class? Can't all teachers win over their students with a seductive combination of command, kindness, charisma, and clarity? Indeed, these are the very motivators that being a firm, fair, and fascinating facilitator deliver.

By the same token, this is why the home environment a parent creates is so very crucial to success. Can't all parents strive to make all of their children perform like "honors" students? Can't parents win over their kids with a similar, seductive combination of leadership, love, laughter, and learning? Indeed, this is the influence the Four Ls of Parenting delivers.

IF ONE ADULT CAN MOTIVATE A CHILD, SO CAN OTHERS

Of course, if this sort of progress can happen at school, then it can definitely happen at home. Similarly, if such cooperation and capability is already happening at home, it can certainly also happen at school. And if it is happening in one teacher's classroom, then can happen in all classrooms. By extension, we can safely state that if success is being cultivated by a single adult with one child in one room, be it a classroom or living room, then it is not only possible, it is highly probable to attain comparable favorable results with every other child in that room—every sibling and every other student.

If we accept the fact that there are many teachers out there who have found effective ways to motivate the very same kids who sleep under your roof, then it is entirely possible for any parent to also have that same sort of advantageous influence on their own children. Hence, if persuading kids to cooperate, participate, engage, and achieve can happen in one setting, then it can happen anywhere, with any kid.

By the same token, teachers must also realize that even in their most difficult to control, apathetic, uninspired, and lowest-achieving classes, some of those same kids are actually obedient, responsive, enthusiastic, and highly intelligent children while at home with their parents or while in other classes with other teachers. None of this positivity is happening by accident, of course. All of these impressive parents and teachers are *actively motivating* these supposedly unreachable, unruly kids to advantageous ends using similar means.

Therefore, it is entirely possible for every single teacher to persuade the vast majority of their students toward positivity, even in the cases when other teachers or parents of these same kids do not share such glowing results. Moreover, the potential for progressive results is always available to all teachers. The only question is if those teachers will take the necessary action to acquire the insight and strategies to turn ideals into reality. Thankfully, the philosophy of the firm, fair, fascinating facilitator is completely grounded in reality.

Similarly, every parent can steer their children toward the same desired goals, even in those cases when their children's teachers are currently not achieving those same goals. Furthermore, the potential for progressive results from all parents is at hand, and there is no question that by the end of this book you will possess the insight and assurance to turn ideals into reality because the philosophy of parents providing leadership, love, laughter, and learning for their children is also completely grounded in reality.

Thus motivating all children toward increasing attainment and contentment, with sometimes astounding results, is no longer a question of "Can I … ?" or "Can this child … ?" These questions instead simply revert back to the parents and teachers in the form of "Will I commit to thoroughly and consistently providing the kids in my care with what every child fundamentally needs so that they will all act in both their own and my best interests?" Obviously, the answer must be an enthusiastic "Yes!"

The quiet truth is that there are many parents and teachers out there who are routinely enjoying their personal triumphs with children all on their own. They have dutifully accepted that even all by themselves they still hold significant influence over kids and are thus determined to take positive action without waiting around for everyone else to get on board.

So, even if parents and teachers do not *absolutely* need each other, the fact remains that cohesion, consistency, and comprehensiveness between the home and school always produce better, more thorough, and longer lasting results. And no adult can argue with "better, more, and longer lasting" when it comes to kids to eagerly responding to their high expectations of them!

DO NOT SETTLE FOR SOMETIMES OR SOMEWHAT

Since all parents and teachers certainly have the capacity to be the agents for such glorious change in every kid, then they can also sustain and even capitalize on these breakthroughs for each individual child. We do not have to settle for temporary, sporadic, or stalled improvement with any child—especially when parents and teachers are motivating them similarly, sweepingly, and simultaneously.

With all the adults using common methods and therefore sharing similar inroads, the possibilities for all children become limitless. This is not hyperbole; it is a tremendous opportunity waiting to be seized by all. Furthermore, with patience and persistence, the benefits will be happily shared by all.

Hence, both parents and teachers must not lower their expectations one whit for any child! Be fooled no longer. Oh, that kid most definitely can behave much more cooperatively and respectfully, both at home and in every classroom. The question is: Will that child *choose* to do so?

More to the point, what environment has the teacher created from the first second of school that makes it most conducive to every student choosing not only to cooperate but to participate, engage, achieve, and even enjoy more than they ever had in any classroom before? Again, this is not hyperbole; it is the routine result of the motivating powers of a dedicated teacher who uses their firmness, fairness, fascination, and facilitation to evoke these pleasant responses in their students.

Likewise, what have the parents reinforced in the home, hopefully well before their children have even reached school age, that actively inspires their kids to perform in ways that are often automatic, entirely appropriate, and eminently enthusiastic in every setting? A child can be unique and special, but how is the rest of the world supposed to notice let alone embrace all of their captivating qualities if that child is not regularly playing by some basic rules, assiduously exhibiting common courtesy, and ardently interacting with adults and peers alike?

You see, once positive precedents are set, why would kids deviate from a norm that is not only omnipresent but deeply satisfying to them on every level? Moreover, if much the same expectations are being influenced in similar ways in the two places they spend the majority of their time, wouldn't children be highly likely to carry those attributes of respect, responsiveness, relish, and readiness into every situation—well beyond the home front and the schoolyard?

Since raising expectations for all children does not succeed in the abstract, these sensible goals must be backed by a clear path and comprehensive means of support and encouragement that both prepares and persuades kids to willingly meet and exceed those demands. This is exactly what the Four Ls of Parenting and the Four Fs of Teaching offer to our children.

THE IMPRESSIVE IMPACT OF HIGHLY EFFECTIVE ADULTS

Of course, in those unfortunate cases when, for whatever reasons, their parents or teachers may not be pulling their weight, kids suffer tremendously. They also act out accordingly in order to fill the void left by that adult. In fact, in these ultimately unacceptable and potentially damaging circumstances where certain important adults in a child's life are not fulfilling their responsibilities, we can only hope that there are conscientious parents ready to intervene and to compensate for substandard teaching or that there are diligent teachers ready to intercede and to offset poor parenting.

Leaving aside outright neglect for the moment, even simple adult passivity hurts children in significant ways. Using the irresponsibility of others as an excuse for not living up to one's own obligations is to forfeit the opportunity to be an important part of the solution. Similarly, sitting back and allowing the illusive quest for perfection to stop us from working toward measurable progress ends up moving no one forward, especially the children.

Do not ever let the enormity of a challenge prevent you from persistently trying your best. This crucial lesson in responsibility and commitment is one adults must convey to kids, so it is one we adults all must learn now and take to heart.

In addition, cultivating the drive, perseverance, and self-confidence for kids to not only carry on but to thrive in spite of the obstacles and inequities that are bound to get in their way is something all parents and teachers must strive to instill in children. This is not easy, however, because children are essentially followers by nature.

No matter how much they may fight us or seem not to listen, all kids look to take their marching orders from the adults in their lives. Children pick up cues for how to conduct themselves based on the explicit and implicit messages adults are constantly sending them, whether or not adults are actually conscious of their impact, both positive and negative. This is why clear intention and careful strategy are so important in properly leading and nurturing kids.

The myriad accounts of even one caring adult who singlehandedly altered the course of a needy or neglected child's life drive home the fact that adults do possess a tremendous power to influence kids and that all children can be resilient. When the responsibility for this potential to persuade children toward worthwhile pursuits is embraced by even one important adult in a child's life, the results are profound and plentiful. When that same responsibility is embraced by *all* of the important adults in their life, these dazzling outcomes increase exponentially!

Therefore, even though we have seen that it is possible for a solitary parent or lone teacher to independently attain remarkable outcomes with kids, this piecemeal approach is unnecessary when the methods for confident, capable parenting and teaching are attainable for all and when isolation is always inferior to collaboration. Being allies in education is indeed important, especially when we realize the "education" of children is so much more than academics alone.

Also, know that providing your children with leadership, love, laughter, and learning automatically connects with and complements the classroom. So, thinking that working in tandem with your children's teachers will somehow be an additional obligation for you to pile on to your already full plate simply is not the case. Rather, the Four Ls of Parenting and being an ally in your child's education is meant to *simplify* what is already the complex, critical, and copious job of raising children.

ALL CHILDREN NEED INTENTIONAL ADULT LEADERSHIP

Of course, if any adults are lucky enough to have within their midst some kids who are already self-motivated, their job will not be nearly as difficult as those who must attempt to positively influence, say, currently rebellious, reluctant, or retreating children. Yet even these fortunate adults, blessed with their seemingly perfect children or students, will still need to use the same four approaches all adults must rely upon in order to ensure continued advantageous outcomes with kids who routinely cooperate, communicate, invest, and achieve.

The parent or teacher who leaves it all up to chance or up to the kids themselves, even with these naturally "good" children, will inevitably be in for a surprise. One thing that is certain about children is they are unpredictable and are capable of large swings in behavior and attitude.

In a single school year, teachers sometimes see marked changes in students, both for the better and the worse. Every parent can also attest to these same kinds of dramatic, often inexplicable shifts in their children's attitudes or outcomes. This proves just how fragile and vulnerable kids are and therefore how much they need strong adult leadership. Furthermore, children need consistent monitoring so we can catch them before they fall too far. This has nothing to do with babying, overprotecting, or prying; this is the proper use of an adult's active attention and intentional intervention before a true crisis takes root.

At the same time, this propensity for sometimes swift and striking change also proves how malleable kids really are and how impressionable they are to external influences, both bad and good. While in one respect the easy susceptibility of your children may keep you awake at night, this should also come as good news to parents and teachers who need to realize that in every child there always resides a great capacity for improvement.

Even though they will not tell you so, it is as if kids are just waiting for us to mold them into the responsible yet independent, productive yet creative young adults we pray they will turn out to be. With this fundamental fact in mind, parents and teachers should be eager to exercise their tremendous power to motivate, inspire, sway, and persuade children because their impact will be profound and lasting. Moreover, we do not have to wait, wonder, or worry how kids will "turn out." Instead, we can actually do our jobs as persuasive parents and teachers and then, more often than not, remain sure and proud of the results.

Therefore, there is much a parent and teacher can do to mitigate any sudden, troubling changes in children, as well as to capitalize on any changes for the better. In fact, a major aim of this book is to provide parents with a reliable plan that smooths out much of the rough edges—if not circumvents many of them altogether—and which leaves parents with the confidence and calm in knowing that they are indeed giving their children exactly what they need.

Again, this parental assurance also feeds directly into their children's sense of security and fulfillment. This way, the kids have no reason to rebel, withdraw, or retreat in the first place—and if they do, it certainly will not be for very long or quite as severely.

In both the little and big ways, children should never be expected to parent or educate themselves. Kids must be taught responsibility and self-reliance in increasing, developmentally appropriate measure, but this book is unwavering in its demand that parents and teachers fully assume their roles as guides, mentors, muses, and coaches for all children. Kids pay too great a price for adult inconsistency, inattention, and abandonment.

At the same, time this book is steadfast in its emphasis that balance is crucial. All extremes in parenting and teaching are to be avoided. We want to actively and strategically nurture and direct all children toward increasing autonomy and independence. We neither want to merely hope for the best and essentially allow them to fend for themselves, nor should we orchestrate their every move and indulge their every impulse or urge.

Especially for all those currently unmotivated, seemingly indifferent children who we absolutely adore yet are absolutely stuck with, the persuasion must come from the adults *first*. For whatever reasons, these kids do not inwardly possess the drive or the will to do more than the bare minimum, if that, in regard to what their parents and teachers require of them—unless it happens to be something the children themselves also want in that particular moment.

Thus, the adults in these most challenging kids' lives must without hesitation step up to be the prime and powerful motivators these children require—before they turn us prematurely gray and before their bad attitudes and bad choices become bad habits! And since we are all essentially stuck with each other—parents, teachers, and children alike—we should all stick together and stick with a plan that is guaranteed to work wonders.

WANTING THE SAME THINGS

So, what is to be done? If children surely can be good, but most are not going to choose to be good all on their own, then both the parent's and the teacher's job is to make them *want* to be good. It is the adults' job to allow kids to get what they want—but to go about it so strategically so that what the children wants becomes exactly what the adults want!

See **Table 1.1: An Overview of the Four Ls of Parenting** for a broad vantage point of what it looks like to be a complete, balanced parent and how the Four Ls interact with and complement each other when supplied simultaneously.

Table 1.1 An Overview of the Four Ls of Parenting

The Four Motivators:	Leadership	Love	Laughter	Learning
The four driving forces an effective parent uses *simultaneously* in order to influence their children toward positive and productive home and classroom attitude and activity.				
By consistently using all four motivators, the parent ...	maintains order and respect by taking charge and establishing rules and routines.	exudes a warm, accepting, and caring demeanor by being supportive and understanding.	creates meaningful family activities by being dynamic and adventurous.	takes their child under their wing by being a source of guidance as knowledge and skills are passed down.
The parent's four-part responsibilities that help motivate their children.	To enforce.	To encourage.	To intrigue, excite, and entice.	To enable and enhance.
	To caution, curtail, and contain.	To coax, comfort, and congratulate.	To captivate, challenge, and provide choice.	To coach, craft, and coordinate.
	To build a home of structure, discipline, and courtesy.	To build their children up with kindness, concern, closeness, camaraderie, and celebration.	To broaden their children's horizons and to awaken and expand their children's interests and goals.	To broaden and build up their children's capabilities.
The parent's roles.	The taskmaster the boss the leader the drill sergeant the "bad cop" the alpha dog the captain.	The nurturer the cheerleader the listener the counselor the "good cop" the advocate the champion.	The muse the spark the participant the energizer the storyteller the enchanter the collaborator.	The guide the trainer the teacher the tutor the intellectual the illuminator the coach.
The parent's motivating demeanor.	Commanding, curt, and composed.	Courteous, congenial, candid, and compassionate.	Compelling and charismatic.	Clarifying, concise, calculating, and contemplative.

(*Continued*)

Table 1.1 An Overview of the Four Ls of Parenting *(Continued)*

The Four Motivators:	Leadership	Love	Laughter	Learning
	Strong, stern, and strict.	Sensitive, supportive, and sympathetic.	Stirring and satisfying.	Scholarly, savvy, and straightforward.
	Regimented and, if necessary, relentless.	Relaxed and develops a close rapport and relationship.	Riveting, relatable, and relevant.	Rigorous yet reachable.
The parent's initial goal for their children.	Compliant.	Comfortable.	Interested.	Comprehending and competent.
The parent's ultimate goal for their children.	*Self*-correcting and cooperative.	Confident.	Invested.	Capable and clever.
Children eventually realize: *I count, I am important, and I matter because my parent is …*	*conscientious enough to make me and my siblings act responsibly and respectfully. I feel focused and freed up so I can enjoy playing, participating, and producing worthwhile projects.*	*caring enough to really know who I am. They notice when I need reassurance, when I try, and when I need help. I feel emboldened because I am included and valued in this family.*	*cool and creative enough to find different ways to keep me engaged with what we do as a family and what personally interests me. I feel inspired and exhilarated. I find purpose, direction, and meaning in my life.*	*clear and calm enough so I can actually do what they teach me. I feel empowered and intelligent because they let me take over when I am ready to prove I have learned something useful.*
The parent builds up their children's sense of:	Self-control.	Self-esteem.	Self-expression.	Self-efficacy.
How? (by either focusing in or drawing out)	By focusing my children in with my consistency and my confidence.	By drawing my children out of their defensive or apprehensive shells with acknowledgment and appreciation.	By drawing my children out with anticipation, animation, and adventure.	By focusing my children in with access to mastering significant life and academic skills.

Rationale:	So their behavior does not jeopardize anyone's safety and does not disturb the serenity of our home.	So they feel noticed and are commended as a vital member of our family and as the unique young people they each are.	So the crucial need for personal meaning and practicality is cultivated within each child as they explore their talents and passions.	So they feel prepared and skilled to accomplish the tasks that school and life will present to them.
Children's possible negative self-beliefs:	*I'm a bad kid.* *I always get in trouble.* *I can't control myself.*	*I'm shy.* *What I have to say is not correct or important.* *No one gets me.*	*I'm lazy.* *I'm always bored.* *I can't pay attention.* *I don't care about anything.*	*I'm stupid.* *I can't understand or do this.* *I am a failure.*
The negative messages above that children may repeat to themselves or to others may begin as excuses for bad behavior and may even be reinforced by peers who hold the same negative self-images. Over time and left unchecked, however, these mere excuses may become internalized and become a belief system that children hold about their home and school life. Why wouldn't kids begin to believe that they are bad, shy, bored, or incompetent if their parents or teachers have allowed them to repeatedly rebel, withdraw, disengage, and/or fail? Belief begets behavior and vice versa. These negative patterns are reinforced when even the adults in their life may be labeling these kids as "out of control, passive, apathetic, slow, or low."				
How an ineffective parent can exacerbate a child's negative mindset and behavior.	A lack of leadership leads to their children acting up and acting out because no limits are set or are consistently enforced.	A lack of true love leads to kids withdrawing and hiding because there is little recognition or listening, all of which indicates the parent does not care enough.	A lack of laughter leads to their children disengaging because their life has little meaning, choice, joy, or usefulness. The parent has fallen short as a collaborator.	A lack of learning leads to constant crisis when it comes to chores, homework, due dates, and report cards.
Children's negative attitudes that a parent must try to counteract:	"I don't have to …"	"I shouldn't …"	"I don't want to …"	"I can't …"

(*Continued*)

Table 1.1 An Overview of the Four Ls of Parenting *(Continued)*

The Four Motivators:	Leadership	Love	Laughter	Learning
In order to steer children toward positivity, their negative mindset …	Becomes: **"I must …"**	Becomes: **"I should …"**	Becomes: **"I want to …"**	Becomes: **"I can …"**
This positive change occurs due to their children's new rationale:	*Because my strong and committed parent will make me do what they require since it is for my own and the family's good.*	*Because my parent has earned my trust, so there is nothing to lose and everything to gain by interacting, communicating, and sharing with them.*	*Because my parent has made this family and my life mean something to me through choice, creativity, and challenge.*	*Because my parent has made what I need to know understandable and doable because everything is clear and connected.*

Because the children of a parent who provides leadership, love, laughter, and learning at home and the students in a firm, fair, fascinating facilitator's classroom are constantly motivated by thoughts of: "I must, I should, I want to, and I can …" these children ultimately decide ***"I will …"***

Must + should + want + can = the greatest possibility parents *will* get all of what they expect from their children.

Conversely, the lack of any or all of these motivators nearly ensures a child will decide *"I won't …"* Thus, consistent and comprehensive motivation is key to success.

Chapter 2

The Parent's Perspective

In our quest to confirm that parents and teachers share similar goals and desires for the children for whom they both share responsibility and devotion, it is informative to first explore the elemental needs of all people, adults and kids alike.

THE FOUR UNIVERSAL HUMAN NEEDS

A short list of universal human needs would include the following:

1. **Physical and psychological needs:** safety, shelter, sustenance, security, routine, structure, predictability, stability, and health.
2. **Emotional and nurturing needs:** hope, positivity, trust, belonging, relationships, respect, attention, involvement, recognition, encouragement, support, caring, concern, acceptance, and understanding.
3. **Soulful and aspirational needs:** autonomy, individuality, control, choice, creativity, ambition, meaning, excitement, adventure, change, challenge, purpose, and direction.
4. **Intellectual and capability needs:** knowledge and skills, as well as the ability to be productive, to function independently, and to contribute effectively and essentially.

Every person has a longing and a basic human right to have these needs met. Needs, wants, desires, wishes, and dreams: These are the foundations of motivation, and motivation is the driving force behind all actions. The best way to get anyone to do something is when it will meet one of their needs.

Sure, it is wonderful when we act selflessly or delay our own gratification, but such altruism and patience are virtues that responsible adult role models cultivate in children over time. Parents and teachers should also foster in children a sense of compassion for others, as well as help them appreciate that the fruits of one's labor may not be reaped immediately and often not until much later. While the adults toil in these noble pursuits, they would be wise to also meet children's elemental needs now so that kids will be the most inclined to do what the adults in their lives ask of them—right now!

THE REASONS WHY PEOPLE CHOOSE TO HAVE CHILDREN

The predominant desires that parents everywhere have for their children basically fall into each of the categories of the Four Universal Human Needs outlined above. In fact, the main reasons why adults decide to have children in the first place, why they commit to raising and nurturing them for at least the first eighteen years, why they endeavor to remain close and involved throughout that child's adult life (including forming relationships with future in-laws and grandchildren), and why they even decide to perhaps have more children is because *all parents want to be the primary providers of these universal needs for another human being*.

Belonging is perhaps the need we all crave most because we are social creatures who depend upon and find fulfillment from each other. As human beings, relationships play a significant role in our lives. Sometimes people seek to find belonging from another in order to feel connected, complete, and relevant. Children certainly look to their parents and teachers for those vital feelings of inclusion, acceptance, and worth.

Other times, people seek less to receive belonging from another and more to furnish belonging to others in order to feel necessary, contributing, and important within themselves. Parents and teachers naturally find intrinsic value and deep satisfaction in giving graciously to children. They know being responsible for a child will be hard work, but they also know there are rewards that await them: simple yet profound perks like the inner joy that comes from inspiring others to believe in themselves, the delight in helping others to grow, and the gratification reaped from playing a significant role in the happiness and success of another.

Therefore, if at its most fundamental core, all parents want to protect, support, inspire, and teach their kids, then they must find sound strategies to continually supply their beloved children with these vital necessities. Providing your children with leadership, love, laughter, and learning is exactly the way to be sure you are meeting your children's most essential needs. Concurrently, if your children's teachers are firm, fair, fascinating facilitators, you can rest easy that this wraparound effect is creating a seamless, supportive bridge between home and school.

HOW PARENTS AND TEACHERS MEET THE UNIVERSAL NEEDS OF CHILDREN

1. A child's **physical and psychological needs** are provided by parents in their **leadership** role and by a teacher's role in **firmness**. Firm leadership implies confidence, command, and control. All kids inwardly look to adults to be in charge because this ensures safety, order, and stability. The soothing effects of certainty, structure, and consistency on a child are essential, and the importance of adult authority should never be underestimated.
2. A child's **emotional and nurturing needs** are supplied by parents in their **loving** role and by a teacher's role in **fairness**. Love and fairness immediately evoke comforting thoughts of support and acceptance, which give kids confidence and courage.
3. A child's **soulful and aspirational needs** are furnished by parents by their **laughter** and by a teacher's **fascination**. Laughter and fascination connote joy, excitement, and personal fulfillment. These qualities supply a positive impetus and meaningful context by which all kids can approach their lives. Maintaining a sense of humor must also be at the forefront of parenting and teaching!
4. A child's **intellectual and capability needs** are fostered by parents providing **learning** and by a teacher's role in **facilitation**. Learning and facilitation signify that growth will be a constant priority as essential skills are developed and knowledge and wisdom are acquired. Becoming capable and contributing sets the stage for a child's future success.

It should now be abundantly clear that the Four Ls of Parenting and the Four Fs of Teaching all fit naturally into the Four Universal Human Needs and that all four aspects are equally important and interconnected. Because of this vital and complementary balance, it is also evident that each aspect must be sustained simultaneously. Parents and teachers who are supplying children with certainty and consistency, confidence and courage, catalyst and context, and capabilities and contribution—almost all at the same time—simply cannot go wrong.

Of course, there will be frequent occurrences when a child's specific needs in one or more areas require additional attention, but with only four general areas of need, it will not be difficult for a parent to pinpoint exactly where to focus their interventions. With such quick and targeted expressions of support, children should readily resume a state of contented, constructive balance. Moreover, if a child's essential needs are consistently and comprehensively met, both at home and at school, those occasions when increased attention is called for or a crisis is on the cusp of brewing will become decidedly less frequent.

WANTS VERSUS NEEDS

When parents are asked what they want for their children, their answers commonly fall into the following four categories:

1. I want my child to be **healthy**.
2. I want my child to be **confident**.
3. I want my child to be **happy**.
4. I want my child to be **successful**.

Again, notice how naturally these wants fit into the Four Universal Human Needs. The problem with defining what you want for your child, however, is that these desires exist primarily in the abstract. There is nothing at all wrong with these desires parents have for their children. Who does not want health, confidence, happiness, and success for everyone, including themselves? It is just that these wishes reside more in the passive and accidental by virtue of the fact that they do not spell out precisely how these desires for children will actually come to fruition.

It is far better to take a more active and intentional approach when you view your parental duties and desires. If you change the question from "What do to want for your children?" to "What do your children *need from you* as their parent?" your answers automatically become more concrete. Taking a concrete, active, and intentional parenting stance makes it much more likely that your fundamental desires of health, confidence, happiness, and success will really happen for your kids, as opposed to taking an approach that is merely abstract, passive, and accidental.

The best parents and teachers are continually self-reflective and self-correcting in order to maintain their high level of support for the kids they care about. However, this healthy looking inward does not entail constantly looking over their shoulders, questioning their every move, or beating themselves up. Instead, these adults are constantly clear about their intentions and actions because they do not just ask themselves what children need from them, they also define exactly *how* they can meet their goals, as well as precisely *why* those goals are important.

The following list delineates the most common parental responsibilities. It is related in terms of a typical parent's point of view and explains how and why a parent supplies each need for their children. Also, recall that among all of these items there still exists plenty of room for parents and children to express their individuality, preferences, and personal styles.

WHAT CHILDREN NEED MOST FROM THEIR PARENTS

1. **My Parental Leadership Provides My Children with Safety, Structure, and Stability**
   - My children need me to make them feel safe and healthy by tending to their basic needs of shelter and sustenance. My primary role is as their reliable protector and provider, so I will also take a proactive approach to keep my kids well by ensuring their proper nutrition, sleep habits, and exercise.
   - My children need me to shield them from as much extreme physical and psychological harm as possible by insulating them against severe danger and unnecessary pain, worry, sadness, and fear. My job is not to babyproof their entire childhood, but their home should be a soothing place of security, even among all the inevitable scrapes, sprains, and strains of youth. Falling down, getting back up, and dusting yourself off serve as necessary life lessons, so I will be comforting without being overprotective or coddling.
   - My children need me to raise them to be well-behaved and courteous by being a positive role model of the adult I want them to eventually become and by setting and maintaining high expectations of decorum. Appropriate structure, limits, and corrections make for a tranquil, happy home.
   - My children need me to create necessary household routines and to teach healthy lifestyle habits by giving them the leadership and examples needed to meet my progressive expectations of their responsibility and self-sufficiency. This sense of order, efficiency, and stability does not control or confine my children, it *frees* them to enjoy a full and functional life.
2. **My Parental Love Provides My Children with Support, Acceptance, and Confidence**
   - My children need me to be a significant, affirmative part of their lives by giving them the attention, patience, support, appreciation, and recognition they each deserve. This consideration forms a close and lasting parent–child relationship which gradually moves them from dependence to independence.

- My children need to feel an unbreakable bond of love, concern, trust, and understanding from me by evidence of the unconditional acceptance I give them as the special people they are and the unlimited potential they possess. They must know that I am always on their side and their greatest champion as evidenced by my unwavering faith and devotion.
- My children need me to guide them to become increasingly outgoing, persistent, and resilient by always believing in them (especially when their belief in themselves is faltering), by stressing the positive in every situation, and by nudging them toward perseverance. This self-confidence will see them through the rough times, even when I am not around, and it will assist them in the forming of healthy, satisfying friendships and relationships with their peers.

3. **My Parental Laughter Provides My Children with Adventure, Passion, and Purpose**
    - My children need me to add excitement to their lives by creating frequent, sometimes spontaneous, fun and interesting family activities and occasions. This diversion and family time helps them approach many aspects of everyday life with adventure, anticipation, enthusiasm, and hope.
    - My children need me to help them on their quest to find a deep sense of personal fulfillment by offering them opportunities and choices that help them investigate or try out activities that may be of interest to them. This exploration of options assists them in discovering their passions and developing their talents. I must enthusiastically share in my children's curiosities and dreams, even when they differ from my own.
    - My children need me to help them find meaning and inspiration in their lives by my active involvement in what they find pleasurable and profound. This parental participation supports them on their journey in seeing that their place in this world has a purpose and direction that increasingly becomes clearer and richer. Actively collaborating in and appropriately supporting the fascination that my children find in their daily lives is a crucial part of my positive impact as their parent.
4. **My Parental Learning Provides My Children with Abilities, Education, and Independence**
    - My children need me to actively expand their life skills by including them in practical activities they will likely be responsible for when they become adults. This close coaching and collaborating also enhances and solidifies the special, loving bond between us and provides more opportunities to praise my child not just for their compliance but for their accomplishment!
    - My children need me to be actively involved with their formal education by ensuring that they attend school daily, on time, and prepared.

Conscientious homework, studying, and reading habits must also be supervised and reinforced. This parental attention and structure give them the best chance at succeeding in college and the workplace.
- Even though a part of me always wants to feel necessary, my children need me to guide them toward independence by sometimes pushing them and by gradually letting go. This occasional testing of their skills and temporary hands-off approach allows them to increasingly become more contributing and self-sufficient, both in and out of school.

THE PARENT–CHILD AND TEACHER–STUDENT PARTNERSHIP

Parenting and teaching are at their core partnerships between the adult and the child. Would that it were true, but there is no parent or teacher magic wand that instantly produces cooperative, confident, contented, and capable kids. Children must always meet adults halfway.

For how can a parent offer guidance or comfort if a kid does not open up and let her parents in, especially when she is hurting? How can a teacher lavish a student with public praise if he refuses to volunteer or participate? How can a parent surprise or reward a child with a special activity if she rarely cooperates with the most basic of household routines? How can a teacher move a student forward academically if he never tries or completes his assignments?

Of course, the beauty of the Four Ls of Parenting and the Four Fs of Teaching is that these savvy adults do not simply wait around for kids to spontaneously show respect, initiate communication, find direction, or get good grades. Instead, they *actively and intentionally* use four very powerful motivators to entice kids to come to them. These comprehensive strategies work in eventually winning over all kids, even those who are the hardest to reach.

Nevertheless, children have to do their part and fulfill their responsibilities, too. This is especially important because the end game for all this leadership and firmness, love and fairness, laughter and fascination, and learning and facilitation is for kids to one day become fully responsible, secure, fulfilled, and accomplished independent adults.

What many fail to realize, however, is that while the adults are coaching and coaxing kids along this journey to self-sufficiency, they often need children to meet them more than halfway, sometimes 100 percent of the way. Parents need their children to be fully responsible every moment they are out of eyesight or earshot. They are counting on their kids to heed their warnings, hear the wisdom they have imparted, and head straight home whenever temptation beckons or danger nears.

Similarly, teachers fully prepare their students to be able to complete their homework and projects independently, yet they have very little control over whether their students will actually make the effort. Then when it comes to testing day, teachers are required to completely back off as they hope their students perform to the best of their current abilities—all on their own.

IN MY CLASSROOM: STUDENTS WHO MEET ME NO WAY

What can a teacher do when the breezes of ambivalence or inattention sweep in and suddenly take over a normally conscientious kid? Why is it now that this take-it-or-leave-it attitude ensues, perhaps then spreading to their classmates as the seductive scent of disregard pervades the air? How many more students can I catch endlessly staring at their split ends or fixated on their fingernail before I completely lose my mind?

More so than any outward defiance, it is my students' absentmindedness and laziness that make me feel the most defeated. To this day, I just do not get it: If a child has the wherewithal to respond to my firmness and to control himself so as not to be disruptive *and* he has to be in class anyway, why doesn't he just do the dang work instead of wasting time with mindless idleness? Why does it now completely escape his notice that he is not acting in his own best interest?

I know this kid can do the work because I have expertly facilitated the lessons that prepared the entire class for this assignment. I also know this classwork is far from pointless because as a fascinating teacher I have infused it with meaning and elements of personal choice. Furthermore, I know for a fact that this boy views me as fair and on his side because I praise him for his frequently insightful contributions to our class discussions.

Moving kids from being passive consumers to active producers, especially when asked to work independently on classwork, can be a huge challenge for teachers. Students going from full attention and participation when I am vibrantly instructing to merely counting the minutes until the bell rings or just pretending to work when I ask them to practice or produce on their own is not only frustrating, this lack of effort is often used as a reflection of *my* teaching efficacy.

Suddenly, no one cares what the students themselves were or were not contributing. They just are looking for someone to blame for low student performance, and teachers have become an easy target. Every failing grade and below-proficient test score always troubles teachers in deeply personal ways, but now teachers have to face that their career itself may be in trouble if too many below-standard, apathetic students happen to be on their class roster.

The fact is, when students do not act in their own best interests, they are also not acting in my best interest as their teacher! So the only thing I can do is to act in *both* of our own best interests and constantly come at my students from four extremely powerful angles. While the Four Fs may be no magic bullet, they are all a teacher has at their disposal in order to motivate their students, kids who at times can be very unmotivated indeed.

Motivation is so much more effective than coercion, however. Force is always limited in its usefulness and reach, while proper, persistent persuasion is unlimited in its effect and scope. Over time, motivation's range can become so broad that it can influence a child to act productively even without constant adult supervision or intervention.

As a Four Fs teacher, I persevere because I know that more often than not my drive and dedication eventually will be adopted by my students. I also know that if my students' parents were all equally as focused on the Four Ls, our collective influence would be even more pervasive, perhaps irresistible.

WHAT PARENTS NEED FROM THEIR CHILDREN

In keeping with the fact that parenting is a partnership between the adult and the child, it is important to turn around the elemental parent question, "What do my children need from me?" Now focus on what you need from your children in return. Also be specific about *how* your child can fulfill those needs and *why* those needs are actually necessary.

The following list describes the most common attitudes and actions parents need from their children and is again related in terms of a typical parent's point of view. As always, feel free to fill in any gaps you may find regarding personal needs you require from your own kids.

1. **I Need Cooperation, Respect, and Responsibility from My Children**
   - I need my children to cooperate with me by meeting my high expectations of decorum and by cheerfully carrying out the household routines I have established. This type of partnership and work ethic sets the stage for every important job they will have to complete, whether succeeding in school or in their careers or one day maintaining their own homes.
   - I need my children to obey me by listening the first time and taking my advice. I cannot keep them safe and healthy if they do not stay within the guidelines I have set.

- I need my children to respect me, especially in public, by acting as shining reflections of my conscientious parenting. This type of automatic courtesy and deference to all adults will draw others toward wanting to help and to interact with my children. Their friends' parents will want my children around, and their teachers will consider them assets in their classrooms.
- I need my children to be responsible by keeping up with their schoolwork, staying organized, and being proactive. I also need them to be responsible in the choices they make, especially when they are out of my direct supervision. This trust I have in them is part of the way I avoid babying or overprotecting them so they can progressively become more independent and self-reliant. Of course, as my constant reminders and being on top of them gradually decrease as they grow older, the more consequences I must impose if they fail to meet their obligations or if they betray my trust.

2. **I Need Communication, Trust, and Trustworthiness from My Children**
   - I need my children to communicate with me by coming to me freely and often for the little things, as well as for the big things, the things that both delight and trouble them. I will pay close attention, but I cannot read minds, so this open line of communication and honesty is the only way I can be there when my children need me.
   - I need my children to trust me by having faith that even if they do not agree with all my decisions or level of involvement, I do know best and always have their best interests at heart. This confidence that I am always on their side is necessary if I am going to truly support and advise my children, as well as assist them in progressively figuring out their own solutions to their problems and predicaments. With this trust, I can also be by their side as they work through their youthful feuds and frustrations.
   - I need my children to be reliable by following my rules, keeping their promises, and keeping up with their grades. This trustworthiness allows me to gladly grant them the increasing privacy and autonomy they crave.
3. **I Need Engagement, Investment, and Ambition from My Children**
   - I need my children to engage with the family by being equal, willing participants in making memories, creating routines, and continuing family traditions that will hold lasting meaning throughout their lives. This is what being a family is about and a large reason why I chose to have children. These synergistic experiences we share will form the special events we will cling to and reminisce about for years to come.
   - I need my children to find joy and significance beyond the family by exploring worthwhile pursuits that they find enjoyable and meaningful. I should not be the sole catalyst for their personal fulfillment or their only partner in their diversion. I can assist and participate, but I must not push

too hard, take over, or take on too much. I need to see initiative and drive come from my children themselves, not always from me.

- I need my children to show determination by working hard to attain their goals and dreams. They are allowed to change their minds, adjust their ambitions, and even to take their time. However, they must keep exploring and experimenting with positive pursuits.

4. **I Need Productivity, Effort, and Achievement from My Children**
   - I need my children to show they have learned what I have taught them by gradually mirroring my abilities, actions, and attitudes. This can only happen if I continually serve as their primary role model of constructive, charismatic adult behavior.
   - I need my children to try hard by giving their best in a variety of aspects and to continually get better so they can lead successful lives. I know that one major way my children develop self-esteem is when they see tangible progress in their self-efficacy. When they learn and do things with me and then increasingly take control of and ownership for that knowledge and those skills, their sense of pride and self-worth increases in return. Of course, none of this will happen for them if they do not make a serious attempt, so their own effort and grit are paramount.
   - I need my children to take their schoolwork and homework seriously by responsibly completing assignments on time and studying without my constant reminders and supervision. They must stay organized, plan ahead, put first things first, and manage their time. This academic achievement will be the cornerstone of how well they succeed later in life, no matter what career they may choose.

The two parental focal points of this chapter should now be clear. First, parents must be precise about what their children need most from them, as well as how and why they provide their children with these fundamental necessities. In addition, parents must actively inspire cooperation, participation, engagement, and achievement in their children so they become equal partners in their own peace and prosperity. The Four Ls are the perfect way to refine your parental game plan and to win over your children!

ADVANTAGE

A natural question parents tend to ask themselves is: *Because I want the best for my kids, what more do my children need from me besides meeting their four essential needs on a consistent, comprehensive basis?*

Oh, your children themselves can come up with a laundry list of "more" that they think they need from you. Yet if you truly are a Four Ls parent, this list will be filled almost exclusively with their *wants* rather than their actual needs, and the items on that list will be mostly material things. There is nothing wrong with kids wanting more and wishing for things, and there is nothing wrong with parents occasionally supplying their children with those things. Just be sure never to confuse a child's needs with their wants, no matter how your kids may try to manipulate you or compare you to other, more overindulgent parents.

It seems today more so than ever that parents are preoccupied with trying to give their kids every advantage. Some parents run themselves ragged and worry themselves sick trying to lavish upon their children every possible perk, position, preference, or protection. One then has to wonder how the children of an exhausted, overwhelmed, and anxious parent are really faring in this "advantageous" bargain. Could less actually be more?

What this book is primarily concentrated upon is restoring measure and balance in parenting and teaching for those adults who seek a calmer, more stable, and surer path—both for themselves and for children. The harsh but ultimately happy reality is that *kids do not need every advantage in order to lead a successful, satisfied life—not at home and not in school.* All they really need is a wealth of fundamental structure and guidance, support and reassurance, direction and purpose, and intelligence, experience, and expertise—both at home and at school.

Rearing a child is not a race, and it is not a rivalry. Similarly, teaching is not a product; it is a process. Maybe the adult world and the workplace may hold aspects of stressfully meeting deadline after deadline, endlessly proving yourself, and constantly vying to outdo others, but it does not have to be so—and each person chooses to jump on or off that hamster wheel for themselves.

Childhood, on the other hand, should never be anything like a hamster wheel. And for those parents and teachers who treat kids in such a way, even if the children are finding some success in such a relentless scramble, they need to stop and allow kids to choose their own path and their own pace.

Moreover, that success the child may be achieving must be looked at closely to determine if all that achievement is in equal balance with what each of the Four Ls seek to foster in children. Overachievers and superstars of all stripes, not just where academics are concerned, often are lacking in one or more of the other crucial components of a balanced youth, and it is up to the adults to spot and address these inadequacies. The Four Ls are a parent's rubric for healthy proportion and reassuring measure for providing their children with all that they need most.

Therefore, if a child freely chooses to compete in an arena where it is the survival of the fittest, it must be because it is *their vision* and not yours. And whenever they want to change direction, slow down, or stop completely, the parents must allow the child the freedom to do so.

What parents must understand is that even without every external "advantage," their children will still be adequately prepared to meet any future challenges, no matter how intense. Their children will even be able to confidently hold their own—no matter what the situation—but only if you have supplied them with what they truly needed from you all along: your leadership, your love, your laughter, and your learning. For how can a child go wrong armed with self-control and self-respect, self-confidence and self-assertion, self-determination and self-expression, and self-efficacy and self-resolution, all of which were actively cultivated by the important adults in their lives?

Then, if the child herself ever happens to express an eagerness to put herself in the realm of fierce competition, you will have the assurance that you have supplied her with what was always most essential for success and satisfaction. Anything else you ever give your children simply pales in comparison to the Four Ls, and any more you give your kids will eventually come to naught anyway if you neglect to constantly supply them with all of the Four Ls.

All the extra doo-dads, lessons, practicing, coaching, and classes you pay someone else handsomely for and shuttle them back and forth to, mean nothing to a child who is in reality being suffocated by all your "structure," shattered by your "support," stifled by your "spirit," and stressed by your "schooling." This book offers parents a way off of the hamster wheel without a shred of guilt or a hint of inadequacy.

Look, we all want the best for our babies. We want them to dream big. We want them to work hard and to achieve more. We want to collaborate in and enhance their aspirations and abilities. Hence, many aspects of the Four Ls of Parenting and the Four Fs of Teaching do place demands and high expectations on children, all the while seeking to maximize their potential. Just be certain that all your pushing and pressure is also always grounded in laughter, is suffused in love, and does not result in feelings of liability and loathing on your child's part.

See, even without all those "advantages" that are perhaps causing more consternation and conflict than joy and fulfillment for you, your child, and your family, there will still be room for your kids to become president, play for the NBA, colonize Mars, perform at the Met, cure cancer, or become CEO of a Fortune 500 company—*if they wish and then will it for themselves.*

And since only a select few ever reach those highest of heights, maybe your child will be just as content and just as triumphant living one part of their very full and rich life as a public defender or as a volunteer for the Special Olympics or as an amateur astronomer or as a community theater director or as a registered nurse or as a small business owner—or even as a teacher's assistant or as a foster parent. Those are noteworthy, advantageous lives, too.

Your children do not need your excessive hovering, handholding, or hounding to be happy or to get ahead. So much more they need your faith, guidance, and influence. Kids do not need an abundance of gifts, gratuities, and gadgets. They mostly need your love, consideration, and time—frequent, sustained bouts of your undivided attention and affection. All of these are the true advantages that your leadership, love, laughter, and learning lavishly and consistently bestow upon your children every day.

Therefore, your children's best advantage is *you*.

Chapter 3

The Teacher's Perspective

The other advantage every child should have in addition to a parent who supplies them with a steady stream of leadership, love, laughter, and learning is a steady stream of teachers who are firm, fair, fascinating facilitators. These four essential, motivating aspects of highly effective teachers work hand in hand with the Four Ls of Parenting. Teachers and parents such as these complement each other in every encounter they have with the kids they care for, and these positive interactions and expectations flow seamlessly from home to school and back again.

THE SCHOOL–HOME OVERLAP

Although the particulars between school and the home may differ in some respects, they certainly overlap in significant ways.

Conscientious parents want their children to be even more respectful and cooperative at school than is expected and reinforced at home because they tend to view the attitudes and actions of their kids as direct reflections of their own leadership abilities. Teachers also take very personally the conduct of their students because they often are proud of or embarrassed by how their students act when other adults are around. Sometimes it is others who judge parents and teachers based on how well-behaved their kids are. Often, however, it is parents and teachers who are judging themselves as they both seek to inspire order and obedience from children.

Parents also want children who actively participate and willingly share with them what they know, think, and believe, just as they are expected to do in school. Through their love and fairness, parents and teachers both nurture responsiveness in kids who trust them to be on their side and who come to them when they need help, both emotionally and academically.

In addition, parents want enthusiastic, engaged, and invested children who find joy and meaning in constructive activities both at home and at school. Through their laughter and fascination, parents and teachers each cultivate happy, motivated kids who are evolving as committed, creative individuals and scholars.

Finally, parents want capable, competent children who can do what is asked of them both in the real world and academically. Through their learning and facilitation, parents and teachers each create proficient, self-sufficient kids who can contribute and compete successfully.

THE MAGIC IS IN MOTIVATION

Obviously, most positive outcomes with children do not happen by accident or of their own accord. There is no "magic touch" that highly effective parents or teachers may seem to possess. It takes constant intention and attention, as well as a significant amount of action from the children in return.

If there is any magic in the Four Ls or Four Fs, it is in the motivational "spell" that is cast by an adult who knows precisely how to persuade children toward positivity and productivity. Any residual fairy dust resides in the kids themselves who are more than willing to be transformed and transfixed as they eagerly allow their fundamental needs to be met by the significant adults in their lives. So, parents and teachers are right to expect some magic and miracles from the Four Ls and Four Fs but only with respect to the potpourri of pleasant surprises that naturally come from highly effective adults who wisely nurture highly motivated children.

Of course, such thoughtful adult diligence and consistent contributions from their kids do not have to be all-consuming or chronically exhausting—not for the parents, the teachers, or the children. Instead, a sound, strategic, and balanced approach always results in adults who are far more at ease and secure while in the midst of carrying out their daily responsibilities. This newfound adult clarity, confidence, and calm is naturally just as comforting and necessary for the children as it is for the parent or teacher.

Furthermore, all this serenity and self-assurance is *doubly necessary* given the fact that we all know there will be plenty of drama, conflict, and crisis with kids—at home, in the classroom, and sometimes everywhere else in between—in even the best of situations. All the more reason, then, to have a solid basis of composure and certainty so that when these inevitable dilemmas and disasters do descend, parents and teachers can meet them with the focus and fortitude necessary to successfully ride out any storm.

Children need authority, encouragement, inspiration, *and* targeted assistance in order to become what we most hope for them—and what they most hope for themselves. They require calculated influence from the adults in their lives. Clearly, in the absence of these motivators and left to their own devices, many children stand little chance for success. Then, when the storm clouds do rain down upon the homes and classrooms of kids who are poorly parented and terribly taught, bad situations become far worse and often catastrophic.

Thus, the Four Ls and the Four Fs were specifically designed to work collaboratively between home and school and are meant to suffuse children with a consistency that provides, protects, and persuades. In fact, when these powerful motivators are viewed through the eyes of children in the next chapter, the triangle of parents, teachers, and kids will be complete, and this formidable structure will be virtually indestructible. For the moment, however, let us see things from the teacher's side.

WHAT STUDENTS NEED MOST FROM THEIR TEACHERS

The same introspection that makes a great parent also creates great teachers. Similarly, teachers must concentrate on what their students need from them, rather than merely on what teachers want for their students. In addition to this concrete and intentional approach, a teacher must also consider *how* to achieve their goals, as well as *why* those are sensible objectives in the first place. Since this chapter now takes the teacher's perspective, the following teacher needs will be expressed from a typical teacher's point of view.

1. **Teacher Firmness Provides a Safe, Secure, and Efficient Learning Environment**
   - My students need me to make them feel safe by creating and maintaining a serene learning environment. This means that as the authority figure, no other student will be allowed touch another inappropriately, take their possessions, or bully them while in my quiet, clean, and organized classroom.
   - My students need me to make them feel secure by virtue of the fact that no one will be allowed to distract them from or diminish the quality education I provide for them. This sense of capable adult protection includes them knowing that no one, neither teacher nor student, will be allowed to embarrass, tease, or humiliate them while in my supportive class community.
   - My students need me to maintain order and efficiency by creating class procedures that maximize learning and time on task. Being the captain

of my classroom means that I must establish and enforce rules, routines, and limits, as well as provide consequences for when rules are breached, because these are the ways I ensure the businesslike flow of educating thirty individuals at a time. This structure also creates a sense of soothing predictability and comforting certainty so my students are fully receptive to, focused upon, and gaining satisfaction from learning.

2. **Teacher Fairness Provides Support, Encouragement, and Recognition**
   - My students need me to support them by proving that I am on their side and a committed partner in their success in school and their development as a confident, contented child. Being fair is about creating a sense of hope and belonging so all of my students' emotional needs are being addressed. Feelings of validation, understanding, and concern from others are of primary importance to kids. Thus, I must be welcoming, friendly, nurturing, and reassuring to all of my students.
   - My students need me to encourage them by making them feel comfortable and included enough to try, to volunteer, and to take risks. As their champion, I cannot ignore these needs or I will never cultivate the necessary relationship in which my students want to participate and please me as their teacher.
   - My students need me to make them feel that they matter by recognizing and celebrating the progress they make—academically, behaviorally, and socially. I focus on and feature my students' positive choices so that this progress is reinforced and capitalized upon.
3. **Teacher Fascination Provides Engagement, Passion, and Purpose**
   - My students need my curriculum to come alive by making it interesting and exciting. Engagement is not just about fun, however. Engagement turns to real investment when I also create chances for curiosity, controversy, challenge, choice, connections, creativity, and collaboration all within the subject I teach.
   - One important aspect of motivation is creating boundaries to keep kids safe and reined in by being firm, but there is no reason why I should not (and every reason why I should) at the very same time strive to engage and interest my students by *freeing them up* to make individual decisions and to formulate opinions that are personally important to them.
   - My students need me to inspire them by providing multiple and varied opportunities for them to make and to find meaning in my class. This frequent quest for personal interest and significance allows my students to interact with my curriculum on the deepest levels and to feel a sense of ownership in what they are learning and doing.
   - My students need me to make their learning and assignments practical by infusing my lessons and assignments with import and purpose. This sense of usefulness and relevance in all they do and learn in my class

will only increase as they see connections and patterns unfolding before them and as everything consequently makes sense.

4. **Teacher Facilitation Provides Abilities, Achievement, and Independence**
    - My students need me to help them to feel smart and capable while in my class and within the curriculum I teach them by making my instruction comprehensible and accessible, even as it gets increasingly challenging and rigorous.
    - While each student works toward proficiency and beyond, my methods of scaffolding and building upon knowledge and skills, as well as differentiating my instruction to meet particular learning styles and needs, ensure that my students are progressively moving forward. I must meticulously craft my instruction so my students find many avenues that lead them to authentic, deep knowledge and necessary skills.
    - My students need me to assist them with the quality of their classwork by not only providing effective instruction but by giving them useful, formative feedback. This method of offering constructive, positive assistance gives them the greatest chance to successfully achieve when summative assessments and final projects are evaluated. Being a facilitator and coach meets my students' thirst for knowledge, skills, and productivity. *Everyone* wants to feel smart and capable, and I will give that gift to each of my students.
    - My students need me to nudge them toward academic independence by gradually allowing them to take charge of their own learning. True facilitation gives students a strong foundation while also pushing them to progressively figure things out on their own, create their own questions, explain their own responses, and provide evidence for their personal opinions.

WHAT TEACHERS NEED FROM THEIR STUDENTS

Teaching, like parenting, is a two-way street. Education is a partnership because no profound and enduring learning is going to occur without students who willingly cooperate, eagerly participate, enthusiastically invest, and diligently strive—if not for excellence, then for a minimum of consistent academic improvement. Teaching is not done in a vacuum. Knowledge and skills must be diligently attended to, absorbed by, and practiced by the students themselves.

1. **Teachers Need Cooperation, Respect, and Responsibility from Their Students**

- I need my students to adhere to my class procedures by being obedient and exercising self-control. This order maintains the physical safety and scholarly focus for all. Cooperation and compliance also create an environment where I can do my job, which is to teach, and my students can do theirs, which is to learn.
- I need my students to respect me and each other by being courteous and deferring to my authority. This decorum and positivity frees my students to take intellectual risks, to share their ideas, and to be open to finding joy and meaning in school.
- I need my students to be responsible by being prepared, punctual, and proactive. This sense of seriousness, commitment, and professionalism is the only way precious learning time is not squandered or stolen from others.

2. **Teachers Need Trust, Attention, and Participation from Their Students**
   - I need my students to be open to trusting me by increasingly embracing the fact that I am on their side and only want them to succeed. Once this faith in my abilities and intentions as a teacher is established, students cease their rebelliousness and reluctance because they realize that this is not a person to fight or to flee from. Once my students are on my side as well, their newfound openness, effort, and energy will buoy their expanding successes.
   - I need my students to be attentive and responsive to the lesson, discussion, or task at hand by maintaining focus and not allowing themselves to become distracted or passive. This concentration and active approach to learning allows them to take full advantage of the education being offered. They then reap the benefits of scholarship and commitment by learning and retaining much more than had they been uninvolved or indifferent.
   - I need my students to contribute to my class and to endeavor by volunteering and sharing their ideas freely and confidently. This eager participation comes from their faith in me and the feeling that they and their ideas matter as a vital part of our class community.
3. **Teachers Need Engagement, Investment, and Ambition from Their Students**
   - I need my students to often express enthusiasm, interest, and curiosity as proof of their engagement in my class. This student excitement proves that they are being equal and willing partners not only in their education but in finding satisfaction in school.
   - I need my students to be active and invested as they endeavor in concepts and activities that hold meaning for them on a deeply personal basis. When excitement turns to commitment, a teacher can be guaranteed

that real and lasting learning is occurring, and this sets the stage for the diligence and tenacity critical for success in life.
- I need my students to develop drive and ambition by following their passions and allowing those strong feelings to help them to be a self-starter and a person who perseveres. This sense of purpose and of constantly being on the lookout for opportunities to improve and to explore will hold them in good stead to achieve their goals and dreams.

4. **Teachers Need Effort, Analysis, and Achievement from Their Students**
   - I need my students to endeavor by sustaining effort and maintaining focus. This willingness to be an active, attentive learner is as crucial to the fruitful interaction between a teacher and student as it is to a student independently interacting with a text.
   - In addition to mere comprehension, I need my students to be analytical, logical, and sharp by delving deeply into what we are studying, by making inferences, and by thinking critically. This type of mental acuity is requisite for quick responses, as well as for more measured consideration.
   - Since it is the main reason why children are in school, I need my students to learn and to accomplish academically, often without my direct assistance. Facilitators are not mere instructors or lecturers; they strategically build up their students' skills and knowledge so that their students become independent thinkers, questioners, and learners.

PARENTS AND TEACHERS PROVIDE SIMILAR NEEDS TO CHILDREN

When viewed through the lens of the Four Universal Human Needs, the Four Ls of Parenting, and the Four Fs of Teaching, we can now easily see that what kids need from their parents and teachers, as well as what these adults need from children in return, are remarkably similar in scope! Parents can now be assured that their children's teachers are wholly committed to supplying all of their students with almost exactly what they themselves are committed to giving their own children at home.

Hence, the pernicious myth of "teacher agendas" being somehow different than what is directly best for students has been shattered once and for all. Do not fall for the ways some politicians try to pit parents and teachers against each other. Teachers (and by extension, teachers' unions) want what parents want because they both want what is the best for children. Case closed.

It is instructive for parents to have viewed these two highly delineated, complementary aspects of what should be going on in any effective classroom, both on the teacher's end and on the student's end. It does not matter in what subject or at which grade level this is all occurring because good teaching always falls into four distinct categories. Positive student behavior also always resides in these same four domains.

Teaching is one of the most demanding and important jobs anyone could have, but, just like parenting, this vital work can be done without a mountain of undue stress and with all the appropriate warmth and wonder all kids deserve. In the end, this peek behind the classroom door should demystify what really should be going on at school. This insight will help parents spot potential problems and deficiencies at the school site, as well as assist them in finding sensible solutions more readily.

IN MY CLASSROOM: THE END OF BLAME

Of course, if we indulge in the blame game, you well know that there are some teachers who often leap to blame the parents for the antics, apathy, and academic shortcomings of their students. Yet I have the advantage of the long view having been at the same school for over twenty years. I have frequently taught entire families, all the siblings and all the cousins, as well as much of the neighborhood.

Where once I gave certain parents full credit for the stellar achievements and model behavior of their child, there were times when I was forced to reconsider their parental prowess. When the younger sibling of these teacher's pets would come along years later, I could not wait to have them in my class! Yet sometimes these new students proved to be the antithesis of their prized older sibling who came before. I would privately wonder: *What happened? Where did this little terror come from?* You see, I had always assumed that great parents were always supposed to produce great kids.

Likewise, I have had too many nightmare students whose younger siblings I later greeted with dread because I figured they would be carbon copies of their challenging older siblings and would directly be influenced by the same lousy parenting. Yet very often these children ended up displaying none of their older sibling's bad habits or academic deficiencies. Some were even remarkably spectacular! Thus, they either overcame their poor parental influence or else (could it be?) their parents were not nearly as ineffective and culpable as I had once assumed.

Therefore, I now know that parents are neither entirely to blame for the worst that their children offer nor can they take full credit for the best that their children offer. Here the word "offer" is used and used twice in order to emphasize a key piece in the motivation puzzle: the willing response and input of the children themselves.

Similarly, I know that teachers cannot be held solely accountable for every single student action or outcome—negative or positive. It is all so much more complex than that, especially when you are dealing with unique human beings who possess wills and personalities that do not always mesh with what the adults in their lives require.

One aim of this book is to open up dialogue, involvement, and interaction between parents and teachers and to do so using a new perspective as to the way we view each other's roles and by taking a common approach to the way we influence the children we adore. Any former prejudices and previous less-than-pleasant or unproductive encounters between parents and teachers should be set aside as we now each view each other as the allies we must be.

Of course, some teachers and parents do already respectfully interact, inform, and advise—usually with the best of intentions—but often with mixed results. This book will attempt to ameliorate these situations as well.

TEACHERS HAVE A SERIOUS JOB TO DO

The bottom line is that great teachers are going to teach well in any situation, often in spite of any potential insufficient parenting. In fact, unless it is a case of clear cut neglect or abuse, these effective educators do not give a lot of thought as to what goes on outside their classroom door. Even though teachers sometimes endure sleepless nights worrying about their students who go home to less than ideal situations, they are more focused on what they can do to move as many students forward as possible while they are in their presence.

In fact, if need be and as pertains to the classroom, a Four Fs teacher is well equipped to mitigate or counteract the effects of poor parenting. These teachers are too busy creating and maintaining a little educational and emotional utopia for all of their students, rather than focusing on changing those parents who they may never even see or who may never see the light.

On one hand, it is no more a teacher's job to educate parents than it is a parent's job to educate teachers. These are adults, after all. They are ultimately responsible for themselves and each responsible for children in their respective domains. Yet this separation between the classroom and the living room does not have to be so, and it absolutely is the job of this book to encourage both parents and teachers to join together in ways that only make their individual jobs easier and kids' lives significantly better.

Thus, parents need to realize that highly effective teachers always do their best and will not relent until they succeed in motivating all of their students.

These teachers simply take the approach that no matter what a parent may or may not be doing at home, while in their classroom their students are going to be unwaveringly persuaded to act in four fundamental ways.

Four Fs teachers do not have time to play around. On a daily basis, they and their students have serious work to do. Oh, there will be plenty of fun and a multitude of pleasurable aspects of those teachers' classes, but their students' gratification will be derived through scholarship not silliness. An intellectual environment can be satisfying and stirring, and it is a teacher's job to instill that aura of professionalism in their students. For those kids who have never experienced the thrill and triumph of academic endeavor and accomplishment, a Four Fs teacher is determined to open their eyes and to win them over!

Know that basic compliance is always a key component in ensuring flexibility, freedom, fun, and function for all, so Four Fs teachers make sure that firmness is established in their classroom from day one. While reading the following list, however, keep in mind that classroom management is always but one-fourth of a teacher's goals and mostly a means to three other more amenable ends. From the get-go, a Four Fs teacher finds multiple ways to motivate all of their students to cooperate, participate, engage, and achieve all at the same time, and each motivator always complements and enhances the effectiveness of the other three.

THE SIMULTANEOUS EXPECTATIONS FOR STUDENTS IN A FOUR Fs CLASSROOM

1. Students will sit down, sit still, sit up, and stay silent, as well as drop any sour attitude they may bring into the teacher's orderly, respectful classroom.
2. Students will speak up, speak intelligently, and speak their minds—and these opinions and ideas will be supported by appropriate logic, evidence, and explanation.
3. Students will see the world from fresh and intriguing perspectives, seek out what is personally meaningful, and share with the world their talents, dreams, and passions.
4. Students will also sustain their focus and drive to actually learn what is being offered to them, scrutinize and think critically about what they are told to believe, and strive and succeed in ways that they never realized they could.

And these students, lucky enough to have a Four Fs teacher, will do all of this with a smile on their faces and a glow in their hearts—not because their beloved teacher forced them do these things, but because they were *motivated* to do so and because each of the Four Fs fulfilled a deep need in them that many did not know was even there. Teachers seek to broaden horizons, open doors, and expand possibilities. They are not interested educating sheep, creating robots, or reinforcing limitations, and they cannot accomplish their goals amidst chaos or carelessness.

Thus, the list above intentionally took a more hardline approach to the job of teaching in order to make it clear that neither teaching nor parenting is always about sweetness and light. Demands and expectations are vital aspects of nurturing children, and finding the correct balance of toughness and tenderness will continue to be explored throughout this book.

In addition, it bears repeating that if teachers can manifest all of this wonderful student progression without parents' help, or even in spite of some parents' hindrances, then at home parents can do the same sort of things too and with the same kids. Just imagine, though, how much more teachers could accomplish for your kids and for all children if they were not working in isolation.

RECIPROCITY

What parents should also expect is that if the Four Ls are being implemented at home, you not only will have primed your children to get the most out of what a great teacher has to offer, your kids' prior preparation as well-behaved, confident, well-rounded, capable learners will bring out the most in their teachers in return. This reciprocity cannot be overemphasized.

Teachers are at their very best when they have respectful, responsive students. Likewise, parents are at their best when their children are being courteous and conscientious. This equal, active partnership between adult and child just makes things a whole lot easier and pleasant. Consequently, these elements of effortlessness and enjoyment cause each party to gladly give each other even more!

Sure, we are the adults, and we will always give responsibly and generously, even during those times when it seems like kids are giving us nearly nothing in return. Do not be surprised, however, when the motivating powers of the Four Ls, especially when combined with the Four Fs, eventually turn parenting into the predominantly joyous endeavor it was always meant to be.

Moreover, if this book is calling for an end to teacher-bashing, then it must call for an end to parent-bashing as well. See, reciprocity works with the parent–teacher relationship too. A teacher who sees parents actively participating in and supporting their children's education is inspired to go the extra mile for people who appreciate and assist in their efforts.

Unquestionably, any dedicated teacher will teach well and give bounteously to all of their students no matter what level of parental backing they receive, but let us not pretend that feeling valued and encouraged does not embolden all people to dig a little deeper and to give a bit more. Four Fs teachers are consummate professionals, but they are human too; and they react positively to motivation just like anyone else.

Certainly, parents who happily discover that their children's teachers are as committed to and conscientious about their kid as they are will be inspired to be even more involved with those classrooms, both physically and vicariously. Therefore, finally understanding and embracing the fact that parents and teachers are each coming from the same place in terms of wanting the very best for all children will only make their newly formed alliances even stronger as the good will and common good is increasingly championed and enjoyed by all.

Chapter 4

The Child's Perspective

Now that you have viewed children's needs from a typical parent's and teacher's perspective, it is time to expand the picture by getting into the heads of the children you are raising, as well as those other kids they are interacting with and being influenced by at school. What is going on in all these kids' heads is not as baffling or even as random as it may sometimes seem! Parents and teachers can need and even demand things from children, but we are working at a disadvantage if we do not take into account what the kids themselves actually say they need.

WHAT CHILDREN SAY THEY NEED FROM THEIR PARENTS

1. **I Need Safety, Security, and Structure from My Parents**
   - I need my parents to make me feel protected, safe, and healthy, especially when I am scared, sad, worried, uncertain, and not feeling well. No one makes me feel as secure as my parents, and I rely on their special comfort when I am hurting.
   - I need my parents to convince me that they know what is best for me and that they are capable enough to intervene when I can no longer handle things myself. If I ever need rescuing or I really mess up, I need to count on my parents to come through for me.
   - I need my parents to give me a strong sense of predictability, routine, order, and guidance so I feel calm and secure. Structure and stability allow me to wake up each morning in a home where I know what to expect and what is expected of me. This certainty allows me to please

my parents instead of disappointing them. This sense of assurance also allows me to feel comfortable enough to express myself in ways I have been taught are safe and appropriate instead of acting out in ways that only anger or worry my parents.
- I need a properly stocked and dedicated homework space and an environment where I can study and read without distractions. If school is really so important, then I need a place all my own where I can concentrate and stay on top of my studies.

And Since You Asked …

- I need you to be the boss because the minute you do not act like the one in control, then I will assume that it is okay to make my own rules and to be my own leader.
- Your nagging and picking at me do not work, but I do need gentle reminders to keep me on track *before* I mess up.
- I know how to distinguish between basic needs and wanting other material things, but I do consider having my own money very important, too.
- And if I ever come to you about something I did wrong before you found out on your own, I need you to appreciate that I am trying to be responsible instead of getting just as mad as if I had not been honest in the first place!

2. **I Need Support, Attention, Recognition, and Autonomy from My Parents**
   - I need my parents to show me an unbreakable bond of love, concern, trust, and understanding—even when I really screw up or say something I do not really mean. This sense of loyalty allows me to feel secure in the knowledge that if I need advice or support, my parents will be on my side. I must be able to trust that my parents will be reliable enough to be there for me emotionally when I need them.
   - I want to always know that I am important and special and that my parents will put me *first* a lot of the time by paying real attention to me—really often. I also need my parents to be fair and to actually consider my needs and perspective, not just their own.
   - I need my parents to let me know that they are always proud of me, appreciate me, and that they notice me not only when I succeed but when I am trying or making progress. I need my parents to let me know when I please them and make them happy, not just when they are mad or let down. I need encouragement and rewards, not just criticism!
   - I need my parents to understand that as I grow up, they have to give me more independence, trust, and responsibility. But I also need them to accept that sometimes I still make mistakes and need second chances.

And Since You Asked …

- I need your patience and respect, which includes being honest with me. I usually know when you are trying to hide something anyway, so just tell me the truth. I can handle anything with your help.
- I need you to actually listen to me and try to understand my point of view when I come to you. It is not always easy for me to come to you when I am worried or have a problem, so I also need you to sense when something is wrong, even if I do not come right out and say it. Help me to communicate better!
- At the same time, I need privacy and space. I need you to trust me when I say everything is fine. Even if it really is not fine, sometimes I need to figure things out on my own or with my friends. You say you want me to be more responsible, so let me handle my own problems once in a while!
- And if I do come to you with a problem, I need to know that you won't freak out on me! You say you want me to talk to you about anything and that you are always on my side, but I need you to really mean it.

3. **I Need Excitement, Purpose, and Participation from My Parents**
   - I need my parents to provide excitement, change, and spontaneity to break up the structure, routine, and rules I know are important but that also can turn boring really fast. I want there to be times when we are more concentrated on family, fun, creativity, adventure, and collaboration than on me just following my parents' orders.
   - I need my parents to motivate and inspire me by helping me find meaning in my life. Purpose and direction are important to me as I make my way through this world, but I can't do it alone. I need my parents to help me to feel good about myself as I explore what I am talented at and what I enjoy.
   - I need my parents to be a part of the activities that interest me so I can show off and make them proud. I want my parents there alongside me or cheering me on from the crowd. I may not say so, but I also want my parents to attend school functions. Parents say school is important, but sometimes they don't act like it. If school should be my priority, then it should be my parents' priority too.

And Since You Asked …

- I do want to be part of fun family activities and traditions, but I need you not to freak out if I want to include my friends sometimes. Other times, I might just want to be with my friends or alone instead, and this does not mean you are any less important to me.
- If I come to you with some crazy idea about something new that kind of interests me, know that this openness is not always easy for me to

share and that I need encouragement, not just reasons why it's a dumb idea or a waste of money! Also, please don't be upset if what I am into may not be what you are into or what you want me to be into. This is my life, not yours.

- I need you to understand that as I discover what I like and what I am good at, I may change my mind several times. It's not the end of the world when that happens, and it doesn't mean I am a weak person or that I cannot commit to things. It just means that I am still exploring and probably onto something new. I need you to give me the time to find my way without the added pressure of feeling that I have disappointed you every time I change my mind.

4. **I Need Abilities, Education, and Assistance from My Parents**
   - I need my parents to help me to feel capable, contributing, and self-sufficient, both in and out of school, by teaching me how to do all sorts of things. I want to help out and to be included in the things my parents do because this makes me feel needed and important. If my parents can make this learning fun and even sometimes reward or pay me for my assistance or accomplishments, then all the better!
   - I need my parents to find out what I am learning in school and to reinforce it at home. They can show me or I can show them how what I learned about stories, information, and opinions relates to TV, movies, magazines, and news; how math is used all the time in real life; how science and testing theories help us understand the world; how historical events influence people and countries even today; how art is so much more than beautiful pictures; and how sports and physical fitness enhance our lives.
   - I need my parents to help me to succeed in school by giving me assistance with my homework and school projects when I need it. I also need them to stay on top of my grades and assignments so I do not fall behind.

   And Since You Asked …
   - Even though I may act as if I like everything handed to me and done for me, I need to feel productive and useful because this is the only way I truly feel good about myself.
   - If I tell you that school or homework is hard for me or that I do not understand, I need your help, not harassment!
   - I need you to be a coach and even to push me to learn the things I need to. I will probably fight you and complain, but just as often I will be enjoying the time you spend with me teaching me things, especially when we do "guy things" or "girl things" together. I also like it when you show me that girls can like "guy things" and vice versa and when you include me in those other things too.

IN MY CLASSROOM: WHAT CHILDREN THINK THEIR PARENTS NEED FROM THEM

At the beginning of each school year, I conduct a quick experiment by asking my middle school students to anonymously write down the top four things they need from their parents. These surveys are always highly instructive because they provide a window into what kids are actually thinking about their parents instead of merely relying on assumptions. (I ask what they need from their teachers as well, and those answers will be found later in this chapter.)

The list above contains my students' most consistent answers as to their parental needs, with their parents providing them with support, love, and help with homework by far being their most frequently listed necessities. After several years of doing this, I have categorized all of their answers as to which of the Four Ls categories they most likely fall under. It is always gratifying to discover that I have never received any child's listed need from their parents that did not fit nicely into one of the Four Ls. These four categories are truly comprehensive!

Also, I am always thrilled that when limited to only the top four things they need from their parents, my students almost never list any material or superficial items. This is significant because we are getting it straight from the horse's mouth here. Kids actually say they most need leadership, love, laughter, and learning from their parents, even when they usually use different words to convey these same four ideas or when their particular needs sometimes gravitate toward only one or two areas—which is a sure sign of parental imbalance in meeting all of a child's needs.

In addition, I have my students list what they think their parents need from them in return. By far, their most frequent answers are that their parents need respect, responsibility, and good grades from them. Coming in next are obedience and cooperation, including helping around the house, and working hard in order to pass classes, to graduate, and to succeed in life.

My students also write about the importance of them possessing time management skills and maintaining focus in school. Thus it should be apparent that the duties children themselves think they most need to fulfill for their parents fall mainly within the two categories of following their parents' leadership and making proper use of their learning.

On one hand, parents should be pleased to know that no matter what may happen in reality, the vast majority of kids well know that all parents expect good behavior, hard work, and academic achievement from their children. Even the children who misbehave and do not try in school inwardly know what they *should* be doing. Kids are not clueless; it is just that far too many are careless.

Therefore, it is the parents' job through the use of the Four Ls to strategically motivate their children to begin to care: to care about their conduct, to care about themselves, to care about their dreams, and to care about their education. Even though **leadership and learning** are equally vital as parent motivators, kids are definitely getting your message in these two areas.

What should also be apparent, however, is that most children are *not* getting the message in terms of your **love and laughter**. I seldom see a student write that their parents need them to have self-confidence, to communicate openly and honestly, or to feel a sense of belonging. I have just as rarely received a student response that their parents need them to find joy, meaning, or purpose in their life. Obviously, all kids want to be self-assured and satisfied, but clearly they do not think their parents highly value those two qualities in their children.

Yet kids need to realize that a parent's love and laughter not only influence them to act more responsibly and to achieve more in school but that these two motivators also make them more certain and more fulfilled. Parents can easily see how confidence and contentment can positively influence their children's behavior and grades, but how come your kids themselves may not be seeing this crucial relationship as readily?

Moreover, how come most kids are not seeing that your love, acceptance, and belief in them is equally meant for them to love, accept, and believe in *themselves*? How come they are not realizing that your inclusion of family laughter, excitement, and adventure is actually meant for them to make their *own* heroic journey toward *personal* meaning, passion, and purpose? Why are they are not getting that this joie de vivre is supposed to transfer to all aspects of their lives, every day, forever more—and even to school?

This de-emphasis or outright neglect of the importance of children believing in themselves and frequently finding personal fulfillment, even fun, concerns me greatly. What I infer from this is that kids are primarily getting the message from their parents to comply and produce. Since those two aspects of parenting and teaching, represented by leadership and learning or firmness and facilitation, compose a full fifty percent of what I absolutely believe children need from adults, I applaud parents for getting those two important messages across.

Yet is strict obedience and academic achievement the only things parents or teachers want on children's minds? I would hope not, because such "old school" goals comprise only half of the picture. And I can assure you, using merely half of a parent's or teacher's means of motivation will not get us very far and may very well end up blowing up in our faces.

Ignoring the importance of comfort and creativity in anyone's life, especially for children, is nowhere near the complete message of the Four Ls of Parenting or the Four Fs of Teaching. Oh, in many ways I would proudly define my teaching style as "old school," but our children need much more than discipline and drill, both at home and in the classroom.

Love and laughter or fairness and fascination must not be dirty little secrets that parents and teachers shy away from or hide from kids. In fact, these nurturing and inspiring motivators should be flaunted! It is crucial that adults do not ignore the touchy-feely and pie in the sky stuff. Emotions and aspirations are equally as vital as, and integral to, regimentation and rigor.

Perhaps the true messages that love and laughter are supposed to bring are not coming across to kids because too many parents do not themselves clearly see the ultimate goals of these two crucial Ls. It could also be that parents are not thoroughly providing and explicitly expressing the core tenets of love and laughter to their children nearly enough. In either case, be aware that you are depriving your kids when you neglect or downplay any of the Four Ls.

WHAT STUDENTS SAY THEY NEED FROM THEIR TEACHERS

It is equally important to reflect on what children need from their teachers. Teachers are surely going to do whatever it takes to get what they need from their students, but they will be fighting a losing battle if they ignore the essential needs of their students.

1. **I Need a Safe, Secure, and Serious Learning Environment from My Teachers**
   - Although I will not readily admit it, I need my teacher to be strong enough to make me and my classmates behave so that while I am in this class I feel physically safe (no one will touch me or take my things), emotionally safe (no one will bully or embarrass me), and academically safe (no one will be allowed to steal my education—not even me stealing it from myself).
   - At the same time, I need my teachers to treat me with respect by not being rude, barking at us, or treating us like we are babies. Respect is two-way street, and sometimes I do not give respect until I am sure the teacher has earned it.

- I need my teacher to be the leader by being organized, confident, and prepared. When I sense disorder, weakness, or neglectfulness, I will know this is not a serious learning environment, and I will act out accordingly.

And Since You Asked …

- I am not very good at focusing on schoolwork all on my own because I get easily distracted and like to talk to and play with my friends. So, I need you be the captain of your classroom who takes charge, maintains order, and is firm. That is really the only way I will behave and learn.
- And if I get up the courage to talk to you in private about a student who is bothering me, I need you to actually do something about it!

2. **I Need Support, Attention, and Recognition from My Teachers**
   - I need my teacher to be on my side by being understanding, kind, and patient. My teacher's guidance, belief, and support give me the confidence and willingness to try, to participate, and to please them.
   - I need my teacher pay attention to me by taking time to get to know me and by not allowing me to fade into the background. I need to feel like I matter in this class and that what I have to offer is important.
   - I need my teacher to notice me by telling me when I am doing right or doing better. My teacher's faith, trust, and positivity let me know that I am on the right track and that they truly care about my success.

   And Since You Asked …

   - Even though I may be shy or lazy, I often know the correct answer, and I also have important thoughts to share. So, I need your encouragement and for you to personally invite me to participate, even when it seems like I do not want to.
   - I need your moral support and to be my champion when I actually volunteer all on my own, even if my answer happens to be wrong.
   - And if I get up the courage to talk to you in private about a personal matter, I need to know that you will really listen to me and not make me feel like I am only disturbing you.
3. **I Need Passion, Purpose, and Direction from My Teachers**
   - I need my teacher to make class interesting by being enthusiastic, giving us intriguing lessons, and assigning exciting projects. My teacher's sense of humor and making learning fun inspire me to find passion and enjoyment in school.
   - I need my teacher to make what we learn and do useful by connecting it to my life and what is important to me personally. This relevance and purpose keep me engaged.
   - I need my teacher to sometimes give me freedom to learn what and how I want by allowing me to make my own choices and to show my

creativity. I also like to be challenged and the chance to work with my friends.

And Since You Asked …

- I know what you have to say is interesting to you, but there are some days when I just need a break. I will still listen respectfully and do what you tell me, but sometimes I just do not feel like giving 100 percent.
- I know I need to get along with people, but there are some students who are not nice, fool around too much, or who expect me to do all the work. So, sometimes I want to be able to make my own choices about whom I work with.
- And if I get up the courage to share with you my personal thoughts and opinions about your class, I need to know that you will accept and encourage me in my excitement and ideas. Maybe you can even collaborate with me on how I can explore my interests and viewpoints further.

4. **I Need Assistance, Explanation, and Education from My Teachers**
   - I need my teacher to make sure I "get it" by going slowly, being clear, and breaking things down into little pieces. This type of thorough explanation and review will prepare me for the next, more difficult steps.
   - I need my teacher to really teach us things by giving us knowledge and skills we will need all year long and in higher grades. I do not like my time wasted, and a real teacher takes my education seriously, even when I may not.
   - I need my teacher to help me with my work by checking that I am doing things right. I also need my teacher to stay on top of me because I might not even know that I am making a mistake. This frequent feedback is the only way I can adjust and improve.

And Since You Asked …

- I know that reading and writing are important, but those are not always the best ways for me to show you what I know or what I think. Sometimes I want to draw, create, perform, present, or build something.
- You have to know that we may never see eye to eye on this homework thing. I will give my best while I am at school, but after school I get lazy and distracted by other interests and obligations. Don't take this personally. Especially if no one is making me do schoolwork at home, I am just not going to always do it on my own.
- And if I get up the courage to ask you for help with an assignment, I need you to really coach me and to explain it until I get it. Please do not brush me off or make me feel ridiculous for asking a real question.

IN MY CLASSROOM: WHAT STUDENTS THINK THEIR TEACHERS NEED FROM THEM

Of course, I am especially eager to see my students' opinions of what they need from their teachers. Heading their lists of needs are respect, real teaching, and academic assistance. Coming in next, and all in the facilitator category, are clear instruction with lots of explanation and examples, going slowly, giving more time but less homework, and providing feedback.

A teacher's fairness is also a popular student need as evidenced by their inclusion of understanding, patience, attention, and kindness. Children clearly need to be noticed by their teachers and to be supported, both academically and emotionally.

As for what students think their teachers need from them in return, respect, good behavior, participation, attention, effort, and achievement are top on their lists. Responsibility, preparation, attendance, punctuality, and honesty are also popular. What I always find interesting is that my students do not often say they need respect from their parents, but they all demand it from their teachers! Thankfully, though, all of my students do think both parents and teachers need respect from children.

Thus, students definitely know that they must respond to their teachers' **firmness, fairness, and facilitation**. Their role as equal partners in cooperation and respect, participation and attention, and effort and achievement are well apparent to them.

What is sorely lacking and almost nonexistent in my students' responses for what their teachers need from them is in the **fascinating** component. Their own part in the purpose, passion, and meaning of school overwhelmingly escapes their notice. This is similar to children not realizing that their parent's role in laughter was crucial to their own happiness and gratification.

Though children sometimes say they need fun, excitement, and enthusiasm from their teachers, they must consider this a rare luxury because it never tops their lists of needs. It is almost as if to be engaged and invested in school were an unreasonable request, so they do not bother to ask. This troubles me on a deeply personal level because I practice what I preach, and a full twenty-five percent of my teacher persona is dedicated to making my instruction come alive in the most enchanting and profound ways possible.

Just as with parents, can it be that teachers are not getting the message across to their students that they actually want kids to find joy, satisfaction, and meaning in school, even while they also behave, participate, and work hard? Can it be as well that teachers themselves are neglecting or short-changing these vital motivators for more time dedicated to teaching to the Test? Are the arts, electives, recess, P.E., and play being replaced by more reading, writing, and math?

The good news is that parents and teachers both have the time and potential to turn things around, to establish balance, and to fully win children over by emphasizing that the whole purpose of school and life in general is to find personal fulfillment, meaning, and direction. The firmness and leadership, fairness and love, and facilitation and learning provided by teachers and parents directly complement and enhance their additional offerings of fascination and laughter, but we all clearly need to do a better job in the giggles and the glee departments.

What I guarantee you will find is that you will enjoy your kids so much more and they will enjoy you in return if you remember not to neglect the sheer joy and excitement of it all!

WE ALL ESSENTIALLY NEED THE SAME THINGS!

It should now be abundantly clear that any of the discontentment, disillusionment, or distrust between parents, teachers, and children referenced in the preface is completely unnecessary because we all essentially need the same types of things from each other. If we expect that kids will fiercely exert their independence yet inwardly yearn for limits and routine, can we as parents and teachers accommodate both needs? If kids think that they already know it all yet are secretly looking to adults for guidance, support, and approval, can parents and teachers capitalize on all of these childhood necessities?

If kids think fun is forbidden in school and that passion is pointless as far as their parents are concerned, can't we feature these motivators in all we do—especially by showing children that learning and perseverance bring myriad rewards? If kids feel pressure to achieve but are also looking for more clarity, explanation, assistance, and feedback, shouldn't we be thrilled to indulge them, even in the midst of increasing rigor and challenge?

Of course, all parties can find satisfaction because we all fundamentally require the same things in the same basic four categories. Coercion, bribery, force, and fights are unnecessary when wise persuasion and strategic influence will suffice. Armed with these insights, you will be much better prepared to meet your children's needs while, unbeknownst to them, your selfsame needs are being met as well!

Chapter 5

The Public's Perspective

Of course, we can extend our examination of elemental needs just a bit further by considering what the public in general is expecting from parents and teachers in terms of how they interact with children and develop our future citizens. The fact is that kids affect everyone they come in contact with, both positively and negatively. Since these kids will be the adults of the future, it is in everyone's best interest to see that all children receive the strong, well-rounded foundation they both require and deserve.

Therefore, the public at large has a sizable stake in how children are raised and educated, especially because their tax dollars help fund all sorts of programs that directly benefit kids. To at least some degree, society also has a right to hold parents and teachers accountable for the behavior and outcomes of the children they are responsible for. So, it is understandable that the public (which includes parents and teachers themselves) has some strong opinions about how kids should be led, nurtured, engaged, and educated.

By continuing to use the Four Ls of Parenting and the Four Fs of Teaching as broad categories, the following list of expectations are the main desires society has for parents, teachers, and schools. Also included are some of the public's possible unspoken, often self-serving, agendas.

WHAT THE PUBLIC EXPECTS FROM PARENTS AND TEACHERS

1. **Be Firm Leaders**
   - We expect parents to control their children, especially in public. We do not want someone else's kid needlessly disturbing us when we are out

and about all because the parent was being lazy or neglectful. We fully understand babies will be babies and kids will be kids—just as long as parents understand that they must responsibly supervise and effectively correct their children when necessary. A parent's job is to keep their kids in check during those times when their kids cannot or will not keep themselves in check.

- Parents need to be on top of their children so that vandalism, graffiti, theft, loitering, violence, and gang activity do not infect our neighborhoods and cities. Parental excuses like "I didn't know" or "I can't control him" are not acceptable. It is the parent's duty to raise their kids right and to do what it takes to get it right!
- The same is true for the classroom; we do not want any child to disrupt the educational environment for the rest of the class, especially when it is our own child who is trying to learn in that class, too. Teachers must actively monitor and manage their students.
- We want our schools to maintain order and to our keep children safe. As our future citizens, we expect kids to follow the rule of law and to respect authority. We want citizens who will contribute constructively and not be a detriment to society. So by all means, teachers and school staff must be firm and be in control so that bullying and harassment are prevented from harming the children who are playing by the rules and just trying to get a good education.

We Won't Admit It, But …

- Some of us also want our schools to somehow control the children who we ourselves cannot control at home. Some of us also simply want our schools to warehouse and keep "those other kids" off of the streets—but in separate schools or separate classrooms—for as much of the day as possible.

2. **Be Fair and Loving**

- We want parents to nurture their children without coddling or babying them. Love should build up confidence in kids, not make them even more dependent. In contrast, we pay a price in society for emotionally neglected and abused children. At best, these kids do not reach their full potential. At worst, they become antisocial, fall prey to corrupting influences, and may become a danger to themselves or to others.
- We want our schools to embrace diversity and to develop a strong emotional foundation that will drive children to their maximum promise. We expect all kids to get along with others, to play fairly, to dissent properly, and to cooperate even when they do not get their way. We want teachers to instill a strong work ethic in our often distracted and lazy youth. So, the adults at a school must be fair and provide each individual what s/he needs in order to mature and flourish.

We Won't Admit It, But …

- Some of us want our own children to receive individualized attention—and we are ready to lawyer-up to do it. Some of us may want rules, consequences, and equity, sometimes even zero tolerance, but we also demand second chances, exceptions, and extensions for our *own* kids. There are also some of us who want our children to attend schools with children of the same class and culture as our own, and we are loathe to interact with parents or children who are different than us.

3. **Be Fascinating and Provide Laughter**
   - We want parents to raise kids who are motivated, resilient, and fulfilled because these children grow up to innovate, to inspire others, and to be altruistic. Perseverant, philanthropic, and passionate parents inspire their kids to similarly contribute to society in fresh, positive, and crucial ways.
   - We want our schools to foster creativity, ingenuity, and the entrepreneurial spirit within our students. We expect our children to think critically and outside of the box. We also value collaboration. So, the courses, curriculum, and instruction a school offers must be engaging, relevant, and meaningful.

   We Won't Admit It, But …

   - The arts, field trips, state of the art facilities, the latest technology, and extracurricular activities are luxuries some of us demand but are willing to fund or to fundraise for only our own children in our own neighborhoods.

4. **Be Facilitating and Support Learning**
   - We want parents who raise capable kids. We need those children to become adults who not only can fulfill the duties of their job but who take pride in a job well done. We are tired of incompetent employees and lousy customer service. We also want kids who can carry on an intelligent conversation. These qualities of a strong work ethic and articulation do not seem too much to ask for because things like reliability, efficiency, eloquence, and courtesy greatly influence the quality of life and productivity for all.
   - Mostly, we want our schools to hold all students to high academic standards so they graduate from high school college- or career-ready. We expect children to attain mastery and possess world-class skills so our democracy can prosper and be propelled forward.
   - We want informed and productive citizens who will not be a burden on society but who will progressively and capably fill open positions as our workforce retires. They also must be on the cutting edge of new technologies and techniques to meet the world's changes and challenges. So, teachers, be excellent facilitators and ensure that your students actually learn and achieve at an advanced level.

We Won't Admit It, But ...

- Some of us are primarily concerned with high test scores so we can maintain our property values. We demand top grades and challenging courses in order for our children to attend the best universities. Even though we know full well that it is impossible for our colleges to accommodate every single student, some of us want what is best for our own kids, and may the most privileged person win!

PROVIDING THE BEST FOR *ALL* CHILDREN

To an increasingly startling degree, all of us involved with children—those holding the stakes, as well as those ready to burn teachers and parents at the stake—want primarily the same things and in essentially in the same four distinct ways. This fact is quite remarkable and easy to miss unless we put ourselves in each other's shoes.

We, of course, know that raising kids right is always a partnership between society, teachers, schools, parents, and children themselves. It certainly takes a village—and perhaps an entire state or nation—but this book focuses primarily on the parent and teacher as the prime motivators for children. If you are reading this book, you are already one of those responsible parents who are eager to do your fair share. Just like you would expect teachers to constantly evolve and improve, you are also conscientious enough to continually find ways you can better support your children's teachers in inspiring your kids toward success and satisfaction.

And if some selfish people want the best only for their kids or their community, then all the more reason to ensure there is a firm, fair, fascinating facilitator in every classroom in every school, rich or poor, high- or low-performing, who are meeting the needs of all the other children. Especially if some of those children have needs that are going unrecognized and unfulfilled at home, they will be ever more dependent on skillful teachers who endeavor to level the playing field for all of their students.

IN MY CLASSROOM: IN PRAISE OF THE TEACHING PROFESSION

Without fail, when I tell people who I meet that I am a teacher, they fairly gush with appreciation for my noble efforts in educating children. And this is before they even know what kind of person I am!

This automatic admiration becomes even more pronounced when I add that I teach middle school. Their compliments then turn to what courage and altruism I have for dealing with the rampant hormones of adolescents, especially as they remark about how hard it is to control kids these days. When they also find out that I have taught for over twenty years in South Los Angeles, my sainthood is all but secured.

Thus my direct experience with members of the public is always that of receiving validation for which teaching is a revered and vital profession. This frequent expression of respect and honor is very gratifying, especially when I am on the tail end of a particularly challenging day in the classroom.

This is why the teacher-bashing, scapegoating, and distrust of educators in general confuses me so. Somehow, teachers lost control of the conversation about education and became the fall guy for a job that has only grown more difficult, more scrutinized, and more constrictive, all the while having grown even more crucial than ever. As far as I can tell, teachers have not lost the allegiance and esteem of the man in the street, but politically we face a constant uphill battle to protect the few rights and privileges we still hold, let alone trying to increase the protections and prestige such an important profession commands.

Being allies in education works both ways. Parents and teachers need each other equally as much. By advocating for your teachers, you are advocating for your children. By teachers advocating for all children, they are advocating for all of us.

Chapter 6

The Concerns of Parents and Their Children

You now have an accurate and expansive view of what children and the significant adults in their lives most need. In order to complete this picture, it is beneficial to step back into each other's shoes in one last aspect, to explore the darker side of what we all do *not* need.

Parents and teachers can now easily agree on a common dedication to motivating children on four complementary and elemental fronts, but their valiant efforts can too often be undermined and stunted by worry and fear. Therefore, the best way to allow confidence to reign supreme is to confront all these concerns and apprehensions with a clarity and honesty that will begin to diffuse the negative and allow the positive to shine through.

Beginning at home with the parents and their children, let us explore the following questions:

- What *don't* parents and their children need?
- What are their main worries and doubts?
- What are the concerns that place parents and children at odds or that create distance and disengagement between them?
- How many parents do you know who feel disconnected from their kids?
- How many parents do you see who repeatedly make what seem to be painfully obvious mistakes when interacting with their children?
- How many kids do you know who go home to a place that does not fulfill their needs, or worse, causes them damage or strife?

KEEPING UP WITH THE JONESES

Parents chronically comparing themselves to other parents or comparing their children to other children sucks the joy out of what should be a journey of love and an adventure in evolution. Parents consumed by, and acting out of, anxiety do not do themselves or their children any good, either.

Although competiveness is sometimes at play, most parents are not consciously trying to outdo or beat out other parents in a contest that necessitates winners and losers. Instead, parents are commonly acting out of worry for their children in order to give them the very best. These frequent parental apprehensions include the following:

- Fears of their children somehow not keeping up or falling behind (as if all children must strictly adhere to a set timeline that dictates every advancement and skill);
- Fears of falling short as a parent because of some regrettable mistake, no matter how naive or well-intentioned (as if not meeting marks on this arbitrary timeline dooms their children to irreversible adversity);
- Fears of forgetting or overlooking something presumably vital (as if not being adequately obsessed with what every other mommy, daddy, and kiddy is doing on this almighty timeline will result in some sort of irreversible omission and disastrous deprivation).

This parental path of anxiety is not a journey of love or an adventure in evolution. Rather, such an emphasis on worry and comparison is crushing many parents and constricting their children, and teachers today routinely field the questions of these frantic parents. Look, there are elements of anxiety, competition, and comparing in teaching as well. Yet all these petty and often selfish distractions only divert our attention from the real goal of cheerfully supporting children on their own journeys of self-expression, independence, and wisdom. There is no joy in fear and no laughter in worry—not for parents, teachers, or children.

For many parents, conventional wisdom and sage advice has been supplanted by a rigid dogma and the notion that if it seems like everyone else is doing something, it must not only be right, but I had better do it too—and fast! This seeming strength in numbers is usually nothing more than a form of collective overreacting. Do not play into the misguided idea that if "more" always must be better, then anything less is tantamount to an invitation to calamity. "More" often is not better, and "less" may be exactly what is appropriate.

As for mistakes and omissions, these are simply part of the growing process for parents, teachers, and children alike. If viewed as an opportunity to learn and grow, mistakes can be accepted as natural parts of development and progress. Teachers improve from year to year, sometimes from class period to class period, and very often based on their own mistakes.

The key is to self-reflect, adjust accordingly, and keep moving forward. This is an important, ongoing life skill you want your children to learn, so it is important for adults to model for kids how one moves past disappointment, mistakes, and setbacks with their head held high and their eyes on the prize.

The Quest for College

Today's overriding parental dread is that they somehow are not giving and doing *enough* for their child to succeed and to get ahead. Thus one must ask: Get ahead of who or what? And why must everything be a race or a contest?

If you think parenting is only about one "L," meaning learning, you are denying your children three-fourths of what they truly need from you. And many parents who put learning first and foremost are not even being truthful about this lopsided approach to raising children. Those parents do not really value learning; they merely value grades, transcripts, and acceptance to their first choice of colleges.

A great education should be an end in itself, not merely a gateway to a top university. Even though there is nothing inherently wrong with striving for a spot in a prestigious college—if that is what the child himself indeed wants—this quest is rarely a prerequisite for landing a plum job or leading a fulfilling life. College is important for many individuals and on many levels, but know that kids can get a fantastic education and make the right connections in many academic settings, including community colleges and technical and trade schools.

Giving Your Children Just Enough

The fear of not doing enough has overtaken the parental fear of the past that doing *too much* for your children or spoiling them ruins them in the short and in the long run. Of course, both approaches are counterproductive extremes in parenting, and this book seeks to provide parents with some much-needed perspective and balance.

In fact, a parent's consistent attention to the Four Ls guarantees they will always give their children *just enough*. If their children ever need more, and they may, you will also know precisely where to temporarily increase your attention. Moreover, this equilibrium will finally absolve you of some of the parental guilt that may be consuming you, allay your anxiety about overindulgence and over-parenting, alleviate your concerns of inadequacy and incompetency, and most of all, allow you to enjoy the fruits of your labor (pun intended) and the time you are privileged to spend with your children.

PARENTS' COMMON CONCERNS

The main worries of parents fall within the four essential parenting components of providing leadership, love, laughter, and learning for their children. This should not be surprising given the fact that the Four Ls are designed to supply parents and their children with their most essential needs, and when any or all of those needs are ignored or overemphasized, distress is ushered into this imbalance.

Parents who worry about or find themselves currently in the midst of the following upsetting scenarios dwell too often in these dark places of dread, discord, and discontentment precisely because they do not have a consistent, comprehensive parenting plan that ensures confidence and calm. Thankfully, dedication to each of the Four Ls is the quickest way out of such dismay and disharmony.

Of course, every conscientious adult worries to some degree. However, use the following list of potential parental fears to begin to let go of what you cannot control and to allow your steady supply of the Four Ls to give you more control over the things you can.

1. **I may worry that my parental gift of leadership will be ignored:**
   - I am concerned that despite my greatest effort, dedication, and caring, my children will be a chronic source of embarrassment and frustration for me, both publically and privately, because they do not listen to what I say or show me adequate respect.
   - I worry that repeating myself, raising my voice, and threatening will have no effect on my kids but will increasingly stress me out. I do not want to constantly nag, but I do not know what else to do when my kids will not cooperate or comply. I seem to be getting louder and more severe with my punishments because the softer and gentler stuff just does not work, yet getting tougher just causes more resentment without better results.
   - Mostly, I am worried that I will either be too hard or too easy on my kids and that both my children and I will end up paying for these two extremes. Will I ever strike the right balance between being a leader and being loose so that my children can follow me yet feel independent all at the same time?
2. **I may worry that my parental gift of love will go unrecognized:**
   - I am concerned that despite my greatest effort, dedication, and caring, my children will not come to me when they are confused, hurting, or in danger. They will hold in their pain and fend for themselves or turn to their peers for advice that, though well-intentioned, may not be safe or sound.

- I am also concerned that some of their peers may be bad influences on my children and that these "friends" will hold more sway over my children than I do. I also worry about bullies who could destroy my children's self-worth and make them chronically miserable.
- I worry that either by giving my children their own space and privacy or by constantly prying and picking at them to open up, both approaches will backfire. When does protection and concern become over-protection and fretting? When do I allow them to make their own decisions and fight their own battles, and when do I intervene? Will I ever strike the right balance between love and letting go so that my children feel close to but not smothered by me?

3. **I may worry that my parental gift of laughter will be dismissed:**
   - I am concerned that despite my greatest effort, dedication, and caring, my children will end up as directionless, apathetic kids who find no interest or joy in the things I think they should. Instead, they will waste time in trivial and shallow pursuits that do not develop their character or talents in any meaningful way.
   - I am concerned that I overindulge and spoil my kids by giving them too many material things, often without regard to how they fulfill their responsibilities at home and school.
   - I worry that either by allowing my children to be who they want or pushing them in pursuits that they only complain about will both result in them further turning to petty distractions as a means of escape. Will I ever strike the right balance between laughter and *laissez-faire* so my children can blossom and grow in productive, meaningful ways but also in ways they find personally meaningful?
4. **I may worry that my parental gift of learning will be ineffective:**
   - I am concerned that despite my greatest effort, dedication, and caring, my children will not realize their potential in school or in the life skills I try to instill in them. Putting behavior aside, I am worried that their lack of effort and initiative in and out of school will become a bad habit. Then, their classwork, homework, and household routines will also be a constant source of concern and battle.
   - I am obsessed with finding the right school and best teachers for my children. Even when I finally make my choice, I worry that my children will not be admitted, the school will be full, or we will not be able to afford the tuition or to live in the proper neighborhood. I am also concerned that even if my children and I do everything right, they still may not get accepted to a prestigious college.
   - I worry that whether I leave the responsibility for my children's studies completely up to them or I exert constant pressure and scrutiny on them for top grades, my children will still not excel in school. Will I

ever strike the right balance between learning for purpose and learning for pleasure so that my children become increasingly self-sufficient and proficient without a burdensome push for perfection?

PARENTS' UNSPOKEN FEARS

As if the previous parental worries were not bad enough, left unchecked these concerns could morph into abject fears. Why wouldn't fear prevail when a parent assumes that their best effort, dedication, and love will get them nowhere? Of course, hard work, persistence, and caring in themselves are never enough without a sensible parental plan in place that provides a way to calmly focus, balance, and maintain all that concerted effort.

Many parents harbor fears that they silently dwell upon and that may eat them up inside. Perhaps they see aspects of themselves or their children reflected in other parents and kids they come in contact with and worry that the worst they see in others could manifest in themselves or their children.

For those parents who rarely think about or encounter such negative situations with their children, this exploration in dysfunction should still help to convince them that great parenting does not happen by magic. This perspective also allows them to see exactly what they are doing right in order to continue to avoid the following undesirable circumstances.

1. **I may fear that my parental gift of leadership will be fought:**
    - I am scared that what began as my children being uncooperative and disrespectful could turn into a completely unmanageable situation where I feel like my children and I are adversaries. My rules and requests will be greeted with distain, and my role as captain will be treated as a joke. Home will be a chaotic place of screaming, discord, and defiance, and this constant battle of wills will destroy our family.
    - As awful as this situation will be for me when my children are in my presence, my real fear is what may happen to them when they are out of my sight and acting in ways that put them in serious jeopardy and danger. A reckless mentality in my children causes my mind to reel with the consequences of them experimenting with sex, drinking, drugs, crime, and gangs.
2. **I may fear that my parental gift of love will be forsaken:**
    - I am scared that my children could come to distrust me and feel like I am not on their side at all. They will think that I do not listen to and could not possibly understand them, which could cause them to think that I do not value them. In turn, this skepticism could also cause them to assume that they do not really need me as their parent.

- I fear that there will be a distance between us that is a deafening silence that will break my heart. As much as my children try to hide it, I know this separation and aloofness will be most hurtful and heartbreaking for them because they still really do need me.

3. **I may fear that my parental gift of laughter will be completely rejected:**
   - I am scared that my children will almost completely withdraw and disengage from family activities (from simple dinners to holidays to vacations), even if I force their attendance.
   - I fear that their peers, electronic devices, social media, and an almost narcissistic obsession with self-exposure will completely overshadow their natural talents and investments in healthier, more constructive quests.
4. **I may fear that my parental gift of learning will utterly fail:**
   - I fear that I am complicit in my kid's dependency on me because I practically do their homework for them and almost everything else in between. I have not taught them any responsibility or life skills they will need when they live on their own—and at this rate, why should they ever forge out on their own when everything is handed to them at home?
   - I am scared that in many important ways my children will be incompetent. They will fail in school, be ineligible for many school activities, and may not graduate high school.

PLACING YOUR FAITH IN YOUR INFLUENCE

We all know too well there are other people and things out there that are frequently attempting to influence your children with their own brands of seduction, so some parental concern and caution is always justified. Some of this corruption of children is purposeful, and some is residual. Some are the perennial temptations that lead to a bit of trouble, and some are the tricksters and traitors that lead straight to torment and tribulation.

Thus, there unfortunately may be a small minority of kids who persist in resisting all that even the best of parents and teachers have to offer because someone or something else is holding sway over them and may be exerting a stronger grip on that child right now. These kids may even blatantly reject or rebel against your positive persuasion and valiant interventions. They may continually withdraw from you, even as you stand right beside them and shower them with all you know they desperately need. And sometimes the parents, the teachers, and the school are not at fault at all. In fact, these adults and institutions may be doing everything right.

Of course, this sad but rare reality does not mean we ever give up. It is never too late to work to get a kid back on your side so she can be back on her own side. This unfortunate scenario is mentioned only to emphasize the delicate balance motivation holds over individuals who ultimately have their own wills and wishes.

All the more reason, then, to be extra proactive and ever ardent in suffusing our most vulnerable youth with leadership, love, laughter, and learning at home and with firmness, fairness, fascination, and facilitation at school. Parents are right to fear external, negative influences, but they should no longer fear themselves or their children's teachers. Instead of allowing dread to paralyze us, we should let it spur us to be those daily positive influences that can and do counteract much of the bad influences that try to steer children in the wrong direction.

Hopefully soon, the similar methods of the Four Ls and the Four Fs will be in such widespread use that even when parents and teachers have not formally come to consensus about such common approaches, they will inherently know they are still working as allies because the kids they share routinely and proudly show the benefits of such a successful, albeit sometimes unspoken, collaboration. In so doing, these lucky children also will likely have the wherewithal within themselves to resist the lures and snares that at times lurk around the corner.

THE VALUE OF KNOWING WHAT CHILDREN DISLIKE AND WHAT DISTRESSES THEM

Part of this vigilance in parenting is strengthened by knowing what children themselves commonly worry about and fear. The success of the Four Ls and Four Fs philosophies is based upon persuading children to make the same healthy, wise decisions that their parents and teachers want them to make because kids do not stray far from the adults who are consistently and comprehensively meeting their fundamental needs.

The additional piece of the puzzle, of course, is for parents and teachers to be insightful enough to also know what concerns and scares kids. Because if we can meet their four essential needs, while at the same time allaying, circumventing, or eliminating many of their greatest fears, children will have no reason to flounder or flee. Especially if you know beforehand what it is about yourself as a parent that concerns and bugs your kids, you can also use this insight to avoid these things that create distance and division, or you can work to counterbalance them.

Remember that the emphasis for all successful parenting and teaching is on motivation, encouragement, and influence. An adult's actions and interactions with children should be designed to get them to come to you and to then remain on your side, precisely because they see that you are always on their side—even when they do not particularly like every one of your expectations or requirements of them.

However, the answer to allaying, circumventing, or eliminating many of your children's greatest pet peeves and perturbations is not to be found in just giving in and giving them what they want! All leaders ultimately fail when they are primarily focused on winning a popularity contest or on catering to people's every whim.

The Four Ls intentionally focus only upon what children *need*, and many kids can be quite clueless as to what they truly need. This lack of awareness is either due to the fact that they are still children and naturally require adults to lead the way or because they have been so over-indulged and over-stimulated they cannot discern for themselves between what is best for them in the long run and what pacifies them in the moment. Remember that the end goal of all this adult guidance, support, inspiration, and education is for kids to become self-actualized so that one day they no longer need their parents and teachers to sustain their most basic needs.

In the meantime, also know that when children finally find that adult who actually attends to all of their fundamental needs, those kids will progressively let go of their rebelliousness, their retreat, their fears, and their fussing because subconsciously they now have everything their little hearts actually always desired. When you are that person who provides this deep inner satisfaction to a child, you will gain their lasting devotion. Of course, if you are only now becoming a Four Ls parent for your growing children, expect a bit of kicking and screaming along the way as they adjust to your new and improved leadership.

CHILDREN'S FRETFUL AND FEARFUL HOME SCENARIOS

Even as a consummate parent, villains and monsters still manifest in everyone's lives. Yet properly parented children will know just who to run to when they are scared—and a Four Ls parent will be the person they will run to, not from. These parents will then be there to appropriately embrace and comfort their frightened kids. Eventually, that embrace will at times be replaced with a pat on the rear as you send your child back to slay their dragons on their own. Over time, your child will even proudly tell you their war stories of how they vanquished one of their foes or fears without having first come to you at all.

The worries of children can be just as counterproductive as those of adults, especially because their imaginations often leap straight from concern to outright fear. Children's silent, inner worries reveal a great deal about how they look to their parents for protection and promise.

This fact cannot be overemphasized because all children need the adults in their lives in very profound and critical ways. No matter how much they may try to hide it, deny it, or fight you on it, every child is counting on adults to take charge, nurture them, embolden them, and strategically guide them—even when in some respects you are annoying the heck out of them or causing them to cringe at how completely uncool and out of touch you are!

Therefore, be aware that some of the most common worries of children are about their own parents. Of course, kids can be dramatic, overreact, and not see past their own limited perspectives, so take some of their possible gripes about you with a grain of salt. Just also know that these same qualities of blowing things out of proportion and not seeing the other person's point of view are some of the things kids most complain about you as their parent!

Nevertheless, you have a great deal of control over the criticisms and concerns of your kids if you adhere to the Four Ls. So now put yourself in your children's shoes thinking about the following range of their possible pet peeves and worst-case scenarios about *you*.

1. **My parent may not really be my leader but is unreasonable, unsure, or erratic:**
   - I dislike it when you make me do endless chores around the house, especially for no allowance, no reward, or no recognition—and especially when you act lazier than I do!
   - I dislike it when you do not treat me with respect. At least you can say "excuse me, thank you, and you're welcome" to me sometimes!
   - I don't like to disappoint you, but I hate it when you get angry for things I did not even know I was doing wrong, did not know annoyed you, or had no idea weren't allowed!
   - I dislike it when you shout at me, get mad too easily, have a fit about nothing, and endlessly lecture, nag, and hound me! I also hate it when I do not even get the chance to explain my side. You never let things go and don't let me live down my past mistakes.
   - I am scared to make any move because whatever I do makes you angry, so why should I behave? You don't respect me, so why should I respect you? By the way, belittling me, cursing at me, and comparing me to my siblings or other kids does not make me respect you or like myself very much.
   - I do not like it when you take away my possessions or ground me. I know that you do not want me to embarrass you when we are in public, but I also do not want you to embarrass me, especially by yelling at or punishing me in front of my friends!
   - I am scared that my life will be always in a state of chaos and uncertainty when I am with you because you never mean what you say, always break promises, and never plan ahead.

- I am worried that because the house is dirty and disorganized, my things will continue to get misplaced, lost, ruined, or broken. Can't you control my siblings so they leave my things *alone*? I also hate it when meals are always a last-minute decision and the refrigerator is always empty.
- I don't worry about listening to you because I mostly do what I want anyway, but I do worry that if I really needed protection, you wouldn't be strong or aware enough to help.
- I don't like it when my parents keep secrets from me or argue with each other, even when you think I can't hear. Separation and divorce are the things that scare me the most.

2. **My parent may not really be giving me true love but is distant, uncaring, or smothering:**
   - I really dislike it when you do not pay attention to me or listen to me. It makes me feel like I do not matter or that all I am is a bother to you.
   - I am scared that I will always come second, especially behind my siblings and your work, friends, and lovers. I hate it when my parents play favorites!
   - I worry that nobody notices me, even when I do something really good or special.
   - I dislike it when you treat me like a baby. I do not need to be overprotected, constantly worried about, or hovered around. You never consider my point of view or remember that you were a kid once too, you know.
   - I feel like a prisoner in this house because I have no freedom. When can I make my own decisions without you automatically shooting me down, criticizing me, or being completely unreasonable?! You say you want me to be responsible, but you never give me any chance to prove to you that you can trust me.
   - I am scared that my parents will invade my privacy. I am scared that they will go through and read my personal things. Don't pry so much!
3. **My parent may not really be dedicated to laughter but is mostly pestering, preoccupied, or is disinterested:**
   - It disappoints me when my parents do not spend enough time with me, especially if they have to work or travel a lot. But when they are constantly on the phone, on the internet, or watching TV instead of interacting with me, that really hurts.
   - I am scared that my parents will continue to suck all the fun out of the things I like to do because they put too much pressure on me to perform perfectly, every time. There is no emphasis on excitement, experiment, or play in this house!
   - I fear that my parents want me to live in their shadow and to only live out their stupid dreams that have nothing to do with my interests or what I care about. Do you even know what I like or who I really am?

- Even when something is actually my dream, I am scared you will try to take over or push me so hard that it stops being fun or interesting.
- I worry that you will continue to make excuses why you can't watch me perform or participate in the things that are important to me and that I have been practicing at. It's embarrassing when other parents show up and mine don't. I hate making excuses for you!
- I want to have some choices about what the family does or where we go. Can't you ask for my opinion sometimes?

4. **My parent may not really be invested in my learning but is a bully who always criticizes me:**
   - I am scared that I am a constant source of disappointment and shame for my parents, especially in school. I hate always being pushed to be my very best every moment! Sometimes, I just want to get by and have that be enough.
   - Once in a while I just need a break! Hard work and perfection isn't necessary every moment, and I need some time to myself after a long day at school. Besides, you have to understand that even sometimes when I do try my best, I will still fall short—and it makes it worse for you to be on me for it!
   - Even with things around the house, I am never good enough. You are too picky! If I never do anything right or good enough, why should I even try? Your constant pressure is making me hate my life!
   - You get frustrated with me too fast when I try to help you or when you are teaching me something. Lighten up! I am just a kid, and I mess up sometimes.
   - I don't bother to help my parents with anything because clearly they would rather do everything themselves or do it for me. In one way, I like being catered to, but I also feel useless and inept when you baby me.

USING THE FOUR Ls TO MITIGATE COMMON PARENT–CHILD CONFLICTS

When you analyze the most common fears of both parents and their children, some startling similarities are exposed.

Common Conflicts with Leadership

If children and their parents demand respect from each other, is there a way for parents to remain the boss yet often recognize and even reward their children for their courtesy and compliance? Recall that appreciation is a major part of being loving and that spontaneous fun and random freebies and freedom are part of a parent's laughter.

If children and their parents want measured and mature reactions to conflict, can the dramatics and overreacting be tempered on both ends? Recall that true love harbors fairness and forgiveness, not resentment and revenge. Kids need their punishments to fit their crimes and deserve endless opportunities to regain trust, privileges, and the chance to return to your good graces. Always remember that your laughter and liveliness has to be equal to or greater than your scolding and strictness. Also recall that you only seek improvement not reasons to punish.

If children and their parents fear embarrassment from each other, can they put awareness of each other's sensitivities at the forefront, especially when in public? Recall that love always means that you *have to* say you're sorry. Love also fosters open communication, and a little cheerful and proactive reminding of what you expect and what you fear from each other before it even happens goes a long way to circumvent unnecessary chagrin. Likewise, a focus on laughter even in the most mundane of situations helps lighten the mood and lower one's guard.

Common Conflicts with Love

If children and their parents both dislike the strain that overprotecting puts on them, can't trust win out over worry and doubt? Recall that love is all about trust. At practically any age a parent can give their children opportunities to earn some amount of trust and choice.

If your whole aim is to gradually nurture your children toward independence, then give them chances to express their autonomy and to earn your faith in them. This letting go must come as much of a relief to you as it certainly will for your children. If this incremental, developmentally appropriate release toward privacy and kids making their own decisions terrifies you, you are nowhere near the realm of love. And where there is no love, there is no laughter because you are too busy structuring, stifling, and stigmatizing your child's every move.

In addition, if feeling like they both matter is paramount to parents and kids, can each give a little more to the relationship to reassure and prove to each other they are highly valued? Recall that love requires frequent listening, interacting, and understanding. This crucial bonding time must be a priority on both ends. Yet if laughter is included in this time, neither parent nor child will consider this time spent together as an intrusion, inconvenience, or onerous obligation. Instead, they will each look forward to sharing time together and thus becoming closer.

Common Conflicts with Laughter

Similarly, if parents and kids dislike being disregarded, dismissed, and directed to death, can't they make an earnest attempt to respect and encourage each other's passions? Love does not mean two people must be exactly alike or spend every moment together, but they do invest the time to find out what makes each other so unique and what they each most enjoy. Besides, true passions are magnetic, even when they may not be your particular cup of tea. Seeing the face of someone you care about light up because they are reveling in what they are doing right now is the delicious comingling of love and laughter that is naturally irresistible and willingly shared.

Common Conflicts with Learning

If parents and their children constantly butt heads over expectations of performance, especially in terms of grades, can't there be a happy medium that places on an equal footing the push for excellence with the realization that too much pressure can be counterproductive? Recall that a parent's love balances unconditional acceptance and constant encouragement with pushing children to reach further, to care more, and to not give up. Laughter provides kids with so much choice, creativity, and change that kids can also tolerate a bit of good old academic pressure and homework hounding without feeling unduly burdened or like a constant disappointment.

THE BENEFIT OF FACING OUR FEARS

It is healthy to confront our fears head on from time to time so we can release ourselves from the power that apprehension can hold on us. Every real problem has a real solution, and you are seeing ever more clearly that the way to parent–child symbiosis is through an equal balance of leadership, love, laughter, and learning. The collective power of the Four Ls is unmatched in winning kids over from their dislikes and fears.

Parents are probably never going to get kids to love cleaning their rooms, washing dishes, mowing lawns, or doing homework. This is okay because life is full of duties, drudgery, and annoyances, and the sooner kids learn responsibility and to fulfill their obligations, the better.

And if children do not like being chewed out, lectures, nagging, or punishments—good! These less-than-pleasant motivators in the parent's leadership toolbox still hold a rightful place and can be quite effective when used in moderation. The key, of course, is for parents to keep it *all* in place and in play so that the rules, routines, and regimentations of life are only one part of what their children experience.

Since this is a book not just about parenting but how the home and the classroom intersect, we must linger in the realm of doubt a moment longer. We move now to the school site to explore how the worries of teachers and their students manifest themselves there.

Chapter 7

The Concerns of Teachers and Their Students

What *don't* teachers and their students need? What are their fears? Which worries paralyze them? What apprehensions would cause a person to act out, burn out, or drop out? You have seen kids exhibit these negative behaviors, but do you know teachers who speak of a career in education as an increasingly disheartening and uphill endeavor? How many children dread or dislike school? How many kids each year check out of school, whether literally or figuratively?

TEACHERS' COMMON CLASSROOM CONCERNS

Teachers' possible worries fall within the four essential classroom components of being a firm, fair, fascinating facilitator.

1. **I may worry that my students will ignore my firmness:**
   - I am concerned that despite my greatest effort, dedication, and caring, my students still will not obey or respect me—or respect each other.
   - I worry that I will not be able to trust my students and will be drained by the constant supervision, corrections, and consequences they require: "Sit up straight. Stop talking. Turn around. No, you may not. Give me that. Sit back down. Eyes on me. Why isn't your book open? Get to work. Take that off. Spit that out. Leave her alone. Stay still. Pick that up. Why are you late? Quiet down. Focus. Why don't you have your . . . . *Stop that!!!*"
   - I especially worry that once I have lost class control, I will never get it back this year.

2. **I may worry that my students will not recognize my fairness:**
   - I am concerned that despite my greatest effort, dedication, and caring, my students still will give me only minimal attention, participation, response, or effort—or none at all.
   - I worry that my students will act aloof and uninvolved because they do not trust that I have their best interests at heart. They will not believe that I am on their sides.
3. **I may worry that my students will dismiss my fascination:**
   - I am concerned that despite my greatest effort, dedication, and caring, my students still will be disinterested and disconnected from my instruction and assignments.
   - Even though I take great pains to create interesting lessons, I worry that my students will find a lack of meaning in my class and will begin to tune out.
   - On the rare occasions my students actually do their classwork or homework, I worry it will only display the feeblest of efforts and not reflect what they are truly capable of.
4. **I may worry that my facilitation will be ineffective:**
   - I am concerned that despite my greatest effort, dedication, and caring, my students still will not achieve or improve academically.
   - Even though I try to teach well and give individual help, I am concerned my students will not learn, retain, or be able to do a fraction of what I taught them or what is expected.
   - I worry that the amount of failing grades my students earn will be less about outright failure and more about a series of zeros for work that was simply never completed.

TEACHERS' UNSPOKEN CLASSROOM FEARS

As if the worries above were not bad enough, things could be even worse. Many times, teachers are reluctant to share their deepest fears with others because they do not want to appear weak or ineffectual. Delving even deeper, here are some teachers' *unspoken* fears:

1. **I may fear that my firmness will be fought:**
   - I am scared that defiance, discord, and danger will reign in my chaotic classroom, and ultimately I will be the one blamed.
   - I fear that an adversarial relationship will develop where my students perpetually and purposely fight me and seek to undermine me—all much to their delight and my dismay.
   - I dread being chronically under stress and at risk of losing control of my reactions.

- I fear I will be embarrassed in front of my colleagues and parents when they see what a miserable manager I am. I especially fear that my administrator will see I have poor class control, and I will receive a bad evaluation.

2. **I may fear that my fairness will be forsaken:**
   - I am scared that my students will not trust me or like me, and this will be common knowledge school wide.
   - I fear that a contentious atmosphere will develop where my students constantly complain and intentionally question my motives and methods.
   - I fear that my students will purposefully withdraw from taking an active part in my class. I am scared that apathy and sloth will become commonplace.
3. **I may fear that my fascination will be completely rejected:**
   - I am scared that my students will dread my class because they are completely turned off by my lessons, activities, and assignments.
   - I fear that my reputation among students, parents, and faculty will be as a lifeless teacher with pointless lessons.
4. **I may fear that my facilitation will utterly fail:**
   - I am scared that ultimately I will be blamed and face the consequences for the amount of failing grades in my class and for my students' low test scores.
   - I fear parents will complain about me, and I will be under continual stress and scrutiny.

IN MY CLASSROOM: MY FEARSOME FIRST YEAR OF TEACHING

Too many of the fearful teacher scenarios above I actually experienced during my miserable first year of teaching. Yet, looking back, my very first day in the classroom was not horrible by any means. Not anywhere near perfect, but in no way a disaster. I did have a window of opportunity to manage those kids, but I was just way too late in taking any effective action. The possibility was always there to reach those students, and I myself had the potential. The only problem was that I did not yet have the proficiency. So by the second day, I was a goner.

Before long, I was so overwhelmed, so overwrought, and so foolishly oblivious that I had absolutely no idea that some of my students were literally jumping out of my second story classroom window onto the covered walkway below, shinnying down the pole, and then running back upstairs to breathlessly knock at my door pretending that they were late. Like the nitwit neophyte I was, I would repeatedly interrupt instruction to answer the door and allow each "tardy" student into the classroom. As the rest of the class inexplicably giggled, I would half-think to myself: *Didn't I* ***already*** *mark him present*?

Little did my students know, it was I who was about to jump out of that window! *That* seemed my only window of opportunity I had left.

Through the two books I wrote for educators and my work as a mentor teacher, I hope to have saved some teachers, as well as their students, from similar untenable and unconscionable situations. Managing and motivating children is not as elusive as it may seem. Even though it took me many years to figure it all out on my own, the Four Fs eventually allayed my fears and allowed my students to act like the responsible, involved scholars I then persuaded them to be.

STUDENTS' FEARFUL CLASSROOM SCENARIOS

By viewing the above list of teacher worries and fears, it was beneficial for parents to see how concerned teachers are when their students are not acting or achieving their best. This is simply more evidence that teachers are on parents' sides every step of the way and that they care about student conduct, responsiveness, enjoyment, and accomplishment just as much as parents do. Those teacher fears had nothing to do with selfishness; they all were rooted in a teacher's earnest commitment to quality.

Thus the teacher concerns and fears outlined above should not be dismissed as merely the complaints of a derelict teacher. They are actually the apprehensions of a teacher who cares deeply and who is trying their best but who may be in a situation where they were insufficiently prepared, are patently ill-supported, or are chronically drowning.

Again, this book makes no excuses for ineffective teachers. The point here is just to emphasize that both parenting and teaching are all-encompassing, arduous obligations even in the best of circumstances. We can all chuckle at ineptitude of some new teachers or at the mischievousness of certain students, but in reality these predicaments are far from funny. The individual teacher, the teaching profession as a whole, and the students themselves pay too great a price for teachers who fail to adequately manage, support, captivate, and educate students.

So while caring for kids and good intentions are vital, they are never enough. There is a vast difference between caring and careful consideration, as well as between good intentions and wise, intentional motivation. The parents and teachers who know these distinctions are the ones who quell the fears of children and whose own fears never manifest themselves. These adults and their happily inspired children are too busy enjoying each other's company and finding deep satisfaction to be bothered by worry and doubt.

Now as you also view the following complaints and fears kids have about their teachers, parents will be able to see just how grinding, grueling, and ghastly school can be for some kids. Seeing these concerns spelled out can help parents guide their children through school and help them spot the ways in which their children's teachers may be lacking in or overemphasizing their firmness, fairness, fascination, or facilitation.

Left unchecked, student worries can easily turn to fear. Besides their parents, all kids look to their teachers for protection and promise. While away from home, children are in many ways dependent upon their teachers to supervise, nurture, engage, and of course, teach them. Kids want to be led and to be inspired to do their best but only for those whom they deem worthy.

Children may indeed have plenty to complain about school in general and about many of their teachers specifically. However, just as with some of their gripes about their parents, teachers must take certain students complaints in stride. Like it or not, punctuality, preparedness, assignments, projects, presentations, participation, deadlines, reading, and writing are part of the program of school, just as chores, rules, and studying are part of the program at home. When kids grouse about having to follow a leader or work hard at something they may not particularly enjoy, well, they are just being kids.

Thus, uncomfortable consequences and unpleasant punishments for not meeting one's responsibilities are also part of the program in both places. When kids begin their caterwauling about being disciplined for their own choice to act irresponsibly or disrespectfully, you can take their whining as proof that they are indeed learning their lesson.

By contrast, your children may constantly criticize or have major issues with one teacher over another. This may show how a Four Fs teacher is able to have high standards yet still win their students over, while a less effective teacher with the same high standards fails to engender the allegiance and affection of those same kids.

Put yourself in a student's desk thinking about the following classroom concerns that range from simple pet peeves to possible worst-case scenarios.

1. **My teacher may not be firm but is actually weak, unsure, and erratic:**
   - I am scared that my teacher will allow me to be harmed in some way by another student (physically hurt, bullied, harassed, stolen from, etc.) in this out-of-control classroom. How can I learn when I am too busy watching my back?
   - This teacher screams at kids all the time, and I am scared I too will be unfairly belittled and picked on. I hate grumpy, mean teachers! Why be a teacher if you hate kids?

- I fear that I will be unjustly blamed, punished, or hurt for something I didn't do, which will also get me in more trouble at home. I do not like it when teachers involve my parents and call home. If you can't handle things yourself, you shouldn't be a teacher!
- I do not like my free time being taken away. Detentions are the worst!

2. **My teacher may not be fair but is distant and uncaring:**
   - I do not like being called on or put on the spot to answer questions out loud. I am scared that my teacher will allow me to be embarrassed or humiliated in front of my peers. I hate teachers who intentionally try to catch students when they are not ready.
   - I fear that my teacher will never take positive notice of me or care how I feel and instead focus all their attention on the worst kids or the best kids. I worry that I will never be an important part of this class, so why should I even try?
   - I worry that my teacher only plays favorites and that there is nothing I can do to win their favor or attention. Why am I always invisible?
   - I hate teachers who punish the whole class for something only a few kids did. Teachers can be so unfair!
3. **My teacher may not be fascinating but is dull, dry, and drones on and on:**
   - I am scared that my teacher will allow me to be bored. All this teacher does is talk at us endlessly or make us do useless worksheets. Doesn't this teacher know that nobody cares about what they are saying?
   - I fear that my time will be wasted because nothing will interest me in this class. How am I supposed to pay attention when nothing in this class matters to me?
   - I dislike teachers who have no personality. I hate teachers who are only strict and serious.
4. **My teacher may not be a facilitator but is incomprehensible:**
   - I do not like a lot of homework, especially on the weekends! Some teachers give work that I know they would not do themselves even if they were assigned the same thing.
   - I do not like it when teachers do not give adequate time to do assignments or when they give pop quizzes. Pressure and surprises only stress me out, and then I don't do my best.
   - I also do not like teachers who do not accept late or makeup work or do not allow extra credit. It's not my fault that I get sick sometimes or don't have time to finish things. Why can't teachers be understanding and flexible?
   - I do not like disorganized teachers, especially when they forget to collect assignments, input grades wrong, or lose my work! Why are teachers allowed to make mistakes, but kids have to always be on point?

- I do not like teachers who are too picky or who always expect perfection. Lighten up!
- I do not like teachers who do not explain well. I am scared that my teacher will allow me to feel confused, lost, and offer no effective help—even when I get up the nerve to ask!
- I do not like teachers who go too fast. I fear that I really must be stupid because I do not understand anything that is going on in this difficult class. There is no way I will pass or succeed in this class. I must really be dumb.
- I do not like teachers who go too slowly. My teacher only focuses on the "low" kids and just keeps re-teaching what I already know.

THE PROACTIVE PROTECTION OF LOVE AND FAIRNESS

Unfortunately, children can have additional fears that exist while at school but occur outside of the classroom door. Often, these very real and upsetting scenarios happen just beyond, as well as far beyond, the classroom teacher's firsthand notice or knowledge, especially when they occur on the way to and from school, before and after school, and during recess or lunch. Teachers may be able to sense or spot trouble in the hallways or during passing periods, but neither teachers nor parents are mind readers.

Therefore, adults need children to come to them when they are uneasy or upset, especially before a problem becomes worse or unmanageable. This is why the strong, open, and trusting relationship that is formed by a loving parent and their children or a fair teacher and their students is so important. These bonds and lines of communication must be long-established so in the inevitable event that there is trouble or concern on the child's part, that child will already be willing to turn to those adults for support or guidance because this has been the longstanding routine in these relationships.

PARENTS AND STUDENTS WANT FIRM, FAIR, FASCINATING FACILITATORS

You can now see how the sets of four fearful classroom scenarios above follow a pattern of what could negatively happen to both a teacher and their students when there is a dearth of teacher firmness, fairness, fascination, and/or facilitation. This is precisely why all of the Four Fs are so vital: When they are present, the Four Fs allow teachers and students to achieve their deepest desires, but when any or all of the motivators are missing, it is not that a neutral environment exists but that a negative (possibly hostile), unproductive, and apprehensive atmosphere is ushered in.

Of course, the very possibility of their own children being subjected to a negative, hostile, unproductive, or apprehensive classroom environment sends parents themselves into worry, fear, and outrage. And justifiably so, for the goal of this book is for every child to receive the same degree of guidance, support, inspiration, and coaching, both at home and at school.

IN MY CLASSROOM: MAKING ROOM TO MEET ALL OF MY STUDENTS' NEEDS

I do not hesitate to point out that as a teacher, I can be a hard ass. Clearly, my learning curve was initially steeper than that of my students, but the days of children running the show in my classroom are long over.

In many ways, I am exacting, demanding, and relentless with my students. My classroom is precise, organized, and orderly. I run a very tight ship, and my students know from the get-go that I am the boss. They all do what I say, when and how I say it, with a respectful, cooperative attitude. I do not ask twice, and my students know better than to question my authority. In fact, every kid at my school knows this is a man who means business and expects respect—and if they do not know it, it will be their choice to learn it the easy or the hard way. But learn it they will.

I also take my students' education very seriously, and I expect my students to do the same. I have high standards for academic growth, and I hold my students accountable for their participation and performance. My curriculum and instruction are challenging and rigorous. We work diligently from "bell to bell," and there is no free time in my class. Laziness and passivity are not tolerated. Homework is assigned, due dates are enforced, and extra credit is limited.

Yet at the very same time, I can say with full confidence that all my students find my class a warm, supportive, cheerful, stimulating, validating, and fulfilling place to be. My particular subject and I as their teacher may or may not be their absolute favorite, but I can safely say we consistently rank very close to the top.

In ways I think parenting is easier than teaching in that the teacher has the obligation of always adhering to academic content standards. Teachers cannot take all their students out for an impromptu ice cream cone, play a game of Monopoly together, or run through the sprinklers with them on a hot day. Yet parents can and should do those types of fun, bonding activities often and spontaneously.

So, if I can find ways to make regimentation, rules, and routines not only palatable but ultimately comforting to kids, then so can parents. And if I can make reading, writing, and academic discussions not only tolerable but mesmerizing and meaningful, then parents can also transform teaching all sorts of useful and challenging things to their children into frequent worthwhile and rewarding endeavors.

The key for teachers and parents to motivate children to cheerfully do the stuff they least like to do is to make sure that the less-exciting stuff is balanced out with the things that are naturally more enticing. If leadership and firmness contain explicit elements of no nonsense, no debate, no hesitation, and no choice, then these limitations and obligations should be balanced out with the freedom and fun that is engendered by laughter and fascination.

See, laughter and fascination revel in delight and recreation. In these aspects of galvanizing your children, their questions, opinions, and changes of mind are most sincerely welcomed and even encouraged. Most of all, these motivators respect individual choices and inclinations. Thus, kids can handle common courtesy and cooperation with an adult leader who *just as often* comforts, cheers, congratulates, creates, captivates, and carouses with them!

Thus, my students rarely feel limited, even in my highly structured class. Instead, they feel inspired and affirmed because I also feature passion and pertinence in all they learn and do. We take function just as seriously as we do fun because we know that respect and rules are key elements of any fascinating game. Kids innately know that obligations and restrictions are simply a necessary part of every life, both for adults and children. If those requirements, drudgeries, and laws are never going away, then at least they can be tempered by equal parts of autonomy, adventure, and amusement that their parent actively emboldens, supports, and participates in.

Similarly, if learning and facilitation do indeed contain elements of oversight, pushing, and "pressure" on kids, then these possibly onerous elements can be tempered by love and fairness. Love and fairness emphasize patience, understanding, and recognition. In these aspects of winning your kids over, parents attend to their children's individual needs and emotions. Thereby they prove they are on their child's side in both their contentment and accomplishment.

Children need to be persuaded to take increasing responsibility for their studies, to push themselves (instead of relying on or complaining about being pushed by others), and to initiate their own high expectations of themselves so their parents are not forced to constantly remind, check, and demand, which are the very things kids say they most dislike about adults!

My students seldom find my class too demanding or my expectations too high. Instead, they rise to my challenges with enthusiasm, attention, and effort because I personally acknowledge their achievements, as well as their valiant attempts. They are sure I am their greatest champion who will also give them a strong foundation onto which they can reach for the stars. They feel respected by my faith in their insights and abilities. I do not give my students baby work or busy work, and this truly inspires them to live up to the confidence I have in them.

Therefore, I practice what I preach. I value each of my needs as a teacher as much as I hold sacred each of my students' needs from me. Since these needs are all essentially the same, I know we both will win out if I focus on these four fundamental needs equally and consistently. Once this positive, persuasive culture of the classroom is set—and an expert teacher can do so in a matter of days and then perpetually reinforce it—the teacher can then get to the business and joy of nurturing and educating a new crop of kids for the next 180 (mostly fabulous) days.

After my first few miserable years of basically failing as a teacher, I never thought anyone, least of all me, could actually find success or satisfaction in teaching—especially teaching the dreaded middle school student! It simply could not be done without a lot of harsh compromises in the caring and conscience departments, as well as tons of giving in, turning a blind eye, rationalizing, making excuses, blaming others, catering, coddling, and dumbing down.

Two decades later, however, I can proudly and honestly state that fulfillment and excellence in education is attainable for all and in all settings *without compromise*. Oh, sure, I adjust, adapt, and evolve all the time, but I consider these as additional positive qualities that keep my teaching fresh, focused, and functioning in today's world. Kids may be essentially the same, but after twenty years in the business, each new generation of youngsters brings idiosyncrasies, attitudes, and abilities that need to be addressed, as well as honored.

Being a firm, fair, fascinating facilitator allows both me and my students to have it all, even as each day we each realize our potentials a bit differently, especially depending how much each person contributes to their fair share in the partnership of education. Much more often than not, however, I feel re-inspired each day to give my best, which in turn inspires my students to give their best. My classroom is typically a happy, heartwarming, hardworking place to be.

As for my students no longer running the show, even that is not altogether true. Now I absolutely want them to run the show but with all the requisite diligence, intelligence, and creativity that I have mustered and developed in them.

MOVING FROM PERSPECTIVE TO PROPORTION

Of course, parents do not have to compromise either. They can create homes that are equally happy, heartwarming, and hardworking as the best classrooms. Just as in the classroom, once the positive and persuasive culture of the home is set, parents can then get to the business and joy of raising their children for the next eighteen mostly wonderful years and beyond.

The first avenues to a solution are always perspective and wisdom because no one can grow or change without clarity and commonsense. This book has provided both through the explanation and examples of the Four Ls of Parenting and the Four Fs of Teaching. You have now gained thorough perspective, and the inescapable conclusion is that in as much as kids need and fear, so do their parents and their teachers—and all in the same four categories and in the same ways.

All the more reason, then, to cease accusing and assuming the worst about each other and to instead work to ensure there is a Four Ls parent in every home and a Four Fs teacher in every classroom supporting and complementing parents at school. Hence, we all should be making continual progress *together* instead of needlessly being at odds or wasting time thinking one side does not have the best interests of the other. We all need and fear essentially the same things, so how could we doubt each other's good intentions or earnest efforts?

In fact, the multiple examples of worries and fears presented in this chapter need never manifest themselves. Precisely because we all now know what could happen on the negative end, we each will take great pains to be sure they never happen in the first place. We will certainly be proactive enough to never let things slide so far that anyone's concerns mutate into fear. Moreover, let us take the "pains" out of the equation entirely and only focus upon calmly and confidently striking the correct balance so that we always feel like we are on a safe and sound course when dealing with children.

Part II

ACHIEVING PROPORTION

Chapter 8

Avoiding Extremes, Insufficiencies, and Inconsistencies

Whether it is your own home or your child's classroom, the adults in both settings require order, communication, investment, and accomplishment from all the kids in the room. It should also now be apparent that an overemphasis or de-emphasis of any of the Four Ls or Four Fs would throw a household or classroom out of balance. Since proportion, consistency, and thoroughness are the three components of effective parenting and teaching, it is helpful to see the negative results of overreaching, underestimating, inconsistency, or incompletion. With such insight, those adult mistakes can be avoided.

TYPICAL PARENTING AND TEACHING EXTREMES

In the often tumultuous, overwhelming world of nurturing children, it is easy for the adult in charge to lose their way and to go too far. Occasionally, parents and teachers provide *too much* for children as they take one of the Four Ls or Four Fs to its counterproductive extreme.

Consider the following possible scenarios that illustrate all too common parent and teacher extremes. The similarities between the home and the classroom are remarkable and just waiting to be used to their proper, proportional advantage.

Extremes in Leadership

Consider the parents and teachers who are way too authoritarian with their fearful or indignant children and others who allow kids to walk all over them. Maybe because you have seen other parents who do not set proper boundaries and whose children routinely throw tantrums and act like spoiled brats, you take your leadership role extremely seriously.

Yet you may have become so strict, inflexible, and forceful that your children are essentially terrorized in your presence and secretly resent your constant domineering and discipline. Maybe your inappropriate cursing and put downs are wearing away their self-esteem and are actually weakening your authority. Although they obey you, your children do not like or trust you, and in time may outwardly rebel against you. In the most extreme cases, these embittered children will withdraw from you through their adulthood.

This type of extreme is common in teachers, too, especially those who are beginning their second year of their career. They may have had an out-of-control first year and have vowed to never lose command again. In one way, they may achieve success in firmness, but in every other way they will have completely lost their students' faith due to their overemphasis with discipline.

Unquestionably, children require appropriate rules, routines, limits, corrections, and consequences. These are the key ways they learn responsibility and respect, and without these core tenets of character, they will never be successful. A firm adult leader's implicit and explicit message to children is: "I care about you so much that I will intervene—unpleasantly if need be—when you do not act in your own best interest or in the best interest of others. I am the adult and you are the child/young adult, and until this relationship changes, I am the boss."

What a balance of the Four Ls and Four Fs quickly teach kids, however, is that all this firm leadership is yet another way in which the adult proves they are on the child's side and are proud of them. The adult conveys through word and deed, "I also want you to have fun, I want to have fun with you, and I want you to feel accomplished and proud of yourself. Yet none of these wonderful things can happen unless I am sure you are acting safely, sensibly, and efficiently—which in many aspects are the ways that I as the one in charge deem appropriate."

Of course, once an adult finally embraces the absolute necessity and distinct advantages of appropriate firmness, they must then find the means to establish, maintain, and reinforce their leadership. No adult actually wants discourteous children who run wild, but they must commit to the effort and attention such management and guidance always require if they are ever going to truly meet a child's needs—and find for themselves some peace and harmony in the bargain.

Remember that this resulting adult cheer and composure allows love, laughter, and learning to flow. In fact, without this adult ease and calm, no child is going to be genuinely encouraged, emboldened, or educated by a parent or teacher. In both instances above, the adult's leadership/firmness needs to be balanced with their love/fairness, laughter/fascination, and learning/facilitation.

Extremes in Love

Think about the parent or teacher who coddles and overindulges and the next whom the children withdraw from because at least in their own minds they are certain this adult does not care enough about or does not truly understand them.

Maybe you too often baby and overprotect your children in a frantic attempt to constantly shield them from any form of upset. Then when they do experience disappointment out in the real world, your kids do not have the appropriate coping skills to manage their hurt on their own.

Or perhaps because your children misconstrue your zeal to be loving, they instead mostly view you as being nosy and overbearing in your desire to be close and involved in their personal lives. They may feel embarrassed and uncomfortable as you constantly insinuate yourself in their activities and conversations with their friends. You do not appear fair to them but instead are viewed as overly needy and smothering.

So it is with teachers who place relationships with their students and meeting their emotional needs as a top priority. In these cases, a teacher's well-intentioned understanding quickly becomes indulgence and unlimited second chances. Their students are not pushed to excel or held accountable but instead are given free passes to not participate, to miss due dates, to zone out, to arrive tardy, and to come unprepared.

All of this then allows what may be legitimate extenuating circumstances to become perpetual excuses for students not to try or to act responsibly. Giving kids what they each need is the true meaning of fairness, and featuring one motivator above all others deprives children of all that they require.

In these cases, the adult's love/fairness needs to reach a state of equilibrium with their leadership/firmness, laughter/fascination, and learning/facilitation. Love is tangible and palpable; it is not a simple idea or mere words. Love is at times tough, often tender, frequently thrilling, and full of teachable moments. Children need all four facets of love in order to mature and flourish. Love is a full-time job, but it is not an adult's only job.

Four Fs teachers know that their fairness is in full effect when a painfully shy and underachieving student finally begins to open up, answer questions aloud, ask for assistance, or assert themselves. Suddenly, these students no longer allow themselves to fall between the cracks or to fade into the background because they now feel a part of the class community this teacher has created. Actually, children neither want to be pampered nor ignored; they just need assurance that someone has their back. This type of love and support is reinforced with equal parts authority, inspiration, and academics, all of which are forms of love in themselves.

Extremes in Laughter

Imagine the home or classroom that caters to the basest of childish proclivities and the one where the kids are bored to a stupor and woefully unfulfilled and indifferent. Maybe because you equate laughter with free rein and an abundance of material items, your children are given too much freedom and are constantly showered with gifts.

However, true laughter is more about experience than possessions. Whether a parent is bonding with their child collaboratively or vicariously, their participation in or encouragement of their child's passions takes much more time and effort than just pulling out a credit card. This commitment always pays off for both parent and child and lasts infinitely longer than a new toy, device, or fashion accessory.

Teachers often take their fascination too far by catering to their students who are often loathe to do the heavy lifting and maintain the focus that striving for academic excellence requires and that acting in a truly professional manner necessitates. They may have their students perpetually seated in what are essentially cooperative groups, as opposed to truly *collaborative* groups, as their students incessantly socialize while "working" on assignments "together."

There may be a lot of flash and fanfare in these classes but, when viewed closely, not a lot of substance. Oh, their students may be supremely happy in these classes, but these teachers regularly sacrifice true depth and scholarship in favor of educational fads and a decidedly casual classroom atmosphere. Challenge and creativity should not be informal affairs; they should be approached with a seriousness and sincerity that only enhances the inherent joys of learning.

In these examples, the adult's laughter/fascination needs to be harmonized with their leadership/firmness, love/fairness, and learning/facilitation. Fun and fulfillment are what make any person's life meaningful. Yet cheap thrills do not last and often do not come free. In addition, a selfish or superficial life is no life at all. In order to lead a life of worth, wisdom, and wonder—which is a life worth sharing with others—one must have a basic toolkit that also includes responsibility, relationship, and readiness. These are the gifts parents and teachers bestow upon children through a steady combination of the Four Ls and the Four Fs.

Extremes in Learning

Consider the teacher who waters down the curriculum and the next who further befuddles their already clueless kids. Think about the parent who does almost nothing to be an active, interested partner in their child's education and the parent who is so relentless in their demand for academic and extracurricular perfection that their child looks upon activities that should be pleasant and gratifying as impossible burdens and continual sources of parental disappointment.

Perhaps your children react negatively to your inflexible push toward perfection in all they do. They may not view you as a parent who provides and supports learning but as a harsh critic who is never satisfied, rarely proud, and constantly raises the bar of unwavering excellence. The stringent work ethic and unreasonable expectations of responsibility and contribution from every member of the family may be wearing your children down and making them feel trapped in an unfulfilling, relentless home environment.

Similarly, some teachers focus only upon teaching to the Test. Consequently, some of their students may indeed produce wonderful results on those tests but lack in critical thinking, creativity, and truly useful capabilities. These teachers may win accolades from principals and parents, but their students often are in for a shock when their college professors do nothing that resembles teaching to a test. In fact, many students are turned off by single-minded teachers who they find cold, colorless, and dismissive of the least bit of student emotion, out of the box thinking, fervent response, or insightful evaluation—all of which make for a fascinating class.

High expectations and demands are necessary parts of nurturing, but like every aspect of meeting the needs of children, they must be brought into balance. Hard work and grit are prerequisites for growth and success and should be actively fostered in children. Yet no aspect of childhood need be devoid of meaning, flair, excitement, and the pride that comes from a job well done—no matter what the results are, win or lose. In fact, every person should endeavor to live a life filled with these qualities, and adults who possess such joie de vivre and eager dedication directly influence children in the very best ways.

In these instances, the adult's learning/facilitation needs to come into proportion with their leadership/firmness, love/fairness, and laughter/fascination. Being proud of anyone does not necessitate perfection, least of all when it concerns a child who needs nurturing, not nervous tension. There are also a lot of qualities in kids for parents and teachers to be proud of besides academic or athletic excellence. Quality of character, sensitivity, altruism, creativity, passion, and progress are traits that must be cultivated and celebrated as well.

Mistakes Lead to Awareness

Not only do all parents and teachers share the same goals and needs, we all can make very similar mistakes! Now that you see the potential results of not being a balanced parent for your children, you are much more capable of spotting these extremes both in yourself and in your children's teachers. This additional insight can be used to keep yourself in check and to pinpoint when and how these extremes directly affect kids in adverse ways. Awareness is an important first step in returning to equilibrium in meeting all of your children's elemental needs.

We all lose their way from time to time, so do not beat yourself up if you see yourself in certain aspects of the previous four examples of adult extremes. Awareness is necessary, but constantly looking over one's shoulder and repeatedly questioning oneself can be exhausting and counterproductive. Parenting and teaching is all-consuming and draining even in the best of circumstances because you are so focused on doing your all to keep that one child (let alone multiple children) safe, supported, stimulated, and succeeding—all at the same time!

Yet with the knowledge you are gaining as to what your children truly need from you and what you need from them in return, this set of four essential components should refine your goals and provide you with a new, more self-assured focus. The Four Ls are meant to simplify and demystify the admittedly complex and often convoluted job of parenting. Worry and fear about not doing the right thing or not doing enough can now be replaced with a confidence and clarity as you consistently give your children an equal combination of what they actually crave.

EXTREMES IN COLLEGE APPLICATION EXPECTATIONS

Colleges now look for well-rounded applicants, and this broadening of the criteria they use to accept the students who have the best chance at success is to be applauded. It is not all about grades and exam scores anymore, and this is a good thing.

Yet being well-rounded should not mean having to be a super-kid either. This broadening has actually become more of a piling on of even more expectations. The demand for top grades and test scores has not been adjusted to meet the additional college demands for evidence of service, leadership, and or extracurricular activities. Instead, the children and their parents who have long had their sights set on a prestigious university now have the added burden of demonstrating that this child has been everything to everyone, at least for the last four years.

This pressure brings unwarranted stress upon children who have barely entered their teen years. This additional onus is ironic given the fact that the very aspects of volunteering, stewardship, and vocational interests that colleges crave are supposed to be inherently pleasant, philanthropic, and passionate. Free expression, helping others, giving back, and versatility are labors of love. Yet the pressure to prove that a child has done it all, whether or not that child actually wants to or has the time or energy for it, sucks most of those noble qualities right out of the endeavors that universities ostensibly seek.

Colleges complain about helicopter parents, but they bear some of the blame for parents who push their kids to go beyond what is reasonable or necessary. No wonder there is imbalance in many parents today, especially where transcripts, exams, extracurricular activities, and college are concerned. Parents feel just as much pressure as their children and often transfer that stress directly upon their kids.

Know that doing well in high school is a full-time job in itself and is decidedly much more rigorous than it was a few decades ago. Heck, Kindergarten is a far cry from the play and nap time of the past. While the educational pendulum will continue in its drastic swings, parents and teachers do not have to be pawns in the game of pedagogy. They should be vocal participants in advocating for what is truly best for kids and in what proportion. While the educational debate du jour rages on, however, the adults should also close their front doors and classroom doors and try to restore as much equilibrium for the children as possible.

TEMPORARY INTENSITY IS TO BE EXPECTED

Of course, with any parent or teacher who is dutifully employing the Four Ls or Four Fs, there will be times when any one of these four normally potent motivators will *seem* to be losing their effectiveness as evidenced by a sudden or gradual lack of cooperation, interaction, involvement, and/or accomplishment on your child's part.

However, calm and confidence will still fill your days as you simply stay the course and perhaps ratchet up your structure and supervision, increase your praise and attention paid, boost your own interaction and involvement, or enhance your training and tutoring—all according to your children's present needs, which their actions and attitudes are clearly crying out for.

There is a difference, of course, between the wise and necessary parental intervention of *temporarily intensifying* one of your four roles in order to fulfill a specific need in your child and chronically going overboard with one of your roles, no matter how innocently misguided or unduly enthusiastic this extreme may be. In fact, this extra motivation is not at all to be confused with taking your parental role to an extreme. Because each child is unique and constantly evolving, you should expect that they will need more from you in certain areas at certain times.

Therefore, do not be surprised to find that you or your child's teacher need to turn on the toughness from time to time. Do not be astonished when your child needs some extra TLC from you or a compassionate teacher. Do not be taken aback when your normally industrious and dedicated child simply needs a break or a change in their daily routine. Finally, do not be startled when your child needs extra assistance with schoolwork that usually comes easily to them. These targeted interventions are what make you a responsive parent who conscientiously attends to their children's individual and varying needs.

Furthermore, these slips and instances of sluggishness in your kids are not causes for extreme alarm or a sign of certain doom. These are simply those natural occasions when a child needs more from you. In fact, a Four Ls parent and a Four Fs teacher are fully prepared to meet these needs because they are already completely fluent with and adept at providing four fundamental sets of needs on a daily basis.

Giving a child a bit more is as easy and a pleasure for these adults as it is for the children who find even their most intense needs dutifully met. In fact, because these adults are so proficient and attentive, they will meet children's extra needs sooner rather than later, and in short order everything will be back to a state of assured balance.

Moreover, by responding sensibly and directly to your child's needs, this adherence to your parental duties will innately and profoundly prove to your child you are indeed that caring, capable parent they can rely upon—even when they may not right now relish doing what is responsible or taking their appropriate medicine. Armed with that deep assurance and bond, your children will ultimately and faithfully follow you everywhere you lead them.

This fact must not be underestimated: Daily attending to your children's four elemental needs will definitely earn their devotion and cooperation. Yet when you occasionally swoop in to anticipate and respond to any specialized needs they may be exhibiting—whether or not they consciously know it yet—you will have proven to them that you are the ally and champion that is indeed worthy of their obedience, honesty, ambition, and achievement!

POSSIBLE REASONS FOR INSUFFICIENCY

In order to achieve balance, it is constructive to further study what imbalance in parenting can look like and the potential reasons behind it. It can be quite easy to stray from one role or the other as a parent, even when you had begun with the best of intentions, and the following reasons for parental disproportion have nothing to do with not caring enough.

Reasons for Questioning Leadership

Perhaps you yourself were raised by an overly and unduly firm parent, and this excessive leadership led you often to fear or despise that parent and to distance yourself from them. So, the last thing you want is for your own children to feel scared of or controlled by you.

Consequently, you may act less as a leader and more like a buddy with your kids. You give them a lot of leeway, warnings, and second chances. However, the fact remains that your children frequently do not obey your wishes or respect your authority, and you feel conflicted, frustrated, and embarrassed by the constant battles you have with them, especially in public.

Reasons for Limiting Love

Maybe lately you have been so busy, distracted, or overwhelmed (no matter how legitimately) that you have not taken adequate time to give your children all the love and attention they need. You may often neglect to check in with them, forget to praise and acknowledge them, and fail to notice and step in when they need you most. At the same time, you can sense the distance and resentment building up in your children who do not view you as fair or truly involved. They may feel like you too frequently put their emotional needs second to other interests and obligations in your life, so your children close off from you in return.

Reasons for Withdrawing from Laughter

Perhaps you had always envisioned a vastly different interaction with your children than what you currently have. Your children may not be good at and may not value what deeply interests you. In turn, you may find it difficult to relate to your children's interests, so you withdraw from laughing and collaborating with them and participating in their personally fascinating pursuits. This distance then spills over into family functions with a disquieting lack of enthusiastic involvement and commitment from everyone involved. Your children feel unimportant and discouraged, and this disconnection is widening.

Reasons for Distancing Oneself from Learning

Maybe it is easier and faster to simply do things yourself without including and relying upon your children's help. This separation and hands-off approach may extend into your participation with your child's homework, school projects, and grades. You may feel inadequate to offer your children useful academic assistance, or you may simply feel that your children are quite capable of fulfilling their responsibility to learn and achieve academically in school all on their own. However, the fights about your children neglecting to do their chores or bringing home unsatisfactory report cards is an unpleasant drama that routinely plays out with no end in sight.

EFFORT IS NOT ENOUGH

If you see aspects of yourself or parents you know in the rationales and examples above, you realize that these parenting insufficiencies have nothing to do with malicious neglect. Parents stray to one extreme or the other, alternately providing too much or too little for their children, because they may be conflicted about the actual necessity of each of the Four Ls. If they were honest with themselves, some also may admit that they are overwhelmed or uninspired by the job of parenting. This sense of frequent frustration or lingering dissatisfaction will be a recurring theme in this chapter because disillusionment happens to the best of parents and teachers.

As stated in the preface, both ineffective and effective parents objectively love and care about their children in equal amounts. The difference, however, between parental smooth sailing and a sinking ship is in how active each parent is in the expression of that love and caring.

It is the same with children in that every child *wants* to be smart and successful (and they are lying if they say they do not), but it all depends on how much actual effort and intention each kid will muster up—and on a continual basis, mind you—to determine if they will ever attain and sustain that academic and personal accomplishment.

Similarly, a parent *merely believing in* the value of providing leadership, love, laughter, and learning for their children falls woefully short of actually meeting their kids' needs. The same goes for parents simply saying they are committed to their kids. Similarly, parents who only sometimes supply their children with the Four Ls just will not cut it.

Again, great parenting never happens passively, casually, accidentally, or magically. Oh, a lucky few kids may end okay despite lackluster parenting and teaching, but know that the vast majority of children most likely will languish and may permanently lose their way without active, attentive, intentional adult motivation, attention, and intervention.

No one is pretending that the work of parenting or teaching is not tough, tiring, or intensive at times. Yet if you are doing it right, it should be thrilling and tremendously rewarding *just as often*. Equipped with the Four Ls, parenting certainly does not need to be routinely terrifying or tension-filled anymore.

The difference between a parent who is merely superficial or only sporadic with providing the Four Ls and one who is serious and steady—and therefore, successful—is all in the amount of intention, attention, and consistency they impart. Effort may also be a distinguishing factor, but you have likely seen parents who work extremely hard at raising their kids but who in reality are only spinning their wheels. Or making things worse. By and large, their exhausting parenting efforts are ineffective because all their exertion simply goes unheeded or unnoticed by their children. These parents do not need to work any harder, they need to work smarter.

So it is with many ineffective teachers. Go into any out-of-control, dysfunctional classroom, and you are likely to see an extremely hardworking, dedicated teacher. They may be drowning, but they can tread water with the best of them. Thus, effort alone is not enough.

EXAMPLES OF INSUFFICIENCY IN PARENTING AND TEACHING

Then there are those other parents who really have no idea what true greatness entails. They were probably parented just as serviceably as they are parenting their own children now and have never taken the time to find out if there is a better way for both themselves and their kids. Blindly going through the motions may seem like the easiest course, but every one of these adults pay for their passivity sooner or later—probably with the same flare ups and crises with children perpetually reoccurring like clockwork.

Insufficiency in Providing Leadership

The passive parents who think they are leaders by merely providing food, shelter, and material items—and throwing in a few rules here and there that are actually given nothing more than lip service—are only fooling themselves. Everyone else, including their children, sees clearly the ramifications and lost opportunities that perfunctory parenting brings. These parents are not completely indifferent to the ways their children ignore their halfhearted calls to "settle down" or to "stop that," but they always tend to tolerate, and therefore perpetuate, their kids' nearly constant dysfunction, disrespect, and disregard.

It is the same with teachers who go over the class rules the first day and then assume they have performed all of their management responsibilities for the year. Their firmness is put aside as they dutifully set themselves to the "real" task of teaching. In these cursory classrooms, of course, most learning is interrupted or corrupted by their unruly, defiant students who have never been truly motivated to cooperate. Since the teacher is bereft of any management tools other than idle warnings and punishments, none of their efforts make the situation any better.

Insufficiency in Providing Love

Those superficial parents who think that love and caring have nothing to do with frequent, focused attention, encouragement, and positive recognition for their children are in for a long, hard road. Their children have no incentive to please their parents because their parents rarely please them in the most profound and personal ways they yearn for.

Similarly, teachers who convey an emotional separation between themselves and their students soon pay the price. Because these teachers think it is not part of their job description to be warm, welcoming, and complimentary, their lack of effort to be understanding, patient, and congratulatory is definitely noticed by every student. In return, these callous, clinical teachers are rewarded with aloofness, unresponsiveness, and even loathing from their students.

Insufficiency in Providing Laughter

Those haphazard parents who think laughing with their children while watching some insipid sitcom is the same as going on family outings, attending their children's games, activities, and teacher conferences, or actively supporting their kids in discovering their talents and dreams, are in for a bracing reality check. Their children are longing for some real adventure and exciting interaction as a family, none of which must be expensive or elaborate. They are confused as to why their parents do not encourage them or invest in their personal interests. Then again, besides TV, their parents do not show much interest in much of anything themselves.

Likewise, teachers who never reveal anything about themselves personally or their passions, especially for the subject to which they have devoted their professional life, are not going to draw their students out to be enthusiastic, committed, or creative learners and thinkers. Whether or not teachers think they are paid to "entertain" their students, their students will be withdrawn and even hostile in a lifeless class devoid of meaning, humor, self-expression, and choice.

Insufficiency in Providing Learning

Those parents who think that buying school supplies each fall, dropping their kids off at school each morning (even if it is sometimes late), and merely saying, "Do your homework," is all that is needed for their children to achieve in school or in life, are simply in for it. Whether or not these parents feel it is solely their children's responsibility to keep up with their studies, children need the *most* motivation for the things they are most disinclined to do.

Just because some parents may not have been good students themselves or may have had little formal education, this is no excuse to be clueless about how much concerted effort it takes a parent and child working in close partnership in order to succeed in school. Parents must educate themselves about the rigors of seeing their children through their school years. They may never be able to provide much direct assistance with their children's homework, but their interest, involvement, and supervision of their children's academic progress is their nonnegotiable duty.

By comparison, the teacher who merely instructs, rather than facilitates learning, is only scratching the surface of what students need. Merely covering the material may be the quickest route, but such cursory teaching does not cut it. Children need multiple avenues to access increasingly challenging material, they need to be strategically provided with a strong foundation of essential skills and knowledge, and they must be increasingly required to take charge of their own learning. None of these elements of facilitating are fast or easy, but they are the only means to authentic and deep learning.

Of course, it is the children who are really in for it when they are saddled with merely serviceable, superficial, or spaced-out parents or teachers. Kids deserve so much more, and this book is dedicated to seeing that the adults finally "get it" so all children get their due.

INCONSISTENCY IN PARENTING AND TEACHING

Finally, there are those parents and teachers who do occasionally exert their leadership and firmness, express their love and fairness, embrace their laughter and fascination, and/or enable their learning and facilitation—sometimes quite appropriately. The problem is, these adults lack consistency in motivating children. They take things for granted, simply hope for the best, put up with the worst, and/or are unwilling to sustain the effort and intention all children need to be inspired to be conscientious for themselves.

This irony should not be lost on you. How in the world could any parent expect consistent cooperation and courtesy, closeness and candor, contentment and collaboration, as well as comprehension and capability, from their children if the parents themselves seldom give their children those things in return?!

You saw this in the complaints that kids have about their parents in chapter 6. Your children will be reluctant to follow your lead if they chronically see that you do not practice what you preach. Relationships are indeed a two-way street, and when it comes to children, they not only need consistency from adults, they need that consistency to be in the form of potent persuasion that constantly entices them to do the right things.

Inconsistent parents and teachers are not horrible; they are just malingering, intermittent, and patently mediocre. They are not abusive or wholly neglectful. They are not completely cold or coddling. They are not averse to fun. They do not even say that learning is not important.

Some parents, however, exert little effort to truly raise their kids right, beyond just working hard at a job to provide the basics, plus some (often unwarranted) material rewards. Being a working parent, especially a working single parent, is admittedly difficult and particularly draining. Yet it is no excuse for not consistently lavishing your children with their four essential needs.

THE TRUE MEANING OF COMMITMENT

Great parents and teachers can cite a laundry list of specific ways in which they routinely provide children with the Four Ls and the Four Fs. None of this active, intentional motivation is a mystery or a secret to them. Every word and deed that comes from these adults can be directly traced to one of their four fundamental means of persuasion. In fact, they can easily explain how and why they interact with and influence kids precisely because they are always so intentional with what they say and do around children. These adults are routinely proactive, self-reflective, and consciously refining the art of parenting and teaching.

Thus, responsible parenting requires real commitment. Whether it pertains to parenting, marriage, friendship, or teaching, commitment means that from the very beginning you freely entered into a relationship knowing full well—nay, *expecting*—there would be tribulations and temptations that would at times entice you to stray from your obligation to this bond.

As far as parenting, you entered this commitment with your eyes wide open because you were well aware of the hardships and hankerings that would inevitably come along. You even knew that these seductive temptations to just give up or give in can cause even the strongest of parents to question or falter. Of course, what you also knew and what ultimately enticed you enter this compact with another human being was that there would be enough joy, belonging, and adventure shared between you and your child to see you both through the occasional tough times.

What you may not have known is that whenever you feel like this commitment to your children is too much of or too frequent a sacrifice—and every parent and teacher has moments of doubt or despair—it is always wrong to become resentful toward your children for how much relentless work this relationship actually requires. You see, in any committed relationship, all obligations you fulfill and sacrifices you make are not made exclusively for the other people in that relationship. The truth is that you are never doing something dutifully or selflessly *for* your children. Instead, you are always contributing to *the relationship itself.*

And remember that this relationship always includes you! You are just as big a part of this as anyone else, with just as much to gain and just as much to lose. Everything you do for your children is done just as much for you because it is done *for the relationship.* You are simply giving to something much greater than just yourself or just your children. Maintaining this perspective of the true meaning of commitment transforms giving into a pleasure and an eager generosity because all parties always reap and share *equally* in all benefits.

Forget forever the insidious internal debates about whose needs are more important, who is giving more, or who comes first and when. In reality, there is no such thing as sacrifice in a true commitment. Approached in the right way, all committed relationships are constantly win-win—even during those times when you fall under the illusion that you are on the losing end.

In all families—big or small, single parent or two mommies, blended or traditional, nuclear or divided, fostered or adopted, guardian or surrogate, and everywhere in between—love makes a family. Of course, true love requires true commitment. Since someone must be the leader, that responsibility falls squarely on the adults in the house. With that leadership and love in place, that house becomes a home. When the parents also provide laughter and learning, that home becomes a haven—not just for the children but for the parents as well.

Also, always remember that this family you entered into and worked so hard to build was done to fulfill a deep longing within you. You craved connection, closeness, and devotion with another human being. You were irresistibly lured by the joys you knew this commitment would bring, happiness that nothing else in your life would or could ever bring.

Therefore, approach your children and your crucial role as parent with all the graciousness, glee, and giddiness as when you first held that infant in your arms or when you first welcomed that new child into your home. Not only is it never too late to get those feelings back and to make up for lost time, it is this relationship that you have always truly wanted and what you need most.

Chapter 9

Addressing Extreme Behavior in Children

It is important to note that when adults take one or more of their four roles too far in either direction, this imbalance plays right into children's main criticisms, worries, and fears of their parents and teachers. Kids loathe an exclusively domineering and punishing adult yet feel insecure and out of control around a weak adult who provides little structure or guidelines. They also dislike feeling ignored, distrusted, or misunderstood by adults yet do not like to be babied or suffocated by them.

Furthermore, kids detest environments that have no elements of excitement, adventure, or joy yet feel stifled by adults who somehow always manage to strip the fun, camaraderie, and choice out of what was supposed to be a child-centered activity. They also despise an adult who is seldom satisfied with their efforts and who constantly puts pressure on them for perfection yet complain about parents who show no real interest in or provide no real assistance with their schoolwork.

As a consequence of a chronic imbalance in having their fundamental needs met, children will either act out, act aloof, or act invisible. Remember that where there is a significant void in consistent and thorough parenting or teaching, kids will either rush in or retreat—and always in the exact direction the adults do not want them to go! Children can smell an opportunity to take advantage or an excuse to withdraw, and sometimes all it takes is a small gap or slight disequilibrium in effective adult motivation. This is why adult vigilance and consistency are key.

If the following possible extremes in a child's behavior scare you (because you either never want to deal with such dysfunction or because you have seen glimpses of such severity in your own children), remember that knowledge is power. Chapter 12 will assist you in using all your insights to bring your parenting approach into proportion precisely so your children regain and retain their own equilibrium. Striking the correct balance and restoring consistency are the only ways to bring back a child who is currently rebelling, withdrawing, or retreating from the extreme, insufficient, or inconsistent treatment the adults in their life are giving them.

The following extremes in classroom behaviors are illustrated in detail in my first book, *The Firm, Fair, Fascinating Facilitator*, along with specific strategies for a teacher to turn these adverse behaviors around. It is beneficial for parents to become familiar with these examples because you may not only have seen your own children acting in such unproductive ways at home but also at school.

Furthermore, some parents have to face the fact that the majority of the time their children's teachers did not create these negative behaviors. Oh, a weak teacher may not help a problem or may even exacerbate a situation, but teachers are mostly responding as well as they can to a challenge that was already there. Nevertheless, Four Fs teachers have vast experience at diminishing or eliminating dysfunction, at least while the student is in their class.

Even though these unproductive student habits often stem from the home, this is not meant as an opportunity for blame. Rather, it is a call to action on both the parent's and the teacher's parts to as quickly and cohesively as possible address and mitigate these extreme behaviors in children so they do not destroy the home environment for the whole family or the educational environment for the entire class!

Therefore, every parent needs to be aware not only of how students who exhibit extreme behaviors in the classroom negatively impact their own child's education, but how these challenging children can unfavorably influence their own child's behavior. These unruly or apathetic students are not the role models or peers you want persuading your children, so it is in everyone's best interest to turn these detrimental behaviors around as soon as possible.

Thus, a parent hopes there is a firm, fair, fascinating facilitator in every classroom who assumes the role of the prime, positive role model and who sets the tone for a productive and pleasant year for every student. Since this book emphasizes education, let us look at how teachers can effectively deal with these extreme student behaviors and also make connections as to how to reinforce solutions at home.

REBELLION: ACTING OUT

These rebellious darlings are the class destroyers who crave any form of attention (positive *or* negative) at all costs, seemingly all the time. In general, their manner of acting out ranges from being annoyingly immature to rudely disruptive to unpredictably angry. Sometimes they manifest all three qualities!

It takes only one of these kids to suck a teacher's sanity and to steal the education from the rest of the class. Stick several in one class, and it can be a year of hell for everyone involved. This is why teachers must approach these children from every motivating angle right from the start with a potent combination of the Four Fs. In the same manner, one child's misbehavior at home is likely to rub off on their siblings, and parents will need the persuasive powers of the Four Ls to promptly redirect that child before all their kids are acting out in the same ways.

Immature

Rebellion can take the form of an irritating immaturity that can cause a teacher to feel more like a babysitter than an educator. These kids have been so over-stimulated, over-praised, and over-indulged (all too often without earning it) that they shut out anything that requires extended attention and effort or that does not provide them with instant, tangible rewards.

They have been spoiled in the most harmful ways and ignored in the ways they needed attention the most. No one took them under their wing, guided, and pushed them. Instead, they were either neglected or babied with not much in between those two damaging extremes. Because they have been shielded from disappointment all their lives, not getting their way is something they do not take kindly to. They incessantly nag because they fully expect that the teacher will eventually give in like everyone else does.

Whiny, lazy, and selfish, they rely on their teacher and classmates for almost everything: for materials (essential items are often missing or a mess), for help with classwork (which they probably could have done on their own had they just paid attention), and for aid during their constant conflicts (which they themselves frequently instigated). They do not take responsibility for their actions and invariably butt into others' business.

They are expert manipulators and sneaky as heck! They will protest to their parents that their teacher is lying and that all adults treat them unfairly or pick on them. They will always claim their innocence (and turn on the waterworks if need be) and swear up and down they do not have any homework.

They can be impulsive, fidgety, squirmy, and squirrely, too. These students are forever trying to get out of their seats and are full of excuses and ailments, complaints and crisis. They do not transition well and are instantly distracted. They rarely make an attempt to act their age or to control themselves, not because they cannot but because they so often choose not to. And why would they if no one before has had the skills or the infinite patience to irresistibly persuade them to act better?

Whether or not they are currently diagnosed with a specific learning disability or ADHD, the fact is that these children do indeed possess a large capacity to significantly improve all on their own should the spirit move them, even without a specialist, an aide, or a prescription. Yet some kids simply refuse (for now) to buy what the teacher is selling and are quite content to wallow in their infantile nonsense. They often take one triumphant step forward then two demoralizing steps backward as teachers constantly chip away at their most disruptive behaviors.

Immature children live from moment to moment, constantly attempting to put what should come first, last—or even better, not at all. This selfishness and subterfuge can wear a teacher down because it is impossible to babysit and to teach (and to teach well) at the same time. Counteracting such ingrained dysfunction can be endlessly exhausting when you are trying your best and they are not trying at all, especially when all they are trying for is what *they* want.

Yet immature students are a mass of contradictions because, in spite of themselves, teachers will suddenly and frequently find these kids endearing and innocently sweet! They would do anything for them. But until these children meet their teachers halfway, teachers are stuck in a love/hate relationship that is turning them inside out and their classroom upside down—not to mention the havoc these hellions are wreaking at home.

Disruptive, Defiant, and Disrespectful

An adolescent mixture of being anti-school, anti-authority, and anti-*everything* creates another type of rebellious child who at best does not take a teacher's rules or their curriculum seriously and at worst purposely undermines and rejects all the positivity teachers generously offer. Chronically disruptive and distracting, these kids incessantly impede the learning process for themselves and everyone else.

Whether they are a class clown or purposely petulant, they are constantly talking, turned around in their seat, or show up late to class. They are too often disrespectful, rude, or blatantly defiant. They are prone to back talk and turn simple requests into a battle. They purposely drag their feet or pretend to have not heard you. They are difficult to trust because they can also be quite destructive by marking, marring, breaking, or stealing precious class materials.

These rebels are too cool for school. They do not hesitate to let everyone know that they are not interested in buying what the teacher is selling and that anyone who does so is patently uncool and the rightful object of ridicule. Thus, it is not so easy to love these kids at all.

Yet Four Fs teachers are not astonished when these children are indeed won over and eventually become their very favorite—and they, theirs. In fact, it is often the parents who are astounded by their child's dramatic turnaround in a Four Fs teacher's class. That teacher must then remind the parents and the child that since such progress is indeed possible, it must be capitalized on and gradually extended to every other class this student attends.

Angry

The last type of rebellious student either requires kid gloves or boxing gloves. Some of these angry students carry chips on their shoulders and can suddenly become quite volatile. They may be fine one moment, perhaps for days, and then be furious or fist fighting the next. Caught up in the heat of the moment, reason does not work on these children.

Responsibility and self-awareness also do not come readily to them. They do not like being told what to do. Deeply angry about *something*, they can take that fury out on anybody at any time, verbally or physically. They do not shy away from challenge or confrontation, and they rarely back down. The other kids know exactly how to push their buttons and do so for the sheer sport of it. So, these seething students allow themselves to get caught in a vicious cycle of inevitably and often losing their temper.

Ironically, teachers can make the most headway with these angry children, so they must resist the urge to write them off as lifelong troublemakers. It may take a while, but once the Four Fs finally convince these kids that not only is their teacher not their enemy but they are in fact their greatest champion, these formerly furious children become a completely new person when in that teacher's presence. Once they let down their guard and let a teacher in, they will leave that teacher and the child's parents with the eternal hope that even the hardest cases can eventually come around when consistently approached in the right ways.

RELUCTANCE: ACTING ALOOF

These reluctant students are the class deadeners who shun attention but secretly seek help and reassurance. Their reluctance spans a continuum that ranges from the guarded, embarrassed, shy, unsure, unprepared, unchallenged, and unconvinced to the lazy, indifferent, dismissive, and skeptical. Either way, it is exhausting to get them to focus, respond, participate, persevere, or produce.

However, teachers would be wrong to write these kids off as lifelong laggards just because they do their best to hide their light under a bushel. Are they naturally timid, or is it because they think it is not cool to be smart? Are they girls who err on the side of being demure, or have they never been actively encouraged to participate before? Are they passive because everything was spoon fed to them in the past?

Left to their own devices, they will not give their teachers their best, and they may not even try. Under the right conditions and given enough time, however, they are likely to strive and engage. Being fascinating and fair will captivate and help to convince them that they matter. Low skills could be one factor that is driving their reluctance, so these children may also need a true facilitator to guide them step by step toward proficiency.

Another reason why parents and teachers have to worry about these withdrawn children is because just a handful of unresponsive students in one class could set a precedent for apathy that could spread throughout the entire class. If a teacher or parent is not careful, these indifferent kids can seduce other children into being equally moody, uninvolved, or just plain lazy. Too many children are just looking for a reason to check out or to be a bit rebellious, even if that defiance is in a form of an adolescent ennui where they passively parade how they are completely "over" anything that has to do with school.

Therefore, parents and teachers have a twofold job. They must be armed with enticing motivators that steer children clear of any negative or unproductive peer influences while at the same time win over those few who have the potential to be the one bad apple that ruins the bunch.

RETREAT: ACTING INVISIBLE

These children in retreat are the class killers who shut down almost completely but who so desperately seek a helping hand, though they would never let others know it. They range from the closed, uncommunicative, and insecure to the most fearful, distrustful, withdrawn, worried, jaded, and cynical.

Someone, somewhere has let them down, possibly multiple times and in the most damaging of ways. Is it home that is hell with its chaos, abuse, abandonment, loss, or neglect? Is it the neighborhood with its violence and uncertainty that is causing this kid such strife? Or is it the school itself with its bullies and alienation that makes learning a mere afterthought?

These children have already written themselves off as lifelong losers who possess a self-defeating outlook on school and on their futures. A strong sense of futility pervades these kids' world view, so they are flat-out unwilling to give their teachers anything. They are often absent, truant, or tardy, which makes it difficult to make any consistent headway with them.

What these children in retreat need first and foremost is a caring, encouraging, and supportive relationship with a fair teacher. If those kids can just stay around long enough, a Four Fs teacher can use this wedge to convince them they are not only welcomed but a necessary part of the class community.

Parents who coddle their children or allow them any excuse to stay home from school are doing much more damage than they realize. The loss of learning these kids receive, however, is only one-fourth of what they lose. In the hands of a Four Fs teacher, every moment that child is not in class also means a profound loss of stability, structure, and routine; warmth, championing, and recognition; and passion, meaning, and involvement. Don't you think a daily dose of these powerful motivators would do these kids in retreat a world of good?

RANDOMNESS: ACTING INCONSISTENTLY

If you have not seen your children in some aspect of the above descriptions, you certainly have seen kids acting in these extremes in your extended family, in friends' families, around the neighborhood, or in the schoolyard. Ultimately, everyone pays the price for counterproductive behavior in children, but gaining insight into these behaviors assists all adults in motivating these children toward more advantageous ends.

Depending on how ingrained these bad habits have become, change can be long, hard work, both on the school front and home front, but it can be done. And it will only be done through the concerted efforts of the Four Ls of Parenting (leadership, love, laughter, learning) and the Four Fs of Teaching (firmness, fairness, fascination, facilitation). Waiting around for a child to "grow out of" a negative phase is to squander precious time which could be used to lure them into leading a contented, constructive life *right now*.

Yet what about the children who are maddeningly inconsistent and who respond to motivation, but only to a point? These are those "random" kids who exist between the lines of being regularly rebellious, reluctant, in retreat, *or* routinely agreeable—because they show signs of *all* of these behaviors at various times, both the good and the bad! Their inconsistency can become an adult's undoing because you never know what they are going to give you from moment to moment.

Here are some questions you have probably already pondered:

- How can a child who can be positive and productive (because you have seen it with your own eyes a million times) temporarily devolve into dysfunction and then later revert right back to his favorable old self?
- Why would good behavior and a pleasant attitude be only hit or miss in some kids?
- When you require them to work or play independently, why do they suddenly abandon all of the self-control, effort, attention, drive, and excitement they were just sincerely displaying during direct interaction with you?
- What is the reason why certain kids will behave only when you yourself are actively and overtly supervising them? But the minute your back is turned or you leave the room …

- What is going on inside these children that they pay attention but only sporadically?
- Why do they respond, participate, and volunteer but only intermittently?
- Why are they only engaged and focused occasionally—even during the times when you are sure they are extremely interested in the task at hand?
- Why when they actually do their classwork or homework is there little quality, only the bare minimum is given, and their effort is only sustained for the shortest of stretches?
- What is distracting or denying them from consistently being their best—the best that you just saw yesterday or the best that you just saw five minutes ago?
- The Four Ls and the Four Fs are clearly working on them to some degree, but why not with any lasting consistency? (Especially in light of the fact that the parents and the teacher are being conscientiously consistent with their motivation!)

As if this sloth, fooling around, and tuning out were not destructive enough, along may blow a different type of ill wind: that of antipathy, aversion, and animosity for all things home or school related—including you. Suddenly, *the parent or the teacher* is the bad guy simply for being in charge—even when they are in charge of giving praise or proposing an exciting activity!

Out of nowhere, now it is cool for all of your formerly loyal children to think that family is for fools and learning is for losers. Out of the blue, there is contention and petulance about their whole world, which right now happens to be the confines of *your* living room or a teacher's classroom. Adolescent angst, sheer awkwardness in knowing who they truly are and what they really need, and consistently awful peer, adult, and media role models may be partly at play here.

The Microcosm of Middle School

Are these just typical, random middle school behaviors? Perhaps, because middle school is a microcosm for how kids generally behave in elementary and high school as well. Broadly speaking, sixth graders display a more elementary school type of behavior of mainly wanting to please their parents and teachers and to be a part of the family or class community.

Seventh graders, on the other hand, want only to fit in with their popular peers. Being perceived as a teacher's pet or a "schoolboy" often runs counter to their growing quest for independence from adults, even as they increasingly depend on acceptance from and inclusion with their peers. Being marked different than the in-group or labeled as odd in any way is an awful curse on those kids who cannot manage to fit in, no matter how hard they may try.

Finally, eighth graders are more high school-like as they wear their burgeoning uniqueness as a badge of honor—just as long as they have a small clique to validate their singularity. They begin to withdraw from family functions and to distance themselves from their more "childlike" past. They want to be treated like a grown up, even when they do not act like one.

Mainly, elementary kids follow the leader (their parents and teachers), middle school kids follow the crowd (their peers), and high school kids follow their own drummer (which is likely the thing you yourself can least relate to!).

And then there's the fact that they are *children*. They are at times simply confused, conflicted, distracted, and daydream-y kids, like we all were at one time or another and to varying degrees. They are also mischievous, manipulative little rascals who delight in confounding and confronting adults from time to time.

They are feeling their way, but the only way through these occasional bouts of randomness is through adult balance and consistency. It cannot be a matter of the blind leading the blind, and it cannot be a hit-or-miss endeavor. Again, what you are doing with these children is obviously working a great deal of the time, so the only thing you can do is to keep at it in order to persuade your sometimes "random" children to respond favorably even more of the time.

IN MY CLASSROOM: REMAINING VIGILANT

All I know is that when any of these counterproductive student attitudes and actions, no matter how chronic or random, cause me to despair and to feel all at sea, it is the Four Fs that always put me back onto the right course, fighting the good fight. I focus on all the favorable influence I do possess with my students—even with the neediest and most notorious—and remain content with the inroads I make.

I calmly remind myself that tightening up on my firmness may be all that is needed to get my normally cooperative students back on track. I recall that with an extra dose of fairness and support, I instantly revive that happy bond I share with my students. I remember that I am still just as excited as my students will be when I teach that fascinating, challenging, and profound lesson tomorrow! Finally, I note that it is directly because of my expertise as a facilitator that my students were able to accomplish the rigorous task before them and are making steady progress, even despite their occasional lapses of attention, effort, or awareness.

In fact, I have come to attribute much of my classroom success to the ways in which I am vigilant, exacting, and proactive in my expressions of firmness because that ever-present order, cooperation, and courtesy allows my fairness, fascination, and facilitation to be featured. My biggest adversary is not my troublesome or troubled students; it is my own potential to fall prey to laziness or distraction.

Therefore, I do not let anything slide or go unaddressed in my classroom, and I do not allow my words and wishes to go unheeded. I rarely make a big deal out of things, however, because I do not have to. Since I dutifully intervene when indiscretions are small, all it usually takes is a look, a gesture, a quick reminder, or a word of caution to get my students back on task.

Some children do need more redirecting than others, yet my painless but pointed interventions cost me nothing and gain me everything. If extra sternness is called for, I summon that part of my teaching persona without hesitation because that is what the student or the class needed at the time. Then I am right back, pleasant as ever, facilitating some fascinating lesson or celebrating and encouraging my students with my fairness.

Nevertheless, I am scrupulous about student conduct, and I am not scared or doubtful of my firmness, procedures, expectations, or demands. I dutifully enforce positive, productive student behavior and attitude, and I am not shy about the validity of my needs as a teacher. I am always on top of things, which in turn persuades my students to be on top of themselves.

The misbehaviors and mischief that most teachers would dismiss as inconsequential, I focus upon and quickly diffuse because I know that if I do not, it will be I who will soon be paying the consequences for my sloth and lack of leadership. I simply know that whatever a teacher or a parent condones, whether explicitly or implicitly, will always reoccur, intensify, and spread. Instead, what reoccurs, intensifies, and spreads in my classroom are only the things that I as their fearless, faithful leader have purposely planned and actively persuaded to happen.

As far as my most challenging students are concerned, I first ensure that the ways they may act out, withdraw, and retreat do not get worse by proceeding to lay down the law *and* lay on the charm. Then I can concentrate on influencing them to act increasingly better while wooing them to the wonders that school can offer—if they will just give me a chance.

This proactive, intentional, and confident approach to my classroom management, my rapport with my students, my unabashed passion for teaching, *and* my challenging curriculum does take constant effort and attention. However, this course of action is far easier than the alternative where my instruction is chronically interrupted and undermined and I am too frustrated or furious to be warm or whimsical. I do not mind working hard, especially when the work I do is so important and when the effort and attention I put in pays off in such fantastic ways for myself and my students.

Chapter 10

Diffusing Conflicts between Parents and Teachers

There are various categories of divisiveness that can occur between parents and teachers. Yet no teacher wants parents to initiate contact only when there is a conflict, just as no parent wants to only hear from a teacher when there is bad news. So, this chapter continues to advocate for balance in that if we all truly accept the fact that parents and teachers share the same goals and high expectations for kids, we must then let reason prevail and not jump to accusations and outrage whenever there is a hiccup in the often "messy" job of nurturing children.

HANDLING MISTAKES IN-HOUSE

While the Four Ls and Four Fs are the best ways to meet children's fundamental needs, these similar, sound approaches to motivating kids do not automatically guarantee perpetually smooth sailing between adult and child. There are bound to be mishaps and missteps on both the adults' and children's parts. When these misunderstanding and mistakes occur, however, the adult must continue to use their four avenues of inspiration to bring harmony back to the relationship.

Since nearly all adult slights and snubs toward children are completely unintentional, many times the adult may not initially even be aware that they made a mistake or that the child felt unduly shamed or upset. Children can be painfully self-conscious, especially around their peers, so misunderstandings can easily occur.

Thus when parents and teachers occasionally mess up, their explanations are readily offered, their sincere apologies are cheerfully accepted, the child's forgiveness is graciously granted, and the matter soon fades, especially in comparison to the usually close bond this adult and child routinely share. The child quickly remembers that this adult has long been on their side as evidenced by the strong feelings of stability, support, stimulation, and success this adult has consistently provided for them.

A Four Ls parent and a Four Fs teacher can deftly handle any mishaps in-house, within the confines of the living room or the classroom. These adults have become experts at mitigating hurt feelings or soothing wounded prides and rarely need outside help or involvement.

BALANCING QUESTIONS AND CONCERN WITH TRUST AND RESPECT

Then there are those other times when the parent or teacher is either directly informed or suspects that something happened or continues to happen outside of their respective domain that needs some explanation. These adults simply care so much about this child that they also care what happens to this kid's life outside of their domain, especially when they see negative effects carry over from school to home or vice versa.

What can be bad about parents caring how teachers treat their children when they are not around or teachers caring how parents treat their students when they are not around? The answer is there is nothing wrong with care and concern—as long as it is done within reason, with mutual respect, and an ever-present reliance on the best intentions of both parties. Also keep in mind that the adult in question may not even be aware they have caused a child discomfort or distress.

In the relations between parents and teachers, we must focus on creating and maintaining an atmosphere of shared understanding where blame and blow ups very rarely come into play. We must also be ever cognizant of the fact that there will always be some minor errors and altercations when parents and teachers interact with children, but that does not mean conflict or crisis must then ensue between parent and teacher as well!

Recall that the way in which a parent and child or teacher and student were brought back into harmony after a blunder or a bump in the road was by the child quickly realizing that this adult was always on their side. This type of rational thinking and benefit of the doubt based on an already-established trusting relationship with each other are what parents and teachers must cling to *before* they jump to conclusions or rush to judgment against each other. This is what being on the same team means, and if you have got this far through this book, you are committed to this strong parent–teacher partnership that directly benefits your children.

COMMON PARENT–TEACHER CONFLICTS

The following are some of the most common issues parents and teachers may have with each other:

1. **Issues with a Parent's Leadership or a Teacher's Firmness**
   - The teacher may need the parent to exert more supervision, structure, strictness, or sanctions at home in order to positively influence their child's behavior, attitude, and accomplishment in school.
   - The parent may need the teacher to explain or justify a consequence, punishment, or action imposed by the teacher. These parental concerns often have to do with the teacher raising their voice, chastising a student, sending the student out of class, issuing detention, or confiscating items that belong to the student. Also, parents may question a teacher using any sort of physical contact to assert, emphasize, or enhance their authority in order to gain compliance from the student.
2. **Issues with a Parent's Support or a Teacher's Fairness**
   - The teacher may need the parent to be less intrusive in their requests for individualized updates and attention for their child. The parent may need to understand and accept that there are multiple demands upon the teacher concerning a multitude of other students and other parents who also need to be attended to. Each child is important but no more or less so than any other, and a teacher must diligently balance all students' specific needs.
   - The parent may need explanation as to why another child received an award, accolade, or privilege instead of their child. The parent also may want to know why certain students get treated differently than their child. They may not understand that being fair is giving what each child needs at the time, rather than always treating each child exactly the same. Conversely, the parent may need to deal with the fact that some classroom rules and routines must remain the same for all and that exceptions will not be granted.
   - The parent may question a teacher using any sort of physical contact to express comfort, compassion, or congratulation to a student, or they may need clarification as to the amount of time or familiarity shared between the teacher and their child.
3. **Issues with a Parent's Pressure or a Teacher's Free Expression**
   - The teacher may need to inform a parent that their child is responding negatively to the pressures the parent is placing upon them because this stress is affecting the child's overall attitude about school and life in general. Whether these parental demands concern grades, extracurricular

activities, caring for siblings, working at a job, or not allowing their child to dream their own dreams, a teacher may have to tactfully give a parent a reality check.
- The teacher may need the parent to offer incentives to their child to behave properly and achieve progressively in school. The benefits of positive reinforcement, from praise to privileges to prizes, may need to be explained to the parent, especially if the parent's exclusive use of punishments is not working.
- Parents may take issue with the ways their children are being encouraged to think critically, question the status quo, express their opinions, be creative, or collaborate with classmates. They may also be concerned or confused that the teacher is expanding beyond the traditional curriculum and wonder if the teacher is crossing a line in terms of professional discretion and academic freedom. Controversial, provocative, or mature subject matter, literature, or media may also be called into question or need explanation.

4. **Issues with a Parent's Participation or a Teacher's Grading**
    - The teacher may need the parent to take on a more active or supervisory role when it comes to their child's homework, studying, being prepared, and staying organized.
    - Teachers may also take issue with how much parents help with homework or projects, especially in terms of essentially doing the work for their child or making corrections that the child is not even aware of, and therefore, not learning from.
    - Parents may place requests on teachers for more or less homework, the type of work and projects assigned, extra credit, makeup work, and extensions for deadlines. They may also question the grades their child earns, both for certain assignments or a final grade.

IN MY CLASSROOM: SEEKING PARENTAL ASSISTANCE

It is probably a combination of fatigue, futility, and frustration that sometimes leads me to be reluctant to call or conference with parents when I am having a recurring problem with a student. Personally, I have had very sparse success after speaking to a parent of a severely disruptive, defiant, or lazy student. Oh, after the phone call or meeting, often things may very well get better—but only at first. Soon after, things commonly erode back to where they were.

Far too often, that concerned and committed parent who had restored my faith in humanity soon returns to their fool's paradise of believing their child whenever he says that he has no homework or that someone else is entirely to blame when he gets in trouble. That parent initially may give supporting the teacher their best shot, but many grow weary of the constant effort it takes to turn around their kid's poor grades, attitude, or behavior—even at home.

It is not that these parents do not sincerely want things to be different. Just like with ineffective teachers, the reality is that parents who struggle with positively influencing their child's behavior would already be doing better if they only knew how! They are simply at a loss for how to contain their out-of-control or out-to-lunch adolescent.

Sheer laziness or lack of caring occurs just as rarely with parents as it does with teachers. Parents are usually doing the best they can with the few strategies they know but are completely overwhelmed by the seemly insurmountable, ever-escalating problems with their child. So when their child is at school, the parent's attitude too often is that it is now all the teachers' problem.

This is why I quickly came to believe that the Four Fs should be adapted for parents and would provide them with some much-needed clarity and direction. Of course, many parents need much more guidance than others, and an all too common teacher complaint about some parents is: "They just don't get it!"

And frankly, some parents really do not get it because they have no true conception of what thorough, consistent parenting entails. Imagine your child stuck with a well-intentioned but woefully ineffective teacher for a whole school year—which admittedly could have been with me twenty-plus years ago. Yet that parental dissatisfaction is the same frustration teachers feel when stuck with a parent who seldom reinforces at home all the positivity and productivity they are working tirelessly to motivate in their students at school.

The simple fact remains that if a child has parents who already provide consistent leadership, then by default the teacher's acts of firmness almost always work well on these kids. Do not think that children such as these do not need a teacher's firmness at all; it is just that these kids have been long-conditioned to respond quickly and often permanently to authority, rules, routines, and the fear of consequences.

Naturally, these parent leaders are usually very willing to assist a teacher with discipline issues. The problem is: These are not the parents a teacher really needs assistance from! What percentage of the parents who teachers desperately need to see do you think actually shows up for parent conferences? Are you surprised when teachers mostly meet and interact with the parents of their best behaved and hardest working students?

BALANCING ACCOUNTABILITY WITH CONFIDENCE

Directly or indirectly, the previously outlined parent–teacher issues are touched upon throughout this book. Of course, the main point is that if parents are properly providing their children with the Four Ls and teachers are supplying their students with the Four Fs, these issues will not manifest themselves very often.

Moreover, when they do, parents and teachers will already have the perspective of the other party clearly in mind and should easily discern between a misunderstanding and blatant malpractice or malfeasance. Most of the questions and potential issues described above usually turn out to be innocent encounters between teacher and student, which were often well-intentioned, were actually exactly what the student needed at the time, and are easily clarified.

Once parents and teachers know where they each are coming from in general—and we now are sure it is from a place of mutual and deep care for children—then it is simple to regain calm and certainty without making a big issue out every little foible or fumble. Furthermore, once parents and teachers get to know each other on a more personal basis—even if it is just shaking hands at Back to School Night—it is even easier to let most things go as trust and good intentions outweigh suspicion and blame.

This close relationship between the home and school is also the way children think twice about intentionally playing parents and teachers against each other. Kids need to know that unless it is an extreme and clear cut instance of adult abuse or malice, their parents and teachers will always be more united than divided in their support of each other.

Not very long ago, this adult alliance and trust was taken for granted. Unfortunately, now its erosion has resulted in the all too common, untenable situations where children rule the roost and rule the school—and the adults are increasingly too powerless or petrified to turn this divisive, disruptive, and often dangerous behavior around.

Please understand that placing the needs of children first does not mean putting parents and/or teachers last. *Parents and teachers can hold each other fully accountable for appropriately providing children with what they need, even while supporting and maintaining faith in each other as responsible, committed allies in the nurturing of children.*

Unquestionably, those few truly evil adults who seek to purposely harm children must be dealt with accordingly. However, scapegoating, witch hunts, and a mob mentality have no place in protecting kids or ensuring justice. These extremes only ruin lives, destroy careers, break up families, and pull the rug out from under children who were perfectly safe and content in a home or classroom that has now been upended by rumor, overreaction, and a rush to judgment.

Should a serious question ever arise about their child's teachers, the best parents will look on this as another opportunity for calm collaboration with the school and not merely an opportunity for expressing outrage. For if a teacher has an issue with you or your child, how do you prefer the teacher to approach the situation: With blame and bitterness or with an open mind that seeks information and a shared solution?

Always give what you want in return.

Chapter 11

Straight Talk from the Teaching Trenches

It is important for parents who seek to be collaborators with the classroom to try to see things from a teacher's perspective, especially when there is an issue where their own child was involved. Four Fs teachers always welcome sincere questions because they have already thoroughly analyzed and explained for themselves the what, why, and how of their instructional choices. Since they have made conscious decisions about everything that goes on in their classroom and how they interact with their students, these teachers are thrilled to answer any parental queries and prove exactly how all of their students are in good hands.

There is a big difference, however, between a parent seeking information, clarification, and confirmation as to the wisdom of a teacher's decisions—many of which must be instantaneous choices made in the midst of twenty-nine other kids clamoring for their attention—and seeking only to condemn or perhaps terminate a teacher for something that was done in the moment with the best of intentions. If you are not aware that teachers are being vilified, attacked, and undermined as a profession and sometimes personally, you need to see things from today's teachers' point of view.

In our litigious, accusatory, "I'm telling!," "You can't do that!," "My daddy said ..." society, teachers will have to be ready to defend their actions from time to time, especially regarding their firmness. Oh, everyone *says* they want teachers to maintain order and maximize instructional time for all; but when push comes to shove, most administrators and school boards will be less concerned with the teacher's rationale and more concerned with covering their behinds and finding anyone to blame besides themselves. In these situations, teachers must go in with their eyes wide open and expecting the worst.

If a teacher is ever called on the carpet, there is only one wise course of action: teachers must not ever let any administrator or parent lose clear sight of the fact that whatever action they may have taken that is now being called into question was done in a rational, calculated response to what *the child* did that necessitated any teacher response in the first place.

TEACHERS DO NOT RANDOMLY PICK ON STUDENTS

It is virtually unheard of for a dedicated teacher out of the clear blue and without any justifiable cause to take an action that may later be deemed questionable. Know that all teachers are already too exhausted and too overwhelmed to expend any extra energy to "pick on" a particular child. This just does not happen.

Teachers do not ever on a capricious whim aim to deliberately harass, insult, or accost an innocent student in any way. Please accept all this teacher integrity as fact. This way, if you ever are in a position to doubt a teacher's action, you can calmly and logically weigh the evidence between what a student or students may have done and what the teacher did *in response.*

In the event there is indeed an issue with a teacher's response, is there a possibility the teacher was indeed mistaken in their action? Absolutely. Is there the chance this one action could objectively be deemed inappropriate? Certainly. Is there the likelihood the teacher now views their action just as unfortunate as everyone else does? Definitely. If the teacher had the chance to do this all over again, would they probably choose a different response? You bet!

However, the probability that this regrettable circumstance was *entirely* the teacher's fault or done out of sheer animus or gross negligence is extremely slim. Therefore, a parent must be ready to accept the fact that maybe their own child was *mainly at fault* and was the *primary instigator* of this whole mess.

DETERMINING RESPONSIBILITY

Sometimes, a parent may need to hear some harsh reality about their child, and a teacher may be forced to state aloud and unflinchingly, "The fact of the matter is this child is a *thief.* No, he does not swipe items from my class. What he does is actually far worse. He chronically steals the education from his fellow students. He constantly robs me of my ability to teach those who want to learn. Your child regularly and wantonly defiles the educational sanctuary that is my classroom, and he does this without compassion or compunction. All he cares about is himself and trying to blame others for his own selfish and destructive choices."

Now, parents of cooperative, responsive, invested, and serious children should be quite pleased that in this example yet another teacher is standing up for the rights of the innocent just as much as that teacher may be defending herself in the process. Know that all a teacher does in terms of firmness is done for one purpose: to protect the learning environment for *all* students.

What people must also realize is that a teacher's reaction is rarely just about the single incident at hand. It is most often a response to the culmination of numerous acts of blatant disregard and chronic distraction from a student. This cumulative effect of the negative actions of a single student increases exponentially when you include all the other disrespectful or defiant students that teachers may encounter, both on and off of their class rosters. Teachers do not act in a vacuum, and nothing that happens in the classroom should be taken out of context.

Thus, it is easy to understand how a teacher can get worn down, her nerves can fray, and she can eventually lose patience. Notice the words "cumulative" and "eventually." Again, teachers almost never fly off the handle for little or no reason.

This is precisely why a teacher's firmness is so important and fundamental. Teachers are not just protecting their students' learning environment, they are protecting their own work environment. How are the students ever going to reap the joys of fairness, fascination, and facilitation if a teacher calls in sick, burns out, or permanently leaves the classroom—not to mention if the students are chronically out of control?!

This is obviously the same case for a parent. All your leadership, rules, routines, order, and structure in the home are maintained and enforced as much for your children's benefit as for yours. You must protect for yourself the sanctuary of the place you call home, or you will find yourself so stressed out that you snap, scream, and shut down just like any beleaguered teacher. In such an aggravating environment, how are you going to have the energy to truly express your love, allow laughter into your home, or assist with your children's learning?

IN MY CLASSROOM: ISOLATED INCIDENTS

In over twenty years, the times I had to face some reactionary parent or self-serving principal have been thankfully minimal. Yet in keeping with my "warts and all" honesty, I will be specific about the few times I suddenly found myself questioned and placed on the defensive.

I have always had a general policy of avoiding most forms of physical contact with my middle school students. I certainly do not engage in any sort of corporal punishment, and I do not accept hugs from my students.

I may infrequently offer a quick pat on the back for encouragement or a hand on the shoulder for emphasis, but that is about it. I also never allow myself to be alone in a classroom with a student, especially not behind a closed door.

These are my personal professional choices, which are made to avoid even a hint of controversy or notion of impropriety. It is just not worth it to me to ever have to explain or defend myself. That having been said, know that there are sound and compelling arguments both for and against teachers *appropriately* touching their students. You may find it interesting to read up on the rationales of both sides, especially concerning elementary school students.

Yet even with my sincere care and wise caution in how I interact with all students, both physically and verbally, there have still been a total of three times when I was accused of either "kicking" a student, "pushing" at student, or "yanking" a student's ear. Of course, these were all extreme exaggerations. Nevertheless, these honest anecdotes are offered to show that even the most conscientious teachers may be forced to explain themselves, even when falsely accused.

The first incident occurred during my third year of teaching. A student was constantly turning around in his seat and socializing with his classmate in the desk behind him. After he completely ignored my repeated, calm requests to stop disturbing the class with his chatter, I finally walked by where his legs were protruding into the aisle and in so doing physically scooted the student around in order to face forward and to focus on his assignment.

He called it a "kick" and promptly reported me. Of course, all that had been injured was his pride. Because he was used to running the show in other classrooms, he mistakenly thought he could escape his own culpability by making his teacher into the bad guy.

Another time early in my career, a student who I did not even know kept pestering my students while my classroom door was opened. When I went to shut the door, this boy placed his body in the doorway to intentionally prevent me from doing so. After he repeatedly ignored my requests that he leave and return to whichever class he was now ditching, I then proceeded to walk slowly and deliberately forward as a physical incentive for him to back away of his own volition. When he chose to remain in my way, I kept moving until the inevitable yet benign connection of our bodies finally made him realize that I was not playing around.

He immediately said I "pushed" him and promptly reported me. Again, all that had been injured was his foolish pride. Because he apparently thought he ruled the school, he too assumed he could escape culpability by making a teacher into the bad guy.

The final time was a sheer misunderstanding. I graciously allowed a student of mine to serve a time-out in my serene classroom when his other teacher had enough of him. I allowed this courtesy a few times before in order to support my colleague and because this was a student with whom I had a wonderful rapport. I knew he was a troublemaker in other classes but never in mine. I had also taught his older brother the year before, and he had been one of my favorite students.

So, when this boy uncharacteristically kept turning around to bother my students, I nicely asked him to get back to the work his other teacher had given him. After the fourth time, I playfully wiggled the lobe of his ear as I gently guided his head back to his assignment.

Two days later, his dad was in the principal's office enraged that I had "punished" his son by "yanking" his ear. I was dumbfounded as to how this boy had given this lighthearted admonishment a second thought, let alone how he had come to tell his father.

In fact, how his dad managed to completely overlook the wonderful rapport I had with his other son mystified me. Then again, how could this parent know anything about me when I had never met him before? Nevertheless, somehow I was the bad guy again, this time with a parent who had squandered multiple opportunities where I could have sung the praises of his *two* sons.

Obviously, these were isolated, in-the-moment incidents. These were the inevitable hiccups every human being encounters while in the midst of trying to be a good person, go about one's daily business, and get from point A to point B. Some people intentionally get in your way and then inexplicably refuse to respond to kindness or reason. For teachers these days, this happens a lot, both in the classroom and out on campus.

Now, as far as parents and teachers are concerned, let me be clear that *being the leader never means an adult can do anything they want in guiding and disciplining children, no matter what the child may have done in the first place, no matter how repeatedly or defiantly*. However, when the adult is the responsible leader, this also means the children are never free to do whatever they want either. Children must always show obedience, courtesy, and deference to authority. If they chose not to, there may be unpleasant consequences to pay.

This is how the world works: Everyone answers and is accountable to someone else. This is a vital life lesson, and one will never survive in the real world or the work world without respecting others and honoring authority. If you are not deliberately teaching your children this crucial fact of life, you are doing them and society a great disservice.

In the first two examples above, I simply chose not to abdicate my authority to a willfully defiant child. I also chose to handle things swiftly and in the moment so that learning could proceed for all involved—including for the child who was stealing the educational experience of others.

Yes, the whole class and I could have waited around while I perhaps called for a campus aide or administrator to come and intervene—if they ever showed up and if the child would even obey them—but again, I had work to do, students to attend to, and a lesson to teach to every person in the vicinity: This teacher means what he says and is not one of those adults who walks on eggshells around children.

We can debate all day long whether my actions in these three isolated incidences were the best choices possible or even appropriate. However, that is not what is at issue here. You can make your own judgments about my long ago actions if judging is what you are wont to do. Just know that I already have thoroughly scrutinized myself for you because I routinely self-reflect on what works and what does not, as well as what I would choose to do again and what I would not.

Firmness expressed in the form of any physical contact is something every parent must certainly reconcile for themselves. Nevertheless, in both the home and the school it should never be the default or first means of leadership. Yet if a child does not respond to the calm and easy way, an intensified expression of firmness may be exactly what that child needs at the time. This occasional, justified intensity fits completely into the definition of being fair and can be also viewed as an expression of love and concern.

As for me, it is worth noting that I never had a problem with any of those three students again. It was not that they then feared me; it was that they finally knew that I did not fear them or my role as the leader of my classroom. They simply learned that I was an adult who meant business, which in turn meant that they best take care of business while in my presence. Moreover, once these three accepted my authority as fact, they were free to fully enjoy the luxury of my fairness, fascination, and facilitation. In fact, that anonymous boy in the doorway became my student the next year, and we are still in friendly communication to this day.

Now as a proud and fully formed Four Fs teacher, by the first week of school all my students know everything they need to know about me: the good, the bad, and the ugly. By the second week and all the weeks thereafter, the good has become great, the "bad" is actually pretty good, and the ugly need rarely if ever be expressed. There is much that teachers and parents can do to prevent potentially volatile or dicey situations almost completely, especially when an adult is proactively motivating children toward the courteous and constructive.

Nevertheless, stuff happens—even in the best of situations and with the best of teachers and parents. This chapter was not pleasant to write, but I found it crucial to be upfront about the rare yet unfortunate parts of teaching. We cannot truly be allies if we do not approach each other with a balanced and honest perspective of the realities of today's classrooms and homes.

RATIONALLY ASSESSING UNFORTUNATE SITUATIONS

Of course, if the shoe were on the other foot and it was a teacher who was outraged and demanding severe consequences for something a child had done to them, both parent and child (and probably the principal) would be begging the teacher for understanding, forgiveness, and a second chance. "Can't we just sweep this under the rug and move on?" would be their implicit message. How sadly ironic it is that some people are so very reluctant to afford others the same leniency and compassion they greedily demand for themselves.

Like the father in the above example, there are far too many parents these days who are only interested in their child's education when one of two situations occurs, neither of which has to do with what the child is actually learning or how they really behave: Either a parent who never was actively involved before suddenly swoops in to try to save their obviously guilty child from some quite necessary negative consequence, or they burst in to express outrage and to cry injustice for some teacher intervention that in fact was completely appropriate and was exactly what that child both needed and deserved at the time.

Of course, as long as weak administrators cater to and cave in to parents who are only out for themselves or out for blood, teachers will never be free to be as firm as is sometimes necessary and as is completely reasonable—and it will ultimately be the students who suffer the most. Please avoid being one of these coddling or condemning parents, both for your children's sake, as well as on behalf of their teachers who are sincerely trying to give your child their best in four fundamental and rather fabulous ways.

What parents must realize in circumstances like those described above is that when parents' emotions run high and things are blown out of proportion or taken out of context, there are some common threads that run through similar situations when a teacher's actions are called into serious question.

Here is a list of frequent mitigating factors and questions that parents must always ask when there is an issue with a teacher's interaction with their child.

- Was the child given several calm and courteous chances to self-correct and to end the issue with their honor and dignity intact had the child simply cooperated the first time?

  How many times do you allow your own children to completely ignore your requests before you decide to take more intensive measures in order to gain their full attention and compliance? What lesson is any adult teaching children when we show them that it is completely unnecessary to heed our warnings or requests the first time—or even the second or third time? How much leeway are we willing to give uncooperative kids?

  Could unlimited, cheerful warnings and pleas actually be telling children that adult authority need not be respected until children themselves are good and ready—and sometimes not at all? How much time is lost, how much damage is done, how much negativity is reinforced—in both that child and every other who is watching—and how are the rights of many innocent others sacrificed when we capitulate and allow children to act defiantly without consequence?

- Were the teacher's actions made in response to what the child not only did first but also repeatedly chose to continue to do in willful defiance? Was it in any way like the teacher was "out to get" anyone?

  As you interact with your children, do you ever purposely look for reasons to embarrass, scold, or punish them? Of course not. Isn't a Four Ls parent too busy recognizing their children for their cooperation and accomplishments, sharing in some fun activity with them, or building up their confidence and capabilities—just like any dedicated teacher does?

- Did the teacher clearly have only the best of intentions? Were their actions actually nowhere in the realm of intentional abuse or impropriety?

  Can't you easily discern between reacting somewhat rashly to what your child did and deliberately being abusive or cruel? Are you able to forgive yourself for your well-intentioned mistakes? You should, and you should extend this courtesy and compassion to your children's teachers.

  Again, no one is giving any adults license to act with wanton impunity. Children and adults alike do make innocent mistakes, but when anyone chooses to make the same mistake over and over, especially in the same ways, it is then no longer a mistake. Now it is a conscious decision to harass another person and to disrupt the tranquility that others are entitled to. Unquestionably, intentional and malicious behavior such as this needs to be stopped, and the favor of kindness and patience toward that perpetrator, be it adult or child, is promptly withdrawn.

- Was the action that is being questioned highly unusual for this particular teacher, especially when viewed in the context of their routinely stellar conduct and conscientious career? By contrast, is the child's challenging behavior chronic and well-known by all?

  Are you ready and willing to be punished and stigmatized for every single momentary, isolated indiscretion you may ever make regarding your children? Does not a well-earned good reputation count for something and speak volumes about a person's true character? Does not a child's bad reputation need to be addressed and corrected sooner rather than later?

- Did the child actually need to learn an important lesson once and for all about what automatically respecting authority really means?

  All human beings have the option to learn things the hard way or the easy way. The Four Ls and the Four Fs proudly offer children the easy ways, and this is precisely why these parents and teachers rarely find themselves in thorny predicaments. Yet tricky situations can happen to anyone. Do you have unlimited time and composure to allow your children to accept your leadership only when they feel like it?

- Was the teacher also balancing the need to protect the learning environment for all of their students with attending to an individual child's antics?

  Try putting yourself in the shoes of the other students (and their parents) who are being denied their education because your child cannot play by the rules. If the shoe were on the other foot and it was your child's learning that was chronically being disrupted by a selfish student, who would you be judging: that recalcitrant child or that dedicated teacher who dutifully attempted to bring the interruption to a resolute closure?

- Did the teacher "escalate" this situation, or was it really that the teacher brought this situation to a swift and decisive end? If anyone did any sort of escalating, was it actually the child who chose to ignore the teacher's repeatedly calm requests for cooperation and courtesy?

  Have you ever felt that somehow you yourself were at fault for finally shutting down defiant, disrespectful, or dangerous behavior on the part of your children, or did you feel that you were faithfully fulfilling your duty as leader? If the child then became angry at the increased but necessary and appropriate intensity of your leadership, did you feel guilty, or were you confident that your child could stew in their own juices for as long as they wanted to pout about something that they in fact brought upon themselves?

PROFESSIONALS AND PARENTS SOMETIMES MAKE MISTAKES AND MISSPEAK

Obviously, mistakes are bound to happen. Parents and teachers are human beings first and never ever dispassionate machines. The sooner we embrace this fact, the sooner we can seek to learn from our mistakes and move on, instead of being reactionary, accusatory, or unrelentingly judgmental of each other.

By the way, this responsiveness is exactly what makes a great parent or teacher. Sensitivity and passion are our best qualities and are crucial for love and laughter to flourish. There is never a need for an adult to express remorse for caring so deeply. Adults can readily forgive themselves for one decision they may or may not choose to make again when it is compared to the *billions of benevolent, beneficial, and yes, loving gestures* that Four Ls parents and Four Fs teachers consistently lavish upon all children—especially when all of their actions are done with their best intentions and intelligence.

Today's teachers in particular are expected to shrug it off or suck it up for nearly every assault, insult, or instance of harassment from their students—be it physical, verbal, or mental; be it purposeful or accidental; be it malicious or playful—but are so seldom granted the same pardon or patience. If you are looking for people in any profession who do not make mistakes and never misspeak, then you are not living in the real world.

A first-time or rare misstep on the part of a teacher (or anyone for that matter) does not a pattern make or a precedent set! Where there is utterly no credible evidence some unfortunate incident will ever happen again *and* a plethora of evidence exists that proves this person has long been a valuable and honorable teacher, then a simple lesson learned is all that is needed for all parties concerned. Case closed. Let's all move forward with clarity, calm, and certainty.

It is high time teachers stop falling all over themselves for the slightest of slips and instead educate the public that they are professionals who demand the requisite respect and trust such a position holds. Teachers as a group are not the bad guys, they are not the enemy, and their every move and word need not be held under a microscope. The few rotten apples that exist in every profession are no reason to treat everyone else with blanket suspect and onerous scrutiny.

No one can do a job well when they are constantly looking over their shoulder, questioning their every action, or fearing that one unfortunate situation can suddenly put their entire beloved and brilliant career in jeopardy. That is no way to work, no way to thrive, and also no way for a parent to interact with their child. Adults being scared of children or the public's reaction is sabotaging the effective rearing of children.

Yes, parents and teachers are the adults and obviously are held to an infinitely higher standard for their conduct than children are. Yet the point is: we are the adults, and they are the children. It is not the other way around, and kids suffer when adults do not take their leadership seriously. Being a leader means that there are followers. This is how we guide kids to responsible adulthood. Firmness is twenty-five percent of what good teaching is about and is just as important as fairness, fascination, and facilitation. If some parents do not accept this truth about what all children need, then perhaps public school is not the best place for their child.

THE DANGER OF WANTON ACCUSATIONS

Hopefully, teachers can completely avoid ever being falsely accused by a student for something they did not even do. Sadly, this also happens more and more these days. Many of today's kids have been given the dangerous idea that all they have to do in order to seek some form of misguided and misplaced revenge or to cast blame away from themselves is to accuse a teacher of some type of trumped up prejudice or malice. As children, they sometimes do not even know the extent of the irreparable damage such false or exaggerated accusations can cause.

Also, some deluded administrators and overprotective parents may actually encourage children to come forward any time they feel the least bit slighted, singled out, or slandered—no matter how much the student's own actions may have warranted some attention or exclusion. Worse yet, there are some administrators who seem to grant kids carte blanche to run to them whenever they feel the smallest bit of "discomfort" around their teachers, especially those teachers who are trying to keep order and to actually educate their students!

Do you want your children running to their teachers every time they feel "uncomfortable" around you? And when did discomfort and corrections become mutually exclusive? By their very nature, *consequences are supposed to be uncomfortable* or else they are useless. Oh, some district bigwigs claim to be putting the needs of the kids first, but in reality they are merely trying to avoid even a hint of a scandal or the possibility of a lawsuit, no matter how ridiculous. The least effective administrators focus on placating pestering parents and dodging negative publicity, not protecting children.

Teachers today are unduly laden with so many demands, so much scrutiny, and an inordinate amount of culpability, yet they are often times not provided with the necessary trust, compassion, autonomy, or authority their responsibilities require. The very worst part is that teachers are often presumed guilty until proven innocent, and even when proven innocent, the stain on their career and their psyche is often lasting and irreparable.

It is not the intention for this chapter to sound like parent or administrator bashing. Parents and administrators are not the teacher's enemies, but some certainly act like it from time to time. True support, understanding, encouragement, and respect for teachers should not be the uncommon exception.

WHY THE TEACHER'S PERSPECTIVE MATTERS

You may be wondering why parents should even care about the teacher's point of view, especially in a book expressly written for parents and when the teacher may have indeed misjudged. After all, teachers are getting paid to meet students' needs, and parents have their own concerns to deal with—one of which is standing up for the rights of their own children.

What you should realize, though, is that this job is *always more than just a paycheck to teachers*. Four Fs teachers do far more than what they are paid for, and they do so gladly and graciously. You can easily spot those teachers who are committed to a serious learning environment, who champion your child as if she were their own, who clearly love their curriculum and craft, and who help your child progress in remarkable ways. In fact, parents seek these teachers out and fight for their child to get a seat in their fantastic classrooms!

Yet if we all are not careful, the very real alternative is that most teachers, even those superstars, will have no choice but to just go through the motions with their students because keeping the status quo is the best way not to make waves, call attention to oneself, or go down in flames. If teachers are constantly being told that they should be dispassionate automatons, then do not be surprised when you and your children get exactly what you have been asking for.

Teachers can merely let things slide with classroom management, even if it means sacrificing precious instructional time with constant disruptions and halfhearted pleas for the class to come to order. In the process of being lax on discipline, a teacher shows children that respect for authority and each other is not all that important. A dangerous lesson, to be sure, but if it ends up safeguarding a teacher's career to merely back down from all confrontation with kids and to look the other way from all misbehavior, from the minor to the egregious, then so be it.

Back teachers into a damned-if-you-do-but-blameless-if-you-don't predicament and see what teacher rushes in to rescue your innocent child should they become the victim of or have to defend themselves against the physical harassment of one or more students.

Do not be surprised when the teacher merely fulfills their legal obligation and shouts, "Please stop fighting!" and then leaves the scene to dutifully find someone else foolish enough to break up the fight and risk personal injury—or worse, risk being sued or dismissed for *accidentally* hurting one of the students in the midst of trying to protect your child.

The one thing no one will be surprised by is that the student who initiated the altercation certainly did not stop fighting when the adult so nicely requested them to do so. If you think children's automatic respect for and attention to authority does not need to be actively taught and diligently reinforced or that its absence in others will not somehow negatively affect your own child, you have grossly misunderstood the vital necessity of adult leadership and firmness.

Teachers can also simply be more aloof, chilly, and mechanical, even if it means their students distance themselves and withdraw in return. Praise, encouragement, and emotional support can be viewed by cautious teachers as potentially suspect and wisely avoided. Perhaps a teacher will simply ignore one of their students who they spy quietly sobbing in the hallway at lunch rather than bothering to get involved during their duty-free time.

And aren't these hands-off approaches to firmness and fairness better than a teacher being accused of being too harsh or too hands on? Isn't it far wiser to err on the side of caution in protecting one's career rather than on concern for kids who could suddenly turn on you?

In addition, teachers can easily put their passions and special activities on hold, even if it means the students do not find class very stimulating or relevant. These days, field trips are fraught with endless compliance issues and required paperwork that many teachers would rather not hassle with. Why accept increased liability and deal with busses and boisterous youngsters straying where they were forbidden when a teacher can just stay in their silent classroom?

Teachers can also merely teach to the test, adhere to the textbook, and never venture an inch beyond what is rigidly and politically "correct," even if it means students never are pushed to grow as critical, independent thinkers and learners. Teachers can also pass all their students, especially those who have clearly earned a failing grade, in order to completely avoid being harangued by parents and administrators for too many Fs on their class rosters.

And aren't these clinical and cautious approaches to fascination and facilitation better than a teacher being accused of being too creative or controversial? Isn't passing the buck and turning a blind eye better than the potential complications of being conscientious?

These dismal scenarios should not be taken as threats but as an increasing and alarming fact because this pulling back and resignation already happens with teachers in overt and imperceptible ways—*not because teachers do not care but because they have been repeatedly taught the horrible lesson that caring can cost them too much.*

Teachers are saddened by this situation just as much as parents, yet many teachers flee the classroom or the profession altogether as they look for an administrative position, find a different career, or retire early. Even altruistic teachers now scramble to get the heck out of low-performing schools, even though those are the places where they are needed the most. Too often today, potentially fantastic teachers never consider the profession at all. Ask any current or former teacher what they would say to a loved one who expressed interest in becoming a teacher. Their answers should cause you grave concern, not just for your children but for our country.

Therefore, this chapter was entirely necessary, warts and all, because you cannot be an ally if you do not understand. If you now see how teachers can feel defeated, attacked, and circumspect in the midst of sincerely giving their best, then please support them equally as much as you expect teachers to support you and your children—even when one of us messes up.

Chapter 12

Achieving Balance

What parent does not long to be calm and confident? What child does not yearn for a calm and confident parent? What parent does not desire their children to be calm and confident?

By extension, what parent does not seek calm and confident teachers for their children, year after year? What child does not want a calm and confident teacher? Finally, what teacher does not work to cultivate a classroom full of calm and confident students?

What this book is teaching you, of course, is that calm and confidence always come from competence. When you know what you are doing and it produces favorable results, you automatically feel relaxed and secure—and now you clearly know what competent parents and teachers who are eager to do their best look like. As a direct result, the children fortunate to be surrounded by such competent adults become capable kids who in turn are significantly more calm and confident throughout their daily lives.

There are progressive benefits to being a Four Ls parent, and once you know these rewards, you will enthusiastically reap them for yourself and for the sake of your children. There is plenty of satisfaction to go around by using this powerful parenting philosophy.

If this seems all too simple, it is meant to be so. Parenting and teaching will always be difficult and dramatic in some ways because life in general and children in particular are full of surprises, both good and bad. Yet parenting and teaching will be decidedly less arduous, less distressing, and mostly filled with an inner tranquility and poise if the Four Ls and the Four Fs are implemented on a consistent, comprehensive basis.

From now on, whenever you feel that anxiety is creeping up on you or that you are starting to question yourself as a parent—and all conscientious parents and teachers occasionally do—please turn this insidious self-doubt into healthy, rational self-reflection by constantly returning to leadership, love, laughter, and learning for re-direction and re-inspiration. These four parental components will be your bellwether to determine if you are doing too little or too much for your children and in which particular areas. Without this specific insight, it would be difficult to pinpoint where you need to refocus or reform your energies to bring your parenting, and thus your kids, back into balance.

If parents place *equal attention* on four motivators, they and their children will find home, as well as school, pleasant places to spend their days. Of course, it is self-evident that a home or a classroom that is lacking in even a single one of the four essential elements above will be chronically working at a deficit. A home or classroom devoid of not merely a competent adult but a *consummate adult* is a place that at best leaves the children's full potential untapped and at worst holds kids back and keeps them down.

PARENTS DO NOT NEED ANYTHING MORE

Parents do not need anything more than the Four Ls in order to begin to inspire their children toward positivity and productivity. In fact, these four essential motivators are all any parent needs to successfully see their children through their school years.

Yet parents in every situation will always need all of the Four Ls in order to influence their children in beneficial ways and to have that potent persuasion carry over to the school setting and beyond. There is simply no other way you can have such a complete and advantageous sway over how your kids behave, grow, hope, and achieve than with leadership, love, laughter, and learning. Similarly, all teachers must be in some fashion a firm, fair, fascinating facilitator. Kids need it all, they need it always, and they need it all at the same time.

List any other needs or worries you have for your children that were not already addressed in previous chapters, and it is guaranteed that anything else you can name will inevitably fit nicely into one of the categories of the Four Ls. Protecting, bonding, adventure, and imparting wisdom are the main reasons why people choose to be parents, and all of the aspirations parents have for their children find a home in one of these four basic elements.

KEEPING PARENTING SIMPLE SO IT BECOMES SECOND NATURE

Therefore, constantly keeping in mind and consistently implementing as few as four avenues of motivation for your children will never be overwhelming or feel unnatural. You can return to the Four Ls any time you need a simple synthesis of what effective parenting entails. No more confusion, no more doubt; just a clear focus of what is most vital in order for children to flourish.

In fact, with practice, the Four Ls will become second nature to you. You will become so adept at suffusing your children with a steady stream of leadership, love, laughter, and learning that you will find an ease and grace to even your most frazzling days. What is more natural than parents automatically guiding, nurturing, mentoring, and teaching their children? Even in the animal kingdom examples abound of parents providing rules, routines, concern, love, play, and coaching to their offspring.

You will also make the manner in which you embody the Four Ls uniquely your own. You have been give the framework, but ultimately it will be you who will fill it up and flesh it out. This book will give you additional guidance for how to don these roles in the form of pointed questions, but it also respects your autonomy and your best judgment. You should wholeheartedly embrace the challenge and resulting responsibility of such independence and again, leave undue worry and doubt out of the picture.

The Four Ls will fulfill your dreams and desires as a parent, while at the same time fulfill the personal dreams and desires of each of your children. They will bring you closer to your kids, even as all children naturally tend to pull away and eventually exert their own independence. As hard as this relinquishing will be, you will also be gratified in the knowledge that this growing autonomy was always your ultimate goal for your children and that everything you gave them was quite intentionally preparing them for this journey in self-reliance and self-determination.

In fact, the way you will know for certain if your parenting has been a success is when your children need you less and less. As much as this may sting, it should also fill you with pride and relief that all your efforts paid off and are now being paid forward as your children affect the world around them in all the advantageous and altruistic ways you influenced them.

The Four Ls will also bring you closer to your children's teachers who will be delighted at your comprehensive parenting skills. You will see these teachers' actions repeatedly reflected in yours and vice versa. You will consider each other colleagues in giving your children what they truly need.

Moreover, if the Four Ls become (or better yet, have always been) an ever-present part of the way you interact with your children, your kids will never know anything different than the calm, confident, capable parent that you continuously embody. Even better yet, your kids will seldom act any differently than how *you* fundamentally want and have guided them to act!

Just remember that in some critical respects, the way you want your children to act is based more on their *own* passions and proclivities and less on

Table 12.1 The Progressive Benefits of the Four Ls of Parenting

All parents, who by nature are responsible for and dedicated to nurturing children, must consistently and comprehensively provide their kids with leadership, love, laughter, and learning. By doing so, these parents will reap the peace and pleasure of the following positive emotions, as well as avoid the corresponding negative emotions.

Positive and productive parental emotions and qualities	**Negative and counterproductive parental emotions and qualities**
These benefits will lead parents to the next level of positivity, which in turn will be naturally transferred to their children to gain from and enjoy.	These undesirable feelings and attributes can be readily replaced by their positive counterparts once a parent commits to using the persuasive power of the Four Ls.
• Clear insight • Broad perspective • Precise direction • Simplified focus • Fundamental wisdom.	• Confusion • Limited outlook • Feeling lost • Information overload • Doubt and questioning.
Which lead to:	
• Planning and being proactive • Preparation and purpose • Effective action and intention.	• Making it up as I go along • Feeling overwhelmed or drowning • Meaning well but which too often backfires.
Which lead to:	
• Productivity • Competence and potency • Efficacy.	• Spinning my wheels • Feeling in over my head • Feeling ineffective.
Which lead to:	
• Esteem • Confidence (without cockiness) • Decisiveness (without acting cavalierly).	• Feelings of inferiority • Worry and anxiety • Hesitancy and reluctance.
Which lead to:	
• Calm • Vigor and poise • Grace and ease.	• Panic • Exhaustion and frustration • Awkwardness and difficulty.
Which lead to:	
• Enthusiasm • Optimism and positivity • Passion and resolve • Perseverance.	• Dread • Pessimism and negativity • Apathy and resignation • Wanting to give in or give up.
Which lead to:	
• Contentment and satisfaction • Success • Joy and pride.	• Dissatisfaction and despair • Failure • Unhappiness and depression.
All of which eventually result in a relationship with your children filled with:	
• Closeness • Connection • Cohesion and trust.	• Distance • Lack of understanding and bonding • Dissonance, discord, and distrust.

the imposition of your particular tastes and talents. Collaboration is a way of working together in harmony, not dictating another's every move. Likewise, coaching is often about stepping back and allowing your children to discover, try, and succeed or fail on their own, without your constant hovering or hounding.

See **Table 12.1: The Progressive Benefits of the Four Ls of Parenting** for the ways the Four Ls make your life as a parent continually better for you and your family. Every parent experiences negative emotions from time to time, but with the consistent implementation of the Four Ls, these counterproductive qualities will no longer be the norm and will not be your default emotion, especially in times of crisis.

YOU CAN'T MAKE ME! (BUT YOU CAN MOTIVATE ME)

By the age of two, children begin to seek control and independence. From then on, too many parents and teachers are forced to deal with increasingly more entitled, ungrateful, greedy children who frequently whine, nag, demand, or throw a fit until their selfish desires are met by frustrated adults who find it easiest to just give in. Inevitably, these parents merely give these kids what they want in order to shut them up—until the next battle of wills devolves into another calculated meltdown performed by a child who knows exactly how to manipulate adults who lack proper leadership and firmness.

There is often a big difference between a child's wants and their needs. This book focuses on giving children what they need, rather than what they want. In fact, the entire philosophy of the Four Ls of Parenting and the Four Fs of Teaching is based on motivation. Coercion may have some effect sometimes, but it is nowhere near as effective (and pleasant) as influence. Thus, adults are wise to continually greet kids with what they need most—before they even ask!

Rewarding Positive, Productive Behavior

See, if children routinely feel fulfilled, their natural, supplementary wishes and requests which drive most other parents crazy, will not manifest themselves in petty or selfish ways. Instead, children of a Four Ls parent often have fully earned any extras they occasionally ask for. Hence, these savvy parents are more than happy to grant their children's additional requests and wishes.

There are no treats for tantrums in these parents' homes, however; there are only goodies for the good behavior and good choices that their children gladly display on a daily basis. Of course, perfection is neither a realistic nor a necessary goal. Rather, consistent positive persuasion from parents brings equally consistent positive responses in their children.

Therefore, what parent would deny their routinely courteous and cooperative child when they once in a while politely ask for a favored item for no special occasion or when they respectfully request a temporary bending of the rules? The fact is that this child deserves a reward sometimes and has earned some increased freedom or leniency.

Likewise, what parent would balk when their child who is frequently communicative and trustworthy asks for a bit more privacy or some increased autonomy? Unquestionably, this child has earned the right to further prove they are responsible and that they are able to make more of their own wise decisions.

Similarly, what parent would refuse their child who commonly approaches life (including family, friends, and school) with enthusiasm and a supportive spirit when they ask for lessons, equipment, experiences, or special backing in order to pursue a personal passion that is well within the family budget? Certainly, this child has proven herself deserving of the same sort of camaraderie and championing they give to others.

Furthermore, what parent would nix a request from their child who takes all forms of learning seriously when they ask for an opportunity or accessory that will only enhance their experience as an educated, well-rounded person? To be sure, this child is taking his learning into his own hands and progressing beyond all of the coaching his teachers and parents have given him, which is exactly what these adults intended for him to do.

Highly motivated kids such as these deserve rewards and privileges from time to time because they have earned them. And parents do not always have to wait for their kids to ask! Surprise your responsible, respectful children with a variety of perks, *the best of which are special experiences and adventures the entire family can enjoy together.* All this appreciation only serves to further motivate your children to be more responsive to your influence!

MONITOR AND MOTIVATE YOURSELF

This part of the book is about parents finding a balance in the way they approach their children, and Four Ls parents find that their kids become balanced right along with them. With four powerful motivators that directly enhance each other, children have little wiggle room to resist the compelling influence of leadership, love, laughter, and learning.

Yet what about some wiggle room for yourself? You must expect that the intensity and importance of being responsible for children will wear you down. This fatigue is natural, but it must be acknowledged and properly dealt with. It certainly should not become all-consuming.

In some very critical ways and on a consistent basis, parents and teachers must put their needs first. The last thing anyone needs is an adult who is so overwhelmed or exhausted that they gradually become unfulfilled, resentful, or embittered. This can easily happen when one gives too much to others and forsakes themselves too often. This is but another example of an extreme in interacting with children. You may be well-intentioned in your selflessness for your children, but if all your sacrifices are only causing you to burn out, shut down, lash out, or break down, who will be there for your kids?

This is an important question to ask because the Four Ls and Four Fs are all about how kids *need* their parents and teachers in four very essential ways. They are counting on you to be routinely enthusiastic, open, aware, attentive, and energetic. Children have the luxury of bouts of skepticism, distance, disregard, and inertia from time to time, but responsible adults have to carefully manage those instances when they themselves need a break so not to fall prey to the same negativity. The recharging of one's batteries is natural and routinely necessary, so do not wait until you are fed up to finally relax and recreate!

The Importance of Planning

Furthermore, please do not ever confuse being consistent with having to be constant—and certainly not with being chronic. Parenting and teaching are not races. There are many demands and deadlines and duties, but in a great many ways parents and teachers hold significant authority and autonomy over what has to be done when.

Prioritizing, planning, and organizing in ways that never ever puts too much on *anyone's* plate at any one time and that always allows for inevitable interruptions and alterations are essential to keeping everyone sane. Exercise your authority to minimize stress and to maximize the value and pleasure out of whatever you yourself have scheduled. You know yourself, your children, and your routines better than anyone, so use that foresight to plan accordingly.

Effective teachers are masters of this type of proactive planning and deftly manage to make sure everyone in the classroom, including themselves, gets the biggest bang for their buck without blowing up or wearing down in the process. A teacher has to sustain their energy and inspiration for a thirty-to-forty-year career. What good is being a super-teacher if all it does is make a person call in sick too often, interfere with their outside relationships that need time and nurturing too, or make them give up teaching altogether?

Things like these happen all the time, yet teachers still routinely receive the ultimately destructive message that they should be martyrs.

Parental Self-Awareness

Watch your children, but also watch yourself. If you find yourself needing a break or a treat, then appropriately attend to those needs—*before* you come anywhere close to reaching your breaking point! You are gradually teaching your children the necessity of self-awareness, so practice what you preach. This is part of being fair to your kids. Do not make them pay any price for you not pacing yourself and knowing when to refresh, refocus, and reflect.

In fact, if you need a respite, chances are your kids need one too! Seize this very opportunity to appear spontaneous and magnanimous, and take some time for family laughter that you are certain everyone will enjoy. Taking a break does not always mean temporary distance from your kids. Adults' nights out and weekend getaways are important, but they are not the only ways to recharge.

Another way to consciously work in some parental down time is to purposely yet temporarily back off from the Four Ls. Sometimes kids need a break too—but they may need that break from *you*. At whatever level is developmentally appropriate for your children, you should sometimes test out how your kids function without your active motivation or supervision. Therefore, stepping back occasionally is not only okay, it is good and necessary for both the parent and the child. Kids' successes, both big and small, can then be acknowledged and praised. Their independent triumph may even be cause for another impromptu bout of laughter and frolic.

Pace yourself, find a happy medium between pure selflessness and pure selfishness, and do not feel guilty for being a person with needs and dreams of your own. There is room for you and your children to each find personal fulfillment. You can take care of your own needs and dreams quite easily, but your children need you to actively guide and motivate them to explore and realize their own ambitions.

Besides, your children will gain so much more from you when you are serene and satisfied because they will take that as a cue for to how to live a life that is both giving and personally gratifying. You do not have to explain this to them; they will clearly see it in your face and in your peaceful, contented demeanor.

Take heart in the fact that with the Four Ls you will always be giving your children exactly what they need to be happy and successful both at home and in school, and that such a comprehensive and consistent approach is always just enough. By the same token, the Four Ls will motivate you to continue to give graciously and appropriately to your children because your own needs are being met as well!

IN MY CLASSROOM: BECOMING A POWERFUL, PERSUASIVE TEACHER

It bears repeating that my career in education began with a very rocky start. In fact, I always say that back then I was the worst teacher ever. My classroom was completely out of control, and my students could not be bothered to participate, engage, or learn because they were too busy running amok. I had no idea how to motivate them, and I was quickly losing my own motivation to continue to pursue a job that was highly stressful, regularly demoralizing, and downright embarrassing.

Of course, I did stick with it, and I am still in the classroom today. So, if there was hope for me as a teacher, then there is hope for any other teacher—and certainly for any parent. If I could grow and thrive interacting with children all day long, then you too can grow and thrive. Most importantly, each day that I walk into my classroom I now feel self-assured and powerful where for far too long I felt anxious and inept.

When I say "powerful," I mean I now possess the means to make *my students* powerful. Because I am finally a complete teacher who consistently uses the Four Fs, my students now have the power *within themselves* to work toward positive and productive pursuits rather than squandering their education on silliness or surliness, which also steals the learning time of others.

In addition, my students now have the power to proudly and publically share their ideas instead of passively staying silent and praying not to be called upon. They also now have the power to focus themselves on something they find personally meaningful as opposed to tuning out with utter boredom and sheer distain. Finally, they have the power to achieve at increasingly more demanding academic tasks rather than falling further behind in bewilderment and despair.

Hence, my current self-assurance and tranquility in the classroom come directly from the fact that I never have to rely on just one mean to those four essential ends. Where my firmness always keeps my students in check and cooperating, my fairness is right there as well keeping them continually confident and comfortable. Where my fascination constantly keeps them compelled and committed, my facilitation is also omnipresent keeping my students ever comprehending and competent.

Since in some fashion all four motivators are occurring in my classroom at the same time, every single day, starting on day one of each new school year, I no longer have to panic if I see one student or the entire class begin to slip. Whether they are starting to slip with their behavior, their responsiveness, their engagement, or their grades, I know that I will soon win them back over if I stay the course and continue meeting all of their essential needs.

The performance of children naturally ebbs and flows, often inexplicably, so patience and consistency now rule my days. Even if a more targeted intervention is warranted, as it often is, I still remain placid as I confidently provide exactly what each student needs. Because the Four Fs have given me the power and the freedom to be the teacher that I always dreamed of being, my students are also free to be the satisfied and successful thinkers, learners, and individuals that they themselves may have never even dared dream of being.

Part III

FINDING ANSWERS BY ASKING THE RIGHT QUESTIONS

Chapter 13

Determining What Is Really Going on Behind the Classroom Door

The title of this chapter will be of great interest to today's parents who at once have too much information about schools and teachers yet still not enough useful information to discern whether their child is actually in the right hands during the school day. Now that you know truly effective teaching is only twenty-five percent about academics, you may have more questions than ever about your children's teachers, even the teachers you already had assumed were great.

Excellent instruction is only enhanced when a teacher also is an expert at motivating student cooperation, participation, and engagement. You may be shocked by how even at the highest-performing schools and even in the cases where a child is earning top grades and test scores, students are often wasting too much time in silliness, socializing, sloth, or senseless assignments. Many supposedly high-performing students also too often fade into the background, do not actively volunteer or speak up, and find much of school uninspiring, even as they dutifully complete the assignments that mean little to them personally.

Of course, the Four Fs maximize both the product and the pleasure of school—without inundating or shortchanging a child's full educational experience. This book began by stating that parents and children can have it both ways, so how can you be sure your kids are receiving a fully effective, enriched classroom experience, no matter their current skills or school?

Using the Four Fs as a guideline, parents now have an efficient way of measuring what really is going on in a classroom when they have the opportunity to watch a teacher in action. However, most parents do not have the luxury of sitting through an entire class period to observe, let alone the time to visit multiple times throughout a school year.

A parent who is able to volunteer in a classroom on a regular basis will know exactly what is happening in that classroom, as well as what their child is or is not contributing to their own education, but such classroom assistance is impossible for most working parents. Attending Back to School, Open House, and parent–teacher conference events do provide parents with a great deal of important information and sometimes allow parents to ask specific questions, but these encounters can be extremely brief and can often still leave large gaps in knowing what really goes on in class.

Therefore, lists of questions that parents can ask their children throughout a school year are offered in this chapter as an efficient, informative means of figuring out what happens for a large portion of their child's day. The answers their kids provide should give parents an astonishingly accurate picture of how effective their child's teacher is, as well as how much the children themselves are helping or hindering that process.

Remember that education is a *partnership*, and what your children do or do not bring to that relationship directly influences the type of experience they will receive while in a particular teacher's classroom. Also recall that teachers will often go the extra mile for students and classes who are especially pleasant, responsive, enthusiastic, and hard working. Teachers are obligated to motivate their students no matter what the kids give in return, but students have the power to significantly motivate their teachers as well.

SEEKING THE POSITIVE

Whether because of past experience or sheer caution, some parents are inclined to be suspicious and distrustful of teachers in general. If you find these tendencies in yourself, the best solution for everyone involved is for you to take a proactive approach by regularly asking your kids about what happens in school. However, do not do so in order to find fault in their teachers; instead, do so in order to find a wealth of reasons to have faith in both your child's and their teachers' positive actions. This newfound classroom transparency should be a wholly agreeable and reassuring experience for you, your child, and the teacher.

In fact, the following questions exclusively focus on gaining positive information about your child and their teachers. They were carefully crafted so that the emphasis would be on what is going right. If one seeks only to criticize and condemn, they will always find something to complain about. No teacher, student, or parent is perfect, but as we have seen, perfection is not a requirement for success or progress.

Therefore, keep in mind that with these questions you are not "out to get" anyone. Instead, you are collecting evidence, gaining knowledge, and shoring up your confidence that both your child and their teachers are fulfilling their duties in four vital areas of education and child development. You will gather far more useful information and garner much more willing participation and candor from your children if you sincerely approach these questions as a chance to recognize and celebrate what is legitimately praiseworthy about school.

Personalize How You Ask about the Four Fs

Since this book honors individuality and creativity in adults and children, use the following questions as a guideline and springboard to initiate frequent conversations about school between you and your child. As with all of the methods contained herein, freely adapt, edit, and add to these basic questions, especially with regard to your child's age and vocabulary. Because many parents do not know how to initiate and maintain a meaningful conversation about school with their child, the following questions will serve as a good jumping off point.

All these questions are open-ended so you can ask your own related follow-up questions as you seek more detail and explanation from your child. The mere fact that you are engaging your children in frequent intelligent conversations regarding school will go a long way to improve how articulate they are becoming, as well as how eloquently they write. These regular academic conversations model for your children what scholarly speech sounds like, and their benefits cannot be overstated.

What is unique about these questions, of course, is that they are categorized by the Four Fs of Teaching so that you will be thorough in your quest for information. As you gain more and more insight from your children's answers, you will become even more convinced that the Four Fs (and by extension, the Four Ls) are absolutely fundamental. You will also see how they are inextricably intertwined and function optimally when used on a consistent, cohesive basis.

IS MY CHILD'S TEACHER HIGHLY EFFECTIVE?

The following questions are the types of things an interested and invested parent regularly asks their children. This constant curiosity and specificity about their time spent at school proves to kids that their education is indeed important to their parents. Consequently, it is reinforced to children that school should be important to them as well.

Doing well in school cannot be some parental mandate that exists in the abstract and too often blows up in everyone's faces every time the phone rings or a report card arrives. Your children's education and conduct at school should be an almost daily, routine exchange of information, ideas, and ideals between you and each of your children. A parent should be genuinely interested in what is happening at school. If you honestly have not been very interested before, it is probably because you were not asking the right questions.

Parents who are on top of what is going on in all aspects of school, not just obsessing about homework and grades, explicitly show kids the four ways in which they are supposed to perform and produce in school. Cooperation, participation, investment, and achievement are each equally important, and each aspect is one part of a whole educational experience that should be joyful and fulfilling just as much as it must be orderly and rigorous. The sooner children fully appreciate both the intrinsic rewards, as well as the serious demands of scholarship, the sooner they embrace all that school has to offer and all that it requires.

Do not, however, turn these questions into a third degree inquisition! What happens in school is absolutely a parent's business, but you would do well to stress sincere curiosity rather than conveying persistent, prying scrutiny or surveillance. When asking your kids about school, take an approach of earnest interest, even excitement, and an ongoing quest toward awareness.

The Best Times to Ask Questions

You may want to set a regular time that you talk with your child about school, such as at dinnertime. Yet this questioning does not always have to be a formal affair. One of the best ways to elicit honest answers and willing candor from kids is to bring up potentially sensitive subjects when you and your child are engaged in something relaxing, casual, or distracting, perhaps while together baking cookies, raking leaves, or shooting baskets.

Over time, the culmination of your child's answers will give you a broad and quite accurate picture of what is really going on behind the classroom door—all with progressively fewer unpleasant surprises. Furthermore, if you have asked these questions often or from the very beginning, these queries will become a normal part of your children's interactions with you.

You determine if these conversations work best just between yourself and one child or with other family members within earshot. Recall that being compared to anyone, especially siblings, is something kids generally do not take kindly to. If these conversations are done with others listening in, just be sure that siblings are not later using any information in order to one-up or put down each other. Because these questions focus on the positive, however, there should be plenty of praise to go around for each child.

Also, ask these questions on a routine basis so that you only need select one or a few questions at a time and can focus on only one or two of the Four Fs each time. These conversations can be relatively brief and refreshingly breezy. The subject of education is serious, but the emphasis should always be on positivity and progress.

If your child has more than one teacher per day, you can also ask specific questions about specific teachers. The more you ask, the quicker you will remember which teacher is which, as well as what and how they teach.

Be Proactive about Potential Problems

Your child's answers about school are all vital facts that every committed parent should know, so consider this questioning as your main means of becoming knowledgeable about your child's school experience. Making the effort to stay informed provides a parent with essential peace of mind, and it proactively prevents small issues from becoming unmanageable or outright crises. Being an ally in your child's education does not happen in the abstract. Like everything with good parenting, it takes intention, attention, and action.

How can a parent who chooses to be ignorant about the specifics of what happens for eight hours of their child's weekday routine justifiably take serious issue with a teacher they essentially know nothing about? Is it okay to care about school only when there is a possible problem? If a parent really cares so much about how teachers treat and educate their children, how come they are not well versed in what has been going on in every classroom since day one of each new school year?

Having faith in teachers should never be a matter of blind trust. In fact, teachers are happy to *earn* a parent's trust. They are thrilled to show off how they are meeting your child's needs on four essential levels. In turn, a parent should be equally as thrilled to hear ongoing good news about their child's teachers. Yet how can you know the good—or the potentially bad—if you do not take the time to find out?

Furthermore, if you are intimately knowledgeable with what is going on with each of your children's teachers, you should be able to spot the potential for a grave problem long before that distressing circumstance would ever manifest itself. This is a crucial advantage of being a proactive and well-informed parent.

Isn't a parent partially to blame when their intentional ignorance abets a situation that could have been prevented had they been more involved from the outset? What is more important: optimizing your child's safe, satisfying school experience by staying abreast of what is going on or idly waiting around and allowing an easily avoidable situation to occur only so you can express outrage after the fact?

Please understand that things never even have to come down to an either/or situation where the only options are to blame the teacher or to blame the parent. The entire point here is for parents to be proactive so that no one needs to be blamed for anything! Of course, there are rare instances when unfortunate things happen to children even in what appeared to an informed parent to be the most ideal of situations, yet staying in the know is never a bad thing—and most often this attention does indeed prevent very bad things from ever happening.

The fact is that most forms of crisis or consternation do not happen without multiple red flags being raised well beforehand. Thankfully, a parent can still be "there" to spot any possible early warning signs by regularly monitoring who exactly is teaching their children and how they are specifically going about it. The following questions are a great place to exercise your obligation to be informed and up to date without leaving your home. Being a conscientious and committed parent does not require constant hovering or being at the school site all the time.

Using Conversations about School to Provide the Four Ls

This quest for positive information about school pays off in multiple ways. A parent must provide the Four Ls anyway, so why not use the act of talking about school for such purposes? Even working parents can make time for this—and enjoy every minute of it! Remember that you yourself are your children's best advantage.

Not only do these conversations about school provide you with tranquility about all the time teachers are assuming a leadership role for your child, these questions also supply you with an opportunity for loving bonding, attention, recognition, and support with your kids. There will also be laughter as you further discover what your child is good at and is interested in.

In addition, become a vicarious learner along with your child as you find out all sorts of fascinating facts and intriguing ideas your child's teachers are exposing them to! Even the parents who struggle with directly helping their child with homework (because either they forgot that stuff long ago or because it is now taught completely differently than how they were taught) can still support their child's learning by showing involvement and curiosity about school.

Therefore, this time you spend learning about school and learning along with your children will never be an added burden. Instead, it will enrich your relationship with your child, keep them safer and happier than ever, and vastly improve their attitudes and accomplishments in school. With all the wonderful things you hear about teachers, you will also become an even more willing and devoted ally in your child's education.

Just How Much Can Your Children Answer about Their Teachers?

Kids need training in positivity, too! Your questions are not an open invitation for them to merely complain about school. Guide them in searching for the positive so that this becomes what they themselves focus on while in school. Rest assured that even if your child has a legitimate concern about or a sincere issue with a teacher, it surely will come out even in the midst of your positive questioning approach.

If there is ever a profound and ongoing lack of positivity that your child can point to about a teacher, heed those signals sooner rather than later and seek further clarification from other parents or with the teacher. There must be some reason why your child cannot find much good to say about a certain teacher, and a conscientious parent wants to know if the disconnect is coming from the teacher, the child, or a combination of the two. The school itself and issues with peers may be a factor that a parent requires more information about. Thankfully, these situations often are easily set right, especially when attended to early in the school year.

However, it must be stressed again that the goal of these questions is not to "catch" anyone, neither teacher nor child. You are actively seeking evidence in order to trust teachers who care deeply about your child, not searching for reasons to doubt them. You are also providing an open forum for your child to sing their own and their teacher's praises.

A worthy goal for both parents and teachers is to inspire children to, if not love, then to like school. The structure, support, stimulation, and success that school can and should provide cannot be overestimated! So if a child is not expressing an abundance of positive qualities about their teachers in particular or school in general, this lack of motivation must be addressed and corrected as soon as possible. The following questions in themselves should begin to turn children's negative mindsets about school into positive outlooks about their entire education.

This questioning will be an ongoing process for both you and your children, so do not be surprised if they initially cannot come up with an answer to some questions. Many kids have never thought deeply about their school experience and may find it hard to begin to articulate what is actually going on in their classroom.

Your children's answers or their lack thereof may show you that they are being much too passive in the way they approach school. They may be consciously or unconsciously allowing themselves to slip through the cracks, fly beneath the radar, or fade into the background in many classes.

Unfortunately, some kids are simply marking time, daydreaming, or doing no more than the bare minimum while at school.

This passivity problem can be exacerbated when even the most responsible teachers may be overwhelmed and distracted by large class sizes, by lots of squeaky wheels that constantly clamor for their attention (parents included), and by the pressure to get on with the lesson. The awful truth is that it can be all too easy for some children too often to go unnoticed, to be neglected, or to be unchecked, especially the reluctant and retreating students who long not to be noticed in the first place. These questions help alert parents to these situations.

QUESTIONS TO ASK YOUR CHILD ABOUT THEIR TEACHERS

A note to teachers: The following questions that parents can ask their children about their teachers can also be used by you as a self-reflective exercise to determine how well you are providing the Four Fs to your students.

1. **Questions Regarding a Teacher's Firmness**
   - How does this teacher show you that they are the boss or leader of their classroom?
   - What does this teacher do that proves to you that they are in charge?
   - How do you know that this teacher means business and means what they say?
   - How do you know that this classroom is a place of serious learning and scholarship?
   - What are the main ways this teacher keeps the class attentive, focused, and working?
   - How does this teacher command respect and also give respect in return?
   - How does this teacher make sure that the class does not get too loud and that students stay concentrated on their work?
   - What does this teacher do that makes you feel safe and protected in this class?
   - What are the most important rules and routines in this class?
   - What are this teacher's procedures for the students to enter and exit this class in a businesslike and calm way?
   - How does this teacher make sure that the class remains orderly and organized? Can you describe where different class materials are kept, how they are passed out and returned, and how they are organized and stay in good shape?

- Who are the best behaved and most cooperative students in this class? What do these students do that proves to you and this teacher that they are helpful and respectful?
- What does this teacher do better than other teachers in order to get students to arrive on time, to come prepared, and to cooperate respectfully?
- What is one thing you need from this teacher that would help you to behave even better?

2. **Questions Regarding a Teacher's Fairness**
   - How do you know that your teacher is on your side?
   - What does your teacher do that proves to you that they believe in you?
   - How does your teacher encourage you to participate, to volunteer, to share your ideas, or to try and think harder?
   - How does your teacher make you feel comfortable, confident, and secure in this class?
   - In what ways does your teacher show that they are warm, welcoming, and caring?
   - What has your teacher done to make you feel at ease, to feel included, and to feel like you are an important part of their class?
   - What is the nicest or most complimentary thing your teacher has said to your recently?
   - What are your favorite things about your teacher as a person?
   - How does your teacher publically and privately recognize, compliment, or thank you for what you are doing right, for progress you are making, or for how hard you are trying?
   - How are you sure that your teacher knows who you are, tries to understand you, takes notice of your feelings, or is willing to adjust certain things so that you can learn better?
   - What does your teacher do that shows you that they are fair and that they support you?
   - Who are the students who participate, raise their hands, and pay attention the most? What do these students do that proves to you that they are actively focused on the teacher and are really paying attention to the lesson or discussion?
   - What is one thing you need from your teacher that would help you to participate, pay attention, or concentrate even more in this class?
3. **Questions Regarding a Teacher's Fascination**
   - How does this teacher show you that the subject they teach and the assignments they give you are important, useful, and meaningful?

- In what ways does this teacher show you that they are enthusiastic, upbeat, and lighthearted? How does this teacher make you laugh sometimes?
- What does this teacher do that proves to you that they enjoy teaching and that they are excited to teach a particular lesson?
- What was the last lesson or activity in this teacher's class that was particularly interesting, meaningful, or exciting to you? Can you describe it for me?
- How does this teacher challenge you to think deeply, creatively, or outside of the box? How do they inspire you to accomplish things that at first seem complex or difficult?
- What are your favorite things about this class?
- When was the last time this teacher asked for your opinion or response to something you read or learned? What was the topic, and what were your ideas?
- Do you feel that this teacher really listens to what you say? Have they mentioned again or made reference to something you had said before so that it validates, acknowledges, or builds on your previous ideas or comments?
- In what ways does this teacher let you make personal choices about what you read, what you write about, how you complete certain assignments, or who you work with?
- How is what you are learning now connected to what you learned last year or what you are learning in other classes this year? Can you explain some ways that these connections help you make better sense of what you are currently learning?
- In what ways does it seem like this teacher has an overall plan and direction for what they are teaching you this year? Can you explain how things you learned before were repeated or necessary for something you learned later in this class?
- When was the last time this teacher had you work with a partner or in a group? What are the best things about collaborating with your classmates?
- Who are the students who are the most interested and excited in this class? What are the reasons why you think that they like this class so much?
- What is one thing you need from this teacher that would help you to be even more interested and engaged in this class?

4. **Questions Regarding a Teacher's Facilitation**
   - How does the teacher prove to you they are organized and prepared for the day's lesson?

- In what ways does the teacher make learning and their assignments understandable?
- How is the teacher good at explaining things? Can you explain something to me that you learned that was confusing or difficult at first? How do the notes that you take help you?
- In what ways do you feel like the teacher allows you to be in charge of your own learning? Do you ever get to create your own questions?
- How does the teacher make this class clear and comprehensible for you so that you never feel like it is going too fast or too slow for you to understand?
- How does your homework connect with what you are learning and doing in class? Can you describe a recent homework assignment that was necessary in order for you to better understand or do the next day's lesson?
- How does the teacher give you feedback on how well you are learning and understanding? Can you name some feedback that was particularly helpful to you?
- How has the teacher made it possible for you to keep track of your grade in this class?
- Is the teacher available and willing to help you when you do not understand something? How and when are you supposed to ask the teacher for help or if you have a question?
- Who are the students who get the best grades in this class? Besides being smart, what are the specific things they do to earn those high grades? *(Take special note of the names of all the students who cooperate, participate, engage, and/or achieve the most. Do not be surprised if your child offers the same names for each of the Four Fs categories. If so, specifically point out to your child how the students who find the most success and satisfaction in school are the ones who intentionally behave, focus, invest, and put in the work. Stress to your child that none of this positivity happens by accident or luck.)*
- What is one thing you need from the teacher that would help you to better understand and to earn better grades in this class?

IS MY CHILD A HIGHLY EFFECTIVE STUDENT?

Since education is a partnership, do not limit your questions to only what the teacher is doing. The best teacher in the world will only have limited success with students who do not do their share in four fundamental ways.

Therefore, give your child frequent opportunities to show off what they themselves are also doing right! This is a main tenet in showing your love, support, and fairness, so let your child proudly explain how they are endeavoring, achieving, solving problems, overcoming challenges, and establishing or maintaining a good reputation in school.

Reputations

Children who view one or more of their teachers as unrelentingly strict, patently unsupportive, mind numbingly boring, and/or completely incomprehensible, often feel these ways because they themselves are outwardly fighting the teacher's noble efforts to motivate them or because they are inwardly refusing to buy what the teacher is selling. The reasons for such defiance or reluctance may be varied and may actually have nothing to do with the teachers themselves. Some kids begin a new class with their walls up, initially refusing to give their new teacher a chance.

While a Four Fs teacher is good at breaking down walls and winning kids over, it still also takes a student letting a teacher in. Sometimes a student may be locked in a battle of wills with the teacher, and a vicious circle develops as each of the teacher's conscientious interventions are only met with more rebellion or retreat by the inexplicably indignant or offended student. This persistent disagreeable student behavior in turn may cause a teacher to harbor an overall negative perception of this child because that is all this child ever shows the teacher.

Thus, parents and teachers should talk a great deal about reputations with kids. Cultivating and safeguarding a good reputation is a child's best way to get what she wants and to shield herself from needless blame. Good reputations should never be taken for granted, so explicitly tell your children how wise they are to have *earned* a good reputation with you or with their teacher. Also explain that maintaining a good reputation is the main reason why people may be given a second chance, granted a special privilege, or gain extra kindness and attention.

Bad reputations, on the other hand, can haunt a person indefinitely. Sure, it is never fun to get blamed and then punished for some foolish thing you did, but it is far worse to get blamed for something you had no part in! Inform your children that it is perfectly natural and to be expected that when a person has been caught misbehaving multiple times, *everyone else* (not only his parent or teacher) is going to leap to first blame this person of ill repute whenever anything suspicious happens in his vicinity.

Therefore, the next four sets of questions attempt to get your children to explore, crow about, and improve their own part of the student–teacher partnership in order to get the most out of their education and overall school experience. With time, repetition, regularity, and some coaching, your children will become eager and accustomed to sharing with you their accomplishments, as well as their earnest attempts at scholarship and citizenship.

Feel free to also mix these questions with the previous questions about teachers. This back and forth between the student's and the teacher's attitudes and actions will only further illuminate to your children the close interplay success in school requires.

Asking specific questions is the best way to elicit specific answers, as well as to subsequently engender specific, desired actions. Merely asking your child, "How was your day at school?" will not get you very far with useful answers or information. With practice, however, your child will naturally come to view the following pointed questions also as your *expectations*, and in time your child will rise to your implied demands—all with those requirements being couched in a positive, even celebratory, parental approach.

QUESTIONS TO ASK YOUR CHILD ABOUT THEIR PARTICIPATION IN SCHOOL

1. **Questions Regarding Your Child's Cooperation, Courtesy, and Preparation**
   - What is one class or school rule that you successfully followed today? Who do you think noticed your act of cooperation? Why is it important to do the right thing even if you think no one is watching? How does this automatic good behavior help your reputation?
   - How did you show a teacher respect today? What is a different way you could also show them respect tomorrow? Why would your teacher say that today you were one of the best behaved and most respectful students in their class?
   - What is one way you helped out a teacher recently? How did the teacher respond?
   - Which classes were you one of the first people to arrive at today? How do you think punctuality improves your reputation?
   - How did you greet or acknowledge your teachers when you first saw them today, when you left the classroom, or when you saw them on campus? What are some other pleasant things you can say to your teachers when you first see them in class and around school?
   - In what ways were you fully prepared for school today? Can you show me how you organize your backpack, binders, and notebooks? What is at least one thing that is unnecessary or distracting that you can leave at home from now on?

- Can you name me all of your personal supplies that you used at school today? Do you need any new or replacement school supplies? Can you show me your school supplies along with any extras you have in case something is lost or stops working?
- Who do you sit next to in each of your classes? If they are your friends, how do you let them know you are serious about learning and it is not okay to socialize or play while in class? If they are not your friends, how do you let them know you want to pay attention and concentrate on your work? How can you be serious about school and still be cool?
- What is one thing you could do to better cooperate with and respect your teachers?

2. **Questions Regarding Your Child's Participation and Responsiveness**
   - What are the first things you have to do once you are seated in each of your classes?
   - When was the last time you raised your hand to ask a question, make a comment, or volunteer an answer? What did you say or what were you going to say?
   - When was the last time a teacher called on you? What was the question, and what was your answer? How did it feel to be called on? How can you make this a more pleasant and successful experience in the future? How does sincerely trying help your reputation?
   - What was one thing your teacher said you did well or intelligently today? If no teacher praised you today, what would you compliment yourself for?
   - How did you show your teachers you were listening, paying attention, or following along today? How does being an active learner affect your reputation?
   - What do you do on a regular basis that proves to your teachers that you are a focused, responsive, and responsible learner? Why are these qualities important?
   - What example can you give me that shows you recently tried your best, did not give up, or worked really hard at something for school? What were the results of your effort and determination? How did it feel to persevere and remain determined?
   - If you could write a note to your teachers which began with "These are the things I really wish you knew about me," what would you include? What are some ways you could actually communicate these things to your teachers so they better meet your needs?

- What do you do when you finish your work early in each class? What are some productive things you can do when you have extra time in class?
- What is one thing you could do to be a more active learner, to pay closer attention in class, to participate more, or to get your teacher to notice you in a more positive way?

3. **Questions Regarding Your Child's Interest and Investment**
    - What was the most interesting thing you learned or did in school today? Can you explain it to me in detail? How does it feel when school is exciting and fun?
    - What is something that you did or learned that you think I might find interesting?
    - Which class are you most eager to go back to tomorrow and why?
    - What was something challenging in class today that you found success with? Was this challenge something that you enjoyed working and thinking hard on?
    - What is one thing that you learned today that you are curious to know more about? Is there something you could read or watch or is there someplace we could visit together that would allow you to learn more about this interesting fact or topic?
    - What is one thing you learned or did today that was personally meaningful or important to you? How could you let your teacher know that you have taken special interest in what you are learning? How would your enthusiasm and openness help your reputation?
    - What was one thing you learned or did today that you found very useful and practical? How might you use this knowledge or skill in school or real life again?
    - What is one thing you could do to find even more interest and meaning in this class?
4. **Questions Regarding Your Child's Comprehension and Commitment**
    - What was the most difficult or challenging thing you had to learn or do in class today?
    - In class, what can you do now you could not do before? What can you do better or faster than before? What is easy that used to be hard? Can you teach me one of these things?
    - Can you show me your completed homework and explain to me how you know you did it correctly? How does turning in homework on time and regularly help your reputation?
    - When was the last time you asked your teacher for help? Did this help allow you to do your work or understand better? What are the best ways and times to ask for help?

- When was the last time you asked a teacher for feedback about something you were working on? How does asking a teacher to check your progress on an assignment help your reputation, as well as make your classwork better?
- Can you show me some notes you took today and explain them to me? How does regularly reviewing your class notes help you understand, retain, and learn more?
- What are the next tests or quizzes that you need to study for? When is the test day? What is your study plan leading up to that test date? Can you create some questions that I can quiz you on? Do you want to try quizzing me on the same questions?
- What and when are the next big projects or assignments that you need to work on? Can you show me your progress so far? Can you show me your action plan to complete these assignments ahead of the due dates? Do we need to buy or get something in order for you to complete this project? Are the technology or research materials you need available and working properly? Do you need a classmate's or my help in order to do this assignment?
- How do you stay organized for school? If I tell you that we might do a special, fun activity, say, next Wednesday evening, how can you prove to me that you will be up to date with homework, projects, and studying so that we can take a school night off?
- Can you name at least two responsible students from each of your classes whose phone numbers you have so that you can call them if you miss something or need help?
- What is one thing that you could do to raise or maintain your grade in each of your classes? What do you need to do in order to learn and achieve more in school?

Chapter 14

Communicating with Teachers

Especially in secondary school, parents must realize that teachers have very limited time to interact with parents because their total number of students may exceed 150. In a two-hour parent–teacher event, that number would leave each student's parents about ninety seconds of personal time with a teacher—and that is if only half of the potential parents show up!

As a result, too many teachers dread parent conferences and too many parents do not bother to show up because these brief meetings can be so unproductive. This chapter, however, endeavors to change these reluctant attitudes and to get the most out of the little time available.

WHAT PARENTS LOOK FOR WHEN INTERACTING WITH TEACHERS

On the occasions during which you interact with your children's teachers, whether in person or electronically, you will acquire the maximum benefit if you are clear within yourself what you are actually seeking. Explained below are the five basic goals parents commonly seek when meeting with or reaching out to teachers. (Since possible conflicts were discussed in chapter 10, the following explanations do not include encounters such as those.)

1. Information, Explanation, or Confirmation

Parents may simply be seeking information, explanation, or confirmation from the teacher about their child's performance or the class requirements. However, parents can most often gain these facts all on their own from the teacher's class syllabus or professional website, from their child's progress reports, or just by asking their child. So, seek basic information only when you have a specific, burning question you have been unable to get an answer for elsewhere. If you have indeed looked and have come up short, then please let the teacher know as this may be an oversight in their communication with parents they will be happy to be made aware of.

Yet if there is a major issue with trusting the information your child provides you (or may be withholding from you) about school, the power of your leadership and love must immediately be intensified so your child clearly understands the perils of lying to you (including lying by omission), as well as the perks of earning your trust. Please take all of the Four Ls seriously, and do not take situations like these lightly. A parent who does not share an open, honest relationship with their child will forever be working at a deficit—and a potentially dangerous one at that.

Look, if you are relying solely upon teachers to discover the most basic information about school, you are going about being an involved parent in a counterproductive fashion. At worst, this makes you look to the teacher like a parent who either has no clue or no control and at best has you constantly playing catch up with your child's conduct, assignments, and grades—often when it is far too late for either you or your child to have any positive effect.

Even a truly informed parent who assumes they are expressing genuine interest in their child's education may actually appear to a teacher like they are asking vague or random questions merely to be saying *something*. Questions like "Do you give homework?" or "How is he doing?" may cause teachers to inwardly cringe as a precious chance to collaborate is squandered. Instead, try focusing your questions on those areas where during your conversations about school your child was sincerely not able to provide you with adequate information.

Sometimes, the parents themselves may also want to explain to the teacher some special need, issue, or circumstance concerning their child. If you think a teacher requires a heads-up about a personal situation or issue, please convey this information tactfully. Teachers do not want to know the intimate details of a family crisis or a nasty divorce; they just need specifics as to your child's current sensitivities and personal needs as they pertain to assisting with your child's behavior, confidence, engagement, and academics.

2. The Teacher's Personal Insight, Advice, or Suggestions

Parents may be seeking the teacher's personal insight, advice, or suggestions regarding their child. Luckily, teachers enjoy being advocates for their students and being asked for their expertise or input. In fact, teachers may notice aspects about your child that you are wholly unaware of or had not paid particular attention to. They also often possess inside advice that can be extremely valuable to parents who are concerned about their child's next level of schooling, enrichment opportunities, or ways to find specific support.

Of course, you can do what you want with a teacher's personal perspective, but teachers will certainly appreciate that you asked for their opinion. If you are not ready for candid answers to your specific questions, then do not ask them. Yet what teachers have to say may open your eyes in ways that may actually surprise and delight you. Teachers may well be inspiring success in your child in ways you personally struggle with achieving for yourself at home, so their ideas, observations, and strategies might open doors for you.

A teacher's answers to these types of "In your opinion" questions below will show you how well teachers actually know who your child is and in four distinct ways. If it becomes apparent that a teacher does not know your child very well, this may because of how early into the school year it is or because of the sheer numbers of students this teacher may be responsible for. These are not excuses; they are harsh realities of how precious little time or opportunity teachers have to get to know your child as an individual so that they can best attend to their specific needs.

Also know that a major factor in how well a teacher knows your child is in how active and responsive your child is. Children must find authentic ways to distinguish and present themselves while in class so they become a featured player in that teacher's day.

This does not take any more than a kid being routinely pleasant, helpful, participatory, enthusiastic, engaged, curious, and committed—all of which the Four Ls at home have well prepared them for and the Four Fs at school will further persuade them toward. None of this is phony or off-putting; it is simply a child being sincere and open about their school experience.

The questions from the previous chapter that you regularly ask your child about their own conduct in school also show them exactly what you and their teachers expect on the child's end.

3. Ways for Their Child to Improve, Progress, or Excel

Parents may be seeking ways their child can improve, progress, or excel in school. If you are already fairly confident that your child is indeed pulling their weight in any or all areas, you can simply ask a few of the "In moving forward …" questions below. These questions pinpoint where your child can improve but still leave room for the teacher to also bring to your attention any concerns they may have. Teachers will readily tell you if there is a problem without you asking, so no bad news is definitely good news.

These "In moving forward …" questions focus on what can be done to either capitalize on what is currently successful about your child or how you and the teacher can work together to motivate and influence positive, productive change in your child. This emphasis on moving forward together will transform your interactions with teachers.

4. Validation, Praise, or Reassurance

Parents may merely be seeking validation, praise, or reassurance for their child's stellar performance or for their own part in successfully raising their child. Similarly, your child may view these parent–teacher events primarily as a means of basking in the pride of their academic or creative accomplishments and flaunting their grand rapport with their teacher.

Neither of these scenarios has anything wrong with them, especially since this book happily validates conscientious parenting and encourages kids to derive self-esteem for hard work and success in school. So if fishing for compliments is the main reason you meet with teachers, be honest with yourself about it without an ounce of shame.

Just be aware that unless you have the luxury of a private appointment with a teacher, there is sometimes a good chance that you will not receive much face time. Also know that the majority of parents who actually show up to these conference events are parents of teacher's pets just like you who are also vying for their chance to hear accolades from the teacher.

The real disconnect comes with the reality that although the teacher probably is perfectly delighted to honor your parenting skills and extol your child's virtues, they do not *need* to talk to you. Instead, they are vying to get a chance to speak to that parent of one of their teacher's pests who they spy coming through the classroom door and whom they desperately need to speak to!

5. A Casual Connection

Parents may only be seeking a casual acquaintance as they briefly socialize with the teacher. Some parents are well aware of their child's shortcomings as far as school is concerned, yet their aim in meeting with teachers is more about conversing as peers and establishing a working relationship. The same is often true of parents of high-achieving students who already know that their child is exceptional. There is nothing wrong with this informal approach, and many teachers welcome interludes of relaxed adult chat in the midst of a very busy night of being the most popular (or unpopular, as the case may be) person in the room.

QUESTIONS PARENTS CAN ASK THEIR CHILD'S TEACHERS

Choose a handful of questions below that resonate with you or that you are anxious to receive feedback about. These questions are merely a means for you to target your inquiry; they are not meant to be a laundry list for which to interrogate or overwhelm a teacher. These questions were also crafted to hopefully elicit positive answers from teachers. Often the child sits in on parent–teacher conferences, so your child will definitely take note of how you are intentionally asking questions that feature your child's best qualities. This way, your child cannot accuse you of purposely seeking to find fault, and you will further prove that you are on their side.

1. **Questions to Ask a Teacher Regarding Your Child's Behavior and Attitude**
   - How does my child regularly show you the proper respect? Can you give me an example of when my child was particularly courteous or pleasant?
   - How does my child show you a positive and cooperative attitude, especially by doing what you ask the first time? Can you give me an example of a time when they were particularly helpful or kind to you or a classmate?
   - How does my child add to the constructive learning environment that supports the educational experience of the entire class? Can you give me an example of when you were particularly impressed with their preparedness, attention, or determination?
   - In your opinion, which classroom management strategies seem to best motivate my child to cooperate with you? Do you think my child responds better to discipline given with a metaphorically stronger hand or a lighter touch? Does my child respond better to reasons, warnings, and words or to confrontation, consequences, and control?
   - In your opinion, does my child respond better to a highly structured, supervised learning environment or one that allows for more independence and choice?
   - In moving forward, what are the changes you need to see in my child to better cooperate with you, to improve their reputation, or to take your class more seriously?
   - In moving forward, is there anything you need from me to support my child in your efforts to motivate them to better behave, show a more positive attitude, and be a more beneficial part of your class community?
2. **Questions to Ask a Teacher Regarding Your Child's Participation, Attention, and Perseverance**
   - In what ways does my child routinely focus, concentrate, and stay on task? Can you provide an example when my child expressed determination and commitment?

- In what ways does my child show you that they are an active and responsive learner?
- Does my child regularly participate in class discussions, volunteer, and raise their hand? Was there a time when you were impressed by an idea, answer, or comment they offered?
- In your opinion, what best persuades my child to express herself, open up more, and come out of her shell so that she can share her ideas and opinions with others? What strategies do you use to inspire increased confidence in my child?
- In your opinion, does my child seem to have a sense of belonging in this class?
- In your opinion, which strategies do you use that seem to best motivate my child to trust you and to seek to please you, rather than continuing to be distant or apprehensive?
- In your opinion, does my child seem to be a natural self-starter who shows drive, initiative, and grit, or do they still need more encouragement, support, and recognition?
- In moving forward, what changes do you need from my child in order to participate and volunteer more? Is this more of an issue of confidence, perseverance, attention, or skills?
- In moving forward, is there anything you need from me to support my child in your efforts to motivate them to focus, concentrate, and remain on task?

3. **Questions to Ask a Teacher Regarding Your Child's Interest, Engagement, and Inspiration**
   - Does my child ever express curiosity or wonder when learning something new? Have they ever talked to you personally about their questions, ideas, or insights about class?
   - In what ways does my child work well and collaborate with their peers?
   - In what ways does my child show you that they are an enthusiastic and engaged learner?
   - Have you noticed that my child responds more eagerly and performs better with certain assignments, activities, or types of books than others?
   - Have you noticed a special talent or spark in my child that you could share with me? If not, what do you think is hindering my child from fully investing in this subject?
   - In your opinion, does my child work better alone, with a partner, or in a small group?
   - In your opinion, is my child more of a leader, a team player, follower, or loner?

- In your opinion, which strategies do you use that seem to best motivate my child to delve deeper, to look below the surface, and to make connections between ideas?
- In your opinion, is my child especially creative, original, or profound in any particular ways? If not, can you give me advice to get them to think more originally or deeply?
- In moving forward, what are the main things you need from my child in order to get the most out of their learning and to more fully enjoy and appreciate what your class offers?
- In moving forward, is there anything you need from me to support my child in your efforts to motivate them to personally invest in their education?

4. **Questions to Ask a Teacher Regarding Your Child's Work Habits, Assignments, and Grades**
   - Does my child ever ask for individual assistance? Is a quick explanation all they need in order to accomplish their assignments or do they often require more tutoring? Do you think this need for extra help or re-explanation is because they do not fully pay attention the first time or because their basic skills need more support?
   - Can you recommend a supplemental book, workbook, or program you think my child would benefit from working with at home, especially when they finish their homework?
   - Does my child speak articulately and express himself intelligently? Are there any ways I can help increase his academic vocabulary, pronunciation, or general way of speaking?
   - Has my child done anything to distinguish herself or to stand out academically? If not, what do you think she needs in order to more fully rise to the occasion?
   - Is there any quality that particularly impresses you about my child's classwork? Can you name one major aspect of their writing that they need to improve upon?
   - In your opinion, is my child working to their potential and giving their full effort?
   - In your opinion, do you think there are any significant gaps in skills or knowledge that are hindering my child's progress toward proficiency? How can I assist in getting my child up to grade level? Where do you think I should start or concentrate?
   - In your opinion, is my child being adequately challenged? How do they rank in terms of their peer group in this class? Are there any enrichment opportunities you recommend?

- In your opinion, which strategies do you use that seem to best motivate my child to concentrate and produce their best work? How can I mirror these methods at home?
- In moving forward, what are the main things that you need from my child in order to improve their grade in your class or to get even more out of their education?
- In moving forward, is there anything you need from me to support my child in your efforts to motivate them to better comprehend and achieve?

STUDENT-LED CONFERENCES

In many schools, parent–teacher conferences have been replaced by student-led conferences. These are opportunities for the students to take charge of their efforts and accomplishments in school and to assume ownership for updating their parents about the specifics of each class, as well as their cumulative performance.

Of course, those parents who are already on the ball with how their child succeeds in school and who routinely ask the types of questions already outlined in the previous chapter may find these student-led conferences redundant. Just know, however, that this time may still be very important to your child as they proudly act as your classroom docent and guide you through their class portfolio, show you their educational habitat, and point out class artifacts.

Be aware that teachers must be particularly careful with how much one-on-one time they give to parents during student-led conferences because once any parent spots a teacher engaging with another parent, every other parent wants their private audience too. There are even instances where teachers give extra credit not only to those students whose parents show up but also to those whose parents do *not* talk to the teacher during these events!

Parent-Led Conferences

If you do have any opportunity to speak with a teacher, prepare beforehand so you make the best use of your brief time together. Remember that the teacher will not hesitate to bring up issues that concern them, but also think of this as *your time* to address any needs you may have.

Think of this meeting as a "parent-led" conference where you are clear about what you are seeking and have a few specific, preplanned questions you want to ask. You may only have time to ask one or two questions, but have some backup questions ready just in case. Sometimes you may get more precious time than planned, or the teacher may invite you to ask more questions. By being proactive, you will never again feel ill-prepared to meet with a teacher, and you will not walk away feeling like you missed something important.

Especially as a Four Ls parent, you are the expert in the room as far as your child is concerned. You have far more experience with your child than the teacher, yet you should be completely open to benefiting from the experiences, insights, and expertise of your children's teachers. This free exchange of ideas based on mutual respect has only one goal, for parent and teacher to better collaborate in providing your child with what they need most.

Chapter 15

Looking Inward

The following final four sets of questions are the kinds of questions parents can ask themselves within the privacy of their own thoughts or together with their co-parent. They are provided to generate healthy self-reflection and to inspire you to fully embrace how you provide your children with the Four Ls.

DO NOT ALLOW THE PRESSURE FOR PERFECTION TO INHIBIT PROGRESS

These questions are not meant for parents to feel less-than, however. Again, no one is expecting perfection—not with adults or kids—so do not panic if through these questions you acknowledge that in some ways you currently are not fully meeting your goals of providing leadership, love, laughter, and learning for your children.

Goals are important things to strive for and to eventually achieve, but each parent's goals differ from others' in their specifics and evolve over time, especially as your children grow. You cannot do it all, so *do not view these questions as a to-do list* and certainly not as something that any parent accomplishes instantly. Instead, focus on the questions that linger in your mind, and gradually figure out ways to turn your greatest ambitions into glorious actuality.

Do not allow the fear of imperfection to sabotage the pleasure and elegance of parenting. You can and should try to do your best for your children (which includes taking care of your own needs so you can continue to give your best), but on those occasions when you or your children fall short of your high expectations or everything *seems to* fall apart, take heart and then take action. If need be, lower the boom with your leadership, further liberate your love, let your laughter be contagious, or lighten the way by providing wisdom and learning. That is all it will take to set the entire family back on course and to continue humming along as before.

PUTTING FAMILY FIRST

Putting family first is a good way for parents to prioritize their goals. This approach is different than simply putting children first. Of course, parents are altruistic and routinely put themselves second to their children. Yet we have seen how if left unchecked, this mindset of perpetual self-sacrifice potentially leads to resentment and even burn out, even in the most loving of parents. This is why clinging to the true meaning of commitment provides parents with balance in the dance between giving graciously and getting abundantly.

Even dedicated teachers often wrestle with not overextending themselves yet dutifully meeting the needs of the whole class. Add to that the demand of differentiating their lessons, assistance, and feedback according to the individual needs of, say, thirty students, and you have a herculean task—sometimes repeated five times each day. And that's just instruction!

A teacher also has to meet the needs of thirty kids at a time who require varying amounts of supervision and management so that instruction can be delivered unimpeded and time on task can be maximized. At the same time, teachers additionally have to attend to the specific emotional needs of each student. Finally, they have to make the whole experience meaningful and engaging for children who all get excited by different things.

Yet it can be done, and it can be done quite well by a firm, fair, fascinating facilitator. Oh, it takes some juggling and a whole lot of planning, but each student, as well as the teacher, can end up invigorated and satisfied by the entire process.

See, when the teacher puts the class first, they make sure they also attend to some of their own needs because as leader of the class, they are a part of that class, too. They have just as much to gain or lose as anyone in that classroom, and they endeavor to make it a win-win proposition the vast majority of the time. There is always some give-and-take, of course, and the teacher and the students alike sometimes have to be patient when they have a certain personal need to be met. Yet in the long run and on balance, everyone feels fulfilled—both individually and as a crucial part of the class community.

So it should be in the home as well. Putting family first means that the persuasion of leadership, love, laughter, and learning simply does not happen if at least one parent and one child are not together occupying the same space, be it the kitchen, the backyard, the car, the park, or anyplace in between.

MAXIMIZING MOTIVATION

In fact, these motivators work best when the entire family is together because the power of the Four Ls increases exponentially with each additional person who is included. When an adult has successfully motivated one child, every other child in that room is now positively influenced not only by that same adult but also by any other kid who is currently following the adult leader, being swept up by love, rolling with laughter, or intent on learning something useful and new. This multiplying effect of a parent's or teacher's persuasion upon the group cannot be overstated. In certain ways, it is not more difficult to motivate more than one child, and it is often far easier.

Therefore, time together with your children must be top priority. Spending time nurturing your children, bonding with them, reveling in hilarity and hijinks, and guiding them to greatness are what made you want to be a parent, so do not deny yourself, let alone your precious kids, a moment of available time! One-on-one time is fantastic and necessary too, but you can expand even the smallest family circle to include relatives close and distant, as well as friends far and near. As long as they are dear, put out the welcome mat, and watch your positive influence create good times and wonderful memories that are shared by all.

Of course, time together does not merely mean time spent in the same house with no interaction. How can an adult motivate if they are not actively participating in some way? Yet do not think that a parent or teacher is the sole

Table 15.1 The Essential Elements of Parenting

The fundamental qualities that parents must either embody or supply to their children on a simultaneous, comprehensive basis.

Leadership	• Logistics, limits, lessons • Modeling, monitoring, modifying • Command, consistency, corrections • Strength, structure, stability.
Love	• Belonging, belief, backing • Acceptance, attention, appreciation • Relationship, reassurance, recognition • Patience, positivity, persistence.
Laughter	• Passion, purpose, perseverance • Drive, direction, determination • Inspiration, intention, investment • Charisma, curiosity, contentment.
Learning	• Empowerment, encouragement, emboldenment • Involvement, improvement, independence • Strengthening, support, self-efficacy • Coaching, clarity, collaboration.

inspiration for children or that they must give children one hundred percent of their time. Not only is such close, constant contact unnecessary, it inhibits the required and sought after autonomy children must have in order to practice, play, and grow all on their own. Give often, but always with proportion and a joyful generosity.

See **Table 15.1: The Essential Elements of Parenting** for a concise illustration of the fundamental aspects of balanced, comprehensive parenting. Refer to this "cheat sheet" any time you need clarity and focused attention to what your children most need from you and the parental roles you must fulfill.

HOW WELL AM I PROVIDING THE FOUR Ls TO MY CHILD?

There is always room for improvement and growth in parenting, but neither of these will happen without perspective and self-awareness, a clear and measured path, and sound strategies to get there. The following self-reflective questions will get you thinking about further strategies you can create on your own or explore further. There is a wealth of information out there for parents, perhaps too much, but now you can refine your research by homing in on which one of the Four Ls you feel you need the most assistance with at any particular time.

These questions were crafted so that they elicit your positive responses and focus upon what you are doing *right*. Each question also asks for specific evidence as proof of how you are providing the Four Ls. Again, if you find yourself short on evidence for some questions, yet the question itself strikes a chord in you, it is there where you should concentrate your parenting focus in going forward.

1. **Am I really providing leadership for my children?**
    - Can I easily list the most important rules, routines, and limits of my home? Can I briefly explain why they are required and the benefits they create, especially in terms of how they expedite the flow of love, laughter, and learning for the entire family?
    - In what ways do I calmly and confidently convey these household procedures to my children so that my home runs efficiently and orderly?
    - Do my children customarily do what I say the first time? In what ways do I ensure that my questions and calls for attention are answered immediately and my requests are accomplished with dispatch and a cooperative attitude?

- How do I conscientiously and cheerfully maintain and reinforce the grace and ease of how my home runs? Do I mix reminders with praise and appreciation?
- Do I annually review these rules and routines for each of my children and adjust, add to, or increase their responsibilities according to what is developmentally appropriate for each child? How do I balance chores and limits with expanding freedom and trust so my children learn that acting responsibly comes with rewards, not all of which are material?
- How have I given my children the proper guidance so that they are progressing in their abilities to exercise self-control and prove themselves reliable? In what ways do I instill in them the skills necessary to put first things first, to sometimes put others first, and to act with patience and decorum? How do I recognize and appreciate their developing maturity, compassion, and dependability?
- How can I directly link the structure and stability of my home with the cooperation, contentment, and creativity that my children express? In what ways do I model and teach precision, planning, and punctuality so that my children find a comforting predictability and productivity while at home?
- In what ways have I established an environment where my children behave respectfully and responsibly so that there is a thoroughness, readiness, peace, and pleasure that pervades our home—even amidst the inescapable chaos and craziness that living with children can at times create?
- How does polite cooperation and conduct also follow us when my children and I venture away from the house? In what ways do I continue to reinforce manners and obedience when we step outside? Am I calm and easygoing with my kids away from home?
- Do friends and family greet my children with a relaxed enthusiasm because they know my kids will conduct themselves appropriately while in someone else's home?
- How does my children's regard and compliance then extend to the classroom and schoolyard when they are expected to obey other adults and to get along with other children?

2. **Am I really providing love for my children?**
   - How do I frequently reinforce my leadership role by using positive reinforcement and praise so that my rules and routines continue to be respected and run smoothly?
   - How do I consistently, out loud, and specifically recognize, encourage, and appreciate my children for the positive and productive things I see

them doing, both in the moment and afterwards? How does it make me and my children feel when I acknowledge and celebrate what they are doing right or what they are doing better? How does that emphasis on the positive pay off with even more good behavior and attitude?
- How specifically do I pay attention to my children? Do I regularly set aside plenty of time to communicate and interact with them without distractions or trying to multitask?
- How have I made every effort to ensure that the entire family sits down to eat dinner together as often as possible and that all electronic devices, including the television, are turned off and are out of sight until the meal is finished and everything has been cleaned up? How have I explored what other home-cooked meals can be planned, shopped for, prepared, eaten, and/or cleaned up as a family unit, including on weekends?
- In what ways do I nurture my children so that they feel supported, listened to, and understood enough to let me into their personal lives, especially alerting me when there are problems that are causing them unhappiness or worry?
- In what ways do I feel close to my children? How do I show them that I love and accept them unconditionally—even as I also chide and correct them, even as I push and persuade them, and even as I set high expectations for them?
- In what ways do I actively promote a sense of belonging for each of my children so that they truly believe they matter, count, and are an important part of this family?
- How does my children's sense of self-esteem transfer from my home so that they seek and form peer relationships that are healthy and fulfilling instead of harmful and ultimately sabotaging? In what ways do I teach the tenets and rewards of true friendship?
- How have I given my children the proper support so that they are progressing in their abilities to express self-confidence? Can I list several specific qualities in each of my children that prove they are developing the proper self-esteem? In what ways do I foster, capitalize on, and add to those qualities?
- In what ways do I show that I trust my children? What specific opportunities do I give them that are developmentally appropriate and allow them to earn my increasing trust?
- In what ways do I objectively think my children are worthy of increased privacy, privileges, and autonomy as evidenced by their frequent honesty and reliability and with regard to what is developmentally appropriate? Do I annually review these factors for each of

my children? How do my children feel when I show that I have faith in them?

- How does the responsiveness of my children then transfer to the classroom where my children willingly participate in and assume ownership for their education?

3. **Am I really providing laughter for my children?**
   - For each of my children, can I list the top ten leisure or adventure activities we both equally enjoy? How do I routinely engage in these activities with each child on a one-on-one basis in order to bond with them as individuals? In what ways do I use these special activities as a form of incentive and positive reinforcement instead of always buying them material items as rewards for their hard work and cooperation? How am I actively teaching my children to value experience over things?
   - How do I teach my kids that disobedience and disrespect are not the proper ways to show that one is unique? How am I actively developing constructive ways for my children to assert their independence, creativity, and originality?
   - Can I list the top ten leisure or adventure activities the entire family enjoys? How do we routinely engage in these activities? Do we at times include relatives in these activities? Do some of those activities include experiencing nature, art, and architecture, as well as attending cultural and community events? In what ways do I make a specific effort to explore and expose my children to all the riches and opportunities our own town or city (or those nearby) has to offer? Regardless of the family budget, do we also engage in simple pleasures that are neither expensive nor elaborate yet are just as engaging and fun?
   - Do we ever do volunteer, service, or charity work together? How does the family feel when we give of our time and our talents? What lasting lessons does such altruism teach?
   - Do we regularly play board games and solve word and number puzzles as a family that inspire creativity, intelligence, and healthy competition? Do we also play outdoor games that feature exercise, flexibility, coordination, fresh air, and fun? How do I make time to practice and develop the skills each of my children need in order to play all these games more proficiently next time? How do I stress the joys of experience over winning?
   - In what ways do I create spontaneity, surprise, and specialness to break up the everyday routine, such as everyone participating in decorating the house for holidays?

- In what ways do I intentionally create traditions that celebrate and teach about our family's heritage and cultural background? Do we regularly visit with relatives?
- In what ways do I help my children discover what they individually are good at and what they truly enjoy? Can I name the top interests and personal passions of each of my children? In what ways do my kids feel my vicarious investment in their passions?
- Do I actively participate in their passions by asking about their activities, attending their practices or events, and exploring options for further growth and development in this and other potential areas of their interest? How do my children feel when I participate?
- In what ways do I give my children the proper inspiration so that they are progressing in their sense of self-fulfillment and self-direction? How am I myself a role model in word and deed for finding personal satisfaction and leading a life of purpose and passion?
- How does that personal engagement, joy, and sense of meaning and direction then shift to the classroom in some significant ways? In what ways are my children finding a sufficient amount of fulfillment, excitement, and curiosity in school?

4. **Am I really providing learning for my children?**
   - Do I annually review the bedtimes for each of my children, especially for school nights? How have I structured bedtime routines and the powering off of all electronic devices so that distractions and delays, as well as temptations and tantrums, are proactively avoided and what should be a peaceful transition to sleep actually occurs?
   - Do I have a morning routine for school days which ensures that everyone awakens with sufficient time to get ready, eat breakfast, gather essential items, and leave with plenty of time to arrive at school early and ready to begin the day?
   - Do we have a calendar that is prominently posted where all family and school activities and events are recorded and daily reviewed and updated?
   - Do I keep a separate folder for each child organized with all their school records, report cards, accomplishments, awards, and activities in which they have participated?
   - Do I annually determine the top developmentally appropriate skills and knowledge I want to impart to and practice with each of my children for that year? In what ways do I make a conscious effort to regularly teach my children useful and meaningful skills, as well as to augment and assist in their academic learning?
   - How do my children and I often learn things together or build, create, or maintain things as close partners? What ongoing, hands-on

projects could we begin that will help us to bond, that we both look forward to, and that we can increasingly learn about together?

- Have I set aside a dedicated homework space that is stocked with necessary supplies for each of my children? Is the sanctity of this space respected and reserved only for my children's education or creativity? How is this study space organized and maintained?
- Do I schedule regular family trips to the library where each person checks out and returns books that are personally interesting to them? Do I read to my children and/or have them read to me? Do I model reading for pleasure by setting aside quiet time where the entire family reads and we often discuss what we each have read?
- Do I ensure that my children have blocks of time for schoolwork free from distractions and other duties? Do I have a menu of supplemental educational activities my children can choose from if they finish their homework before their scheduled study time is over?
- In what ways do I supply my children with the proper guidance so that they are progressing in their self-efficacy in a wide variety of ways, including vital life skills?
- How does that learning and proficiency then move to the classroom where my children not only are capable but diligently apply and expand their skills by achieving frequent academic proficiency and success?

EMPOWERED AND EMBOLDENED BY THE FOUR Ls

The Four Ls is an entirely practical approach to parenting that is applicable and fully adaptable to all family situations, and this book takes both an inspirational and an aspirational approach to parenting. One aim is to awaken within you your own potential and to spur you to maximize the promise each parent inherently possesses. Another objective is to prod you to reach even further and to dig ever deeper as you discover that as a parent you are capable of much more than you may have initially assumed—all without any of these parental duties ever becoming all-consuming, overwhelming, or overbearing.

Thus, allow the Four Ls to empower you, and then let your newfound parental prowess embolden you to progressively refine your own artistry and grace in parenting. This parental dexterity and style will be your lodestar in determining if you are on the right track. If you allow equal measure and aplomb in parenting to forever replace excess and agitation, you can rest assured that you and your children are doing just fine.

Afterword

Looking Forward

If you have not already noticed, everyone seems to be an expert on parenting. At the very least, everyone has an opinion on how to (or how not to!) raise kids. It is much the same when the subject turns to teaching. When it comes to education, everyone also wants to put in their two cents. Since you are reading this book, you are probably as guilty as I am in both respects.

Of course, this inclination to naively assume, to harshly judge, or to interject uninvited one's notions about the living room and the classroom is as natural as it may be annoying. You see, every person can at least to some degree speak quite articulately as to what constitutes good parenting and good teaching because every person has been a child who was parented and has been a student who was taught—regardless of whether they have ever parented their own children day-in and day-out or have taught a new classroom full of youngsters year after year.

On a deeply personal basis, each can attest to what they liked and what worked, as well as what they loathed and what went wrong, when it came to their own parents and each of their teachers. Yet what you now know that most people do not is that every one of these people's commendations and complaints that pertain to their childhood can be categorized quite easily into four distinct yet closely intertwined components of what constitutes effective parenting and teaching.

Before reading this book, if you had never consciously and specifically approached your children's needs from four fundamental avenues, then placing every one of your parenting moves and beliefs into the context of the Four Ls should be a transformative experience for you. If you also had never considered exactly what you expect your children's teachers to provide for them, then looking at education through the lens of the Four Fs should be a revelation.

Ultimately, I hope the Four Ls of Parenting have come as a great relief to confused, overwhelmed, and frustrated parents, just as the Four Fs of Teaching saved the career of this formerly confused, overwhelmed, and frustrated teacher. If you were already a confident parent, I hope your curiosity about the connections between the classroom and the living room was met with useful insight and fresh perspective. Mostly, I hope these four sets of essential attributes in motivating children profoundly resonate for you as you continue to strive to influence your children adequately and appropriately.

I assure you that these motivators certainly resonate with all children. Even after now completing my third book on inspiring and persuading kids, I never cease to be astounded and deeply pleased by how my students positively respond to the four main ways in which I interact with them. To know that I play a significant role in how they enjoy and excel in my class—and quite likely how that enthusiasm and accomplishment then transfers into their daily lives—this advantageous impact fills me with an honor and gratitude that transcends paychecks, pension, and profession.

Don't get me wrong, though; those three things are extremely important to me as well. I am no martyr. Teachers definitely deserve more respect, trust, and autonomy, including compensation that rivals that of doctors and lawyers.

What I have found after nearly twenty-five years of working with kids, however, is that it is not only unnecessary, it is counterproductive to think that to be effective, to be worthy, or to attain satisfaction while nurturing and educating children one has to give up everything else. That neither does the adult any good, nor does it allow the children themselves to rise to the occasion and to do their fair share. Self-sacrifice does not motivate; it inhibits potential on both sides.

As you generously supply your children with a balance of leadership, love, laughter, and learning, you will only become more invigorated, committed, and contented. In return, your children will reap and mirror these selfsame rewards. Feeling depleted, doubtful, or depressed is not what the Four Ls deliver to parents, even when in the midst of working really hard!

Through the leadership you supply for your children, you will know the satisfaction of true duty and service to others. Through the love you lavish on your children, you will discover the enduring warmth of true connection and unconditional acceptance. Through the laughter you share with your children, you will simultaneously revel in your personal passions and find what the sheer joy of family is all about. Through the learning you provide for your children, you yourself will learn things you never could have known and cannot ever live without.

These are the same gifts students bestow on their teachers. They are also the reason why teachers return year after year to greet with excitement and anticipation a new group of students. Can you imagine if every child had a Four Fs teacher each year, beginning in Kindergarten? What would the children and the country, as well as parents and teachers, be capable of if adults acted as allies and nurtured kids who increasingly and in the most fundamental ways exhibited self-control, self-confidence, self-expression, and self-efficacy? Our collective promise would be unbounded, and the mutual contentment would be palpable.

Thus, with my personal classroom focus placed squarely upon delight and fulfillment, it is obvious that I cannot teach out of dread or fear. I simply refuse to take that dark path. Some would say it would be understandable, even wise, to do so in this age of judging, blaming, and shaming of teachers. But I cannot always be looking over my shoulder, afraid of misspeaking or being misconstrued. I also cannot be so constantly wary of students, parents, and administrators—and myself—that I second-guess, censor, or constrain my every move.

That sort of perpetual panic and relinquishment is exhausting, joyless, and soul-killing. None of those negative attributes are welcome in my classroom because they will adversely influence and infect the enthusiastic, ebullient, and soulful educational environment my students not only deserve but require in order to learn and flourish.

Parents as well cannot raise their kids in fear or in a furious scramble to safeguard their children's every move—present and future. Neither the Four Ls nor any parental approach can guarantee that your children will be protected from every conceivable harm or can even ensure that they will lead prosperous or rewarding lives.

Frankly, in too many ways parenting and teaching are unpredictable, even impossible endeavors. We all try so hard and care so much and have the best of intentions, but we also have so little actual control. As we have seen, exerting too much control will only blow up in our faces. Yet a profound lack of oversight and involvement will end up doing much the same.

Of course, we do not even want total control over kids because that would negate the specialness we adore and seek to actively foster in each child. True parenting and teaching is about nurturing and guiding, not discouraging or forcing. Besides, your idea of fortune and fulfillment may be vastly different from those of your kids, especially when they will live their adulthood in a world that in many ways will be vastly different from the one you know now.

If the real control resides mostly within each individual child and if their success and satisfaction depend greatly upon their own attitudes and actions, then what parents do absolutely have control over is themselves. You are completely in charge of your part of the parenting bargain, what you bring to the relationship with each of your children and the family as a whole, and how committed you are to providing four deceptively simple yet infinitely complex, seemingly obvious yet eternally important, necessities for your children.

You also always possess the power to change what heretofore has not been as effective, as well as to adapt to what your children may need in the future. Whether we like it or not, kids are ultimately in charge of their own destinies. And again, we *should* like this because our entire end game is for children to take what their parents and teachers have given to them and use these core self-beliefs and skills as the essential tools for them to lead worthy, independent lives.

Your job as parent is neither to constantly save your children nor to surrender them too soon. As long as they are children, they are your charge, and you are charged with furnishing them with the proper care and attention. This book has endeavored to show you what that type of care and attention should look like, whether it is a parent or teacher who is charged with nurturing and educating a child. You do not need all the answers because now you have the elemental questions, of which there are but four. These four indispensable questions are all you need to reliably set you on your parenting quest.

Simply, honestly, and thoughtfully ask yourself how you are providing your children with leadership, love, laughter, and learning. Then have confidence that through this occasional yet crucial self-reflection you will indeed figure out and fill in the details on your own and in due time. And you and your children will enjoy every minute of that journey. Parents and teachers must embrace that exploration and accept its fluidity and chaos as part of the supreme adventure of it all.

So forget control, and put your parental stock in influence. And motivation. And inspiration. And persuasion. Not only do those work, your children will eagerly respond when you suffuse them with what they fundamentally require, especially when you entice and allow them to come to you as willing participants in their own amusement and achievement.

Parents and teachers can and do influence much more than we even know—for better or worse. So it is best for all adults to take advantage of their inherent potential and seize the always-available opportunity to intentionally influence our children in the ways they need us most. Therein is our collective power, our fortitude, and our rock.

About the Author

For over two decades, **Robert Ward** has taught English language arts and English language development to a diverse population of students at a public middle school in Los Angeles. He has also mentored over two hundred teachers at various stages of their careers. His additional leadership roles include a two-year appointment by the State Superintendent of Public Instruction to the Student Learning Subcommittee at the California Department of Education in Sacramento and graduate-level teaching experience at California State University, San Bernardino as an adjunct instructor in the College of Education.

He is also the author of *The Firm, Fair, Fascinating Facilitator: Inspire Your Students, Engage Your Class, Transform Your Teaching* and *The Teacher Tune-Up: A Workbook and Discussion Guide for How to Become a Firm, Fair, Fascinating Facilitator*. He can be contacted through his website at www.RewardingEducation.com.